DIGITAL AESTHETICS

Theory, Culture & Society

Theory, Culture & Society caters for the resurgence of interest in culture within contemporary social science and the humanities. Building on the heritage of classical social theory, the book examines ways in which this tradition has been reshaped by a new generation of theorists. It will also publish theoretically informed analyses of everyday life, popular culture, and new intellectual movements.

EDITOR: Mike Featherstone, *Nottingham Trent University*

SERIES EDITORIAL BOARD
Roy Boyne, *University of Duham*
Mike Hepworth, *University of Aberdeen*
Scott Lash, *Lancaster University*
Roland Robertson, *University of Pittsburgh*
Bryan S. Turner, *Deakin University*

THE TCS CENTRE
The Theory, Culture & Society book series, the journal *Theory, Culture & Society* and *Body & Society*, and related conference, seminar and postgraduate programmes operate from the TCS Centre at Nottingham Trent University. For further details of the TCS Centre's activities please contact:

Centre Administrator
The TCS Centre, Room 175
Faculty of Humanities
Nottingham Trent University
Clifton Lane, Nottingham, NG11 8NS, UK, e-mail: tcs@ntu.ac.uk

Recent volumes include:

Undoing Aesthetics
Wolfgang Welsch

Simmel on Culture: Selected Writings
edited by David Frisby and Mike Featherstone

Nation Formation
Towards a Theory of Abstract Community
Paul James

Contested Natures
Phil Macnaghten and John Urry

The Consumer Society
Myths and Structures
Jean Baudrillard

Georges Bataille – Essential Writings
edited by Michael Richardson

DIGITAL AESTHETICS

Sean Cubitt

SAGE Publications
London • Thousand Oaks • New Delhi

First published 1998

Published in association with *Theory, Culture & Society*,
Nottingham Trent University

 SAGE Publications Ltd
6 Bonhill Street
London EC2A 4PU

SAGE Publications Inc
2455 Teller Road
Thousand Oaks, California 91320

SAGE Publications India Pvt Ltd
32, M-Block Market
Great Kailash – I
New Delhi 110 048

British Library Cataloguing in Publication data

A catalogue record for this book is available from the
British Library

ISBN 0 7619 5899 1
ISBN 0 7619 5900 9 (pbk)

Library of Congress catalog record available

Typeset by M Rules
Printed in Great Britain by The Cromwell Press,
Trowbridge, Wiltshire

For my teachers

CONTENTS

PREFACE:
THE UNIVERSAL TOURING MACHINE

The contemporary global and networked society incurs a new ethics, but one which is comprehensible, perhaps only comprehensible, as the gift of beauty; because, in our time, and for a materialist analysis, there is no other name for that utopian longing for the distant, the absent, what appears to us obscure and clouded, as though through a glass, and darkly. For St Paul, the connection between the immanence of salvation, the ethical imperatives of missionary work and the imitation of Christ were utterly given, the donations of a personal God. What the Western heritages from the cultures of the Book have not lost is their sense that that yearning for a higher, better, greater state of being is bound together with the practicalities of sharing the planet and the world with others, as inseparable as a river and its flowing.

The pursuit of the European mind has been to identify the world, to see in it the whole of what can be. Yet in what exists and most of all in what has been made by human hands and human cultures, we find not only what is but what might be. Over and again our technologies and our cultures, scientific and artistic, discover in the raw material of the world we inhabit instabilities that indicate the limitations of the present: its politics, its knowledges, its economics, its beliefs. Even the dreams of the present are a source of profound dissatisfaction, and we displace onto the future a better, clearer, brighter, a more definite and more admirable state of affairs. If we can no longer place our faith in such a state existing on the further side of death, and if it is true that progress and emancipation are no longer credible teleologies, then we are forced to find what we can of that desire for a better state not hereafter, not after the revolution, but in our daily worlds. What we are condemned to seek is evidence of those broken movements between the world and ourselves, disturbances of the existing brutality of the given, stars puncturing the continuum of the dark, pinpricks of illumination that suggest how the world might be otherwise. The aesthetic is this pursuit of an ethical mode of being in despite of the conditions in which we find ourselves.

There is some kind of absurdity in looking for ethics in a technical device: the invention and propagation of digital technologies. The fastest and widest impact that computers have had is in deepening the class structures of contemporary society on a global scale. We have to confront the demolition, not just of jobs, of communities and of cultures, but of hope itself as a direct or indirect effect of the electronic communications that have enabled the entirely destructive expansion of finance capital. How could we find an artwork as complex, as effective, as engrossing as the worldwide nexus of transnational capital?

Kant's piercing and ascetic conceptualisation of the aesthetic – as that in which we should not and perhaps cannot have an interest, but which should transcend our ordinary greed, lust, gluttony – suggests why we should seek in art exactly what is not engrossing, what does not engage us wholly as what we already are, but rather what might let us find an other way of being human. If, in Kant, this drifts towards individualism, in our times, and not just in Europe, the imperative is social. Finance capital, professionalisation, the cultures of risk and trust, the whole drift of urbanisation, technologisation and specialisation sweep us towards our social selves, our mutual dependence. Computers are only an element in this process, but they are more than intensely symptomatic; they are our partners and, like any technology or any lover, increasingly they are ourselves. Where they open up the necessary accommodation between us and the social at a new level, in which our media are intricately identifiable with our relationships, they introduce a new scale of instability, a new uncertainty as to how, and indeed if, we should relate to one another, not just with those we know and meet, but those faceless millions on whom we depend for our wealth and our oppression.

A certain kind of 20th-century art announces only that it exists. Another devotes itself to its own eradication in the act of becoming present. Yet another concerns itself with its own impossibility, its illusionism or its bad faith, and by implication with the infamy of faith in the fact, the real, the event. This book is concerned with art that communicates, or that poses itself as communication, and questions whether any communication is possible that is not already aggression, command, power, submission. Shall we ever speak again? Shall we listen? Shall we love? Must we dream, or shall we face the total domination of what is. The debate is caught in two critical moments: Wittgenstein's 'The world is all that is the case' (Wittgenstein 1961: 5) and Adorno's 'What is essential about a work of art is what is not the case' (Adorno 1997: 335). Aesthetics, beginning in the material of art, is utopian realism, possessing 'an expectable not-yet-existence; it does not play around in an unoccupied potentiality and does not go astray but anticipates a real potentiality in a psychical way' (Bloch 1988: 105), a utopianism grounded in the material (unlike daydreams) but directed towards the future. The purpose of inquiry into the digital arts is not to affirm what is, but to promote the becoming of what is not-yet, the grounds of the future as they exist in the present.

Is the space between the world and us irredeemable? Or is it the source of our most radical motivation? Art in our time is the most profound meditation we have on the sources and purposes of being human, and this book aspires to register those artistic investigations, but also to work as itself a work – of criticism, which like any decent and honest criticism, seeks to emulate the movement of the works on which it depends.

This book is then critical rather than theoretical (see Cubitt 1995). It is structured around the media which compose the human–computer interface. Chapter 1 discusses forms of reading and the devices that surround them, the catalogue, the pile of magazines, the private pleasures of the novel. Chapters 2 and 3 investigate, respectively, the realist and the spectacular aspects of visual media, suggesting that perspective is best understood as a special effect, while realism's favoured form is the map. Chapter 4 attends to the transformations of sound in the arts of recording and broadcasting. Chapter 5 then looks towards the problems of convergence, and the implications of networked communications. Some readers will recognise criticisms of some shibboleths of cultural studies, especially of theories of resistance and subversion. Resistance is a manner of coping with the day-to-day. This book is dedicated to more than refusal: to the building of alternatives that owe nothing to the structures of domination. Nothing less is worth fighting for.

ACKNOWLEDGEMENTS

Though I always try to avoid reprinting previously published materials, the lengthy gestation of this book has allowed me to explore some of its themes in draft with a variety of audiences. In particular, Chapter 1 draws on 'Cyberbooks: Read Only Memories', public lecture, Bookworks/University College London/Slade School of Art, 23 March 1994 and 'Read Only Memories', paper given to the Linguistic Representations of the Subject Conference, Liverpool University, 7 July 1994, published in Karl Simms (ed.), *Language and the Subject*, Rodopi, Amsterdam, 1997, 207–16. Chapter 4 draws on 'Online Sound and Virtual Architecture (Contribution to the Geography of Cultural Translation)', paper given at the ISEA Conference, Rotterdam, Holland, September 1996, published in Michael B. Roetto (ed.), *ISEA 96 Proceedings: Seventh International Symposium on Electronic Art*, ISEA 96 Foundation, Rotterdam, 1997, 17–21, published online by *Leonardo Music Journal* (1998) and in *Leonardo Music Journal*, vol. 7, 1997, 43–8; 'Sound: The Distances', paper given at the Modernist Utopias conference, Musée d'Art Contemporain, Montreal, 9–10 December 1995, published in Chantal Charbonneau (ed.), *Utopies Modernistes* (= Colloques + Conférences 4), Musée d'Art Contemporain, Montréal, 1996, 97–111; 'Video Installation and the Neo-Classical Soundtrack', paper given at the *Screen* Conference, University of Strathclyde, Glasgow, July 1996, published in *Essays in Sound* (Sydney), vol. 3, 1997, 8–20; and 'Pygmalion: Sound for Sculptors', Sound Matters/Live Arts Symposium, Birmingham Art School, University of Central England, 30 November 1996. Chapter 5 draws on 'From Global Transmission to Diasporan Translation', paper given at the Consciousness Reframed: Art and Consciousness in the Post-Biological Era conference, CAiiA, University of Wales College, Newport, Gwent, 6 July 1997; 'Flow: Networks, Transmission and Translation', MA seminar, London College of Printing, 14 March 1997; and 'The Courier: Virtual Realism and Networked Subjectivity', Ruskin School lecture, Oxford University, 11 February 1997.

I am also grateful to the following for support, advice, discussion and criticism: Dudley Andrew, Rasheed Araeen, Eddie Berg, Homi Bhabha, Bryan Biggs, Simon Biggs, Lachlan Brown, Pavel Büchler, Ron Burnett, Chris Byford, Lisa Cartwright, Janice Cheddie, Susan Collins, David Connearn, Rosemary Coombes, David Cross, Felix de Rooy, Eugenio Dittborn, Dimitris Eleftheriotis, Film and Video Umbrella, the Foundation for Art and Creative Technology, Sera Furneaux, Chrissie Isles, Alfredo Jaar,

Pervaiz Khan, Carol Knight, Jim Lastra, Greg Lee, Lev Manovich, Janine Marchessault, Trevor Matthison, Kath Moonam, Iliana Nedkova, Aedín Nolan, Sadie Plant, David Rodowick, Mirek Rogala, Chris Rojek, Robert Rojek, Javier Sanjines, Zia Sardar, Terry Smith, Vivian Sobchack, Mike Stubbs, Philip Tagg, Jez Welsh; participants in the Nettime, Rhizome and Ars Electronica online discussions; and students, colleagues and members of the public who have discussed these issues with me in conferences, seminars and galleries in two continents, especially at Liverpool John Moores University, who also allowed me sabbatical time to commence and to complete the research. A special debt of gratitude is owed to the Rockefeller Foundation and the Chicago Humanities Institute for the fellowship that allowed me to undertake major research on this book in 1995. As ever, none of this would have been possible without Alison Ripley. Many other people have contributed directly and indirectly, and to them this book is dedicated.

1
READING THE INTERFACE

When my father died it was like
A whole library had burned down

(Anderson 1994: 227)

Cybercafé

In small rooms in clubs, and in customised bars where a quarter buys a few minutes of connection, you can log on to the matrix. You don't spill your coffee, and you don't smoke because it damages the hard drives. There's little to observe, except the absorption, and nothing to understand unless you are absorbed. No two screens show the same thing, quite often not even similar things. And yet there's something familiar. Several things familiar. The book is dead, so the graffiti on the wall says, though there are books on sale here, million-selling titles on netsurfing, virtual homesteading, cyberpunk and hacker theology. Someone is searching an archive; on another screen there's a little illuminated manuscript where quicktime figures flicker gently in the video breeze (what a shame that this beautiful effect will be superseded by next-generation liquid crystal displays with a transistor for every pixel). There's an online Shakespeare, *Moby Dick*, dictionaries and a Bible left by electronic Gideons. Elsewhere, you browse through search engines to unearth the themes and concatenations of themes that lure you. Someone is writing a letter. In the myriad worlds of digital comms, reading and the architectures of reading persist and will persist, even after shopping-'n'-fucking novels and comic books become props in costume dramas. The world is at your fingertips, but which world and whose is scrolling through what geographies of mind? Through which detours do the universal claims of writing recycle the histories of globalisation through the silent intimacies of these absorbed and transfixed netreaders in this transfigured local?

Hypertext and the Colonial Dialectic

In a heartfelt defence of theory in the context of the 'new literacy' of post-literate, electronically mediated education, Wlad Godzich writes:

> As the designers of the Macintosh and Windows interfaces have discovered, images have a greater efficiency in imparting information than language does. What is important for our present purposes is that [such] developments entail

a diminution in the role played by the type of language that the culture of literacy is built upon: the so-called natural language as universal mediator. In addition, we need to take into account the fact that the claim to universalism for language has suffered setbacks with the expansion of the market to a global scale, whereas mediated images and electronic messages, backlit by the aura of advancing technology, have overcome local resistances far more efficiently. (Godzich 1994: 11)

Godzich's 'present purposes' centre on the struggle for humanistic learning in English and English Literature in the North American education system. It is then not so shocking that, guarded though his use of the term 'natural languages' is, he has not the same perception of English as the Kenyan novelist Ngugi wa Thiong'o, appealing for the use of Kiswahili as a Pan-African language:

> To know a language in the context of its culture is a tribute to the people to whom it belongs, and that is good. What has, for us from the former colonies, twisted the natural relation to languages, both our own and those of other people, is that the languages of Europe – here English – were taught as if they were our own languages, as if Africa had no tongues except those brought there by imperialism, bearing the label MADE IN EUROPE. (Ngugi 1993: 35)

Ngugi's argument is not only that an oppressor language ends up carrying racist terms and structures, nor simply that the meeting of emergent and dominant languages can never be on the basis of equality, but centrally that 'the rural and urban masses, who had refused to surrender completely in the political and economic spheres, also continued to breathe life into our languages' (Ngugi 1993: 35). The Gikuyu from which this essay is translated, and the Kiswahili lingua franca of East Africa, are far more capable of voicing the experience of anti-colonial and post-colonial struggles than a tongue which has historically become the medium of national elites and the international English-speaking bourgeoisie (Ngugi 1993: 37). Writers as diverse as Ranajit Guha (1988) and Jimmie Durham (1993) demonstrate the geographical spread of English as a racist instrument of exploitation, oppression and genocide, and the core role of other languages in the resistance to colonialism. The status of English as standard language of the net merely accelerates an historical process initiated long ago.

What is perhaps more surprising is that Godzich presumes that everyone, everywhere is universally at home with the window–icon–menu–pointer (WIMP) interface of the Mac and Windows, a culturally specific and, in the event, interculturally normative visual vocabulary as powerful as colonial English. The North American provenance of this most familiar of human–computer interfaces (HCIs) is famous: imagined by Vannevar Bush in the 1945 *Atlantic Monthly* essay 'As We May Think'; unveiled as windows and the mouse by Doug Engelbart at the US Department of Defence Advanced Research Project Agency in 1968; picked up by Alan Kay at Xerox PARC in the mid-1970s; raided for inspiration by Steve Jobs and Apple in 1979; and universalised with the 1990 launch of Microsoft Windows. There was the conscious intention, experienced as inspiration, to reduce the opacity of existing command-driven interfaces, to make the HCI user-friendly, comparable to familiar workplaces, and simple: 'If the computer is only a vehicle, perhaps you can wait until high school to give "driver's ed" on it – but if it's a medium, then it must be extended all the way into the world of a child' (Alan Kay cited in Levy 1995: 58). But who is this user? Friendly after the manners of which culture? Familiar to whom? Simple for the child of the wired suburb or the peasant village? The commercial and ideological analogy with corporate bureaucratic work patterns determined a global technology. At the same time as glamorising through clean technology, bureaucratic capital deskills its labour force, and while offering the appearance of naturalness and emancipation from onerous chores, introduces new orders of supervision and surveillance.

The HCI is the lived experience, the phenomenological apparition, of the 'third office revolution' that follows the reorganisation of clerical-secretarial work from handcraft – copperplate and double-entry bookkeeping – to the mechanised office – typewriters, file cabinets and adding machines – and finally into the digital networked office of the 1960s (Diani 1989: 67–9). Office organisation is closely linked with the evolution of management, and has a particularly swift response to changes in the mode of expropriation. Not only does the technologisation of the clerical workplace proletarianise and feminise a previously white-collar and male job (see Braverman 1974; Aronowitz 1992, 1994 – Aronowitz's second essay markedly less optimistic than his first), in the process shifting women from the position of idealised consumers to ideal promulgators of textuality; it also opens the office trades to a new mode of control, even as it replicates in office after office the serried ranks of desks Bob Cratchit would have recognised. The progressive technologisation of the workplace cannot disguise the fact that the knowledge professions are engaged in vital labours of information inputting, filing and management, distribution and exchange, billing and banking, as they have been since *A Christmas Carol*.

At least one element of the interface remains intensely unfriendly: the QWERTY keyboard, invented by Christopher Latham Sholes, 'father' of the typewriter, during the 1870s as a way of ensuring that the bars connecting the keys to the letters would not jam when used at any speed. This delaying strategy designed to slow down the pace of typing was marketed quite bogusly as a 'scientific arrangement' of the keys: QWERTY bears no relation to the proximity of common combinations or the frequency of occurrence of individual letters, and is notoriously difficult to memorise (Beeching 1974: 39–43; see also Bliven 1954). Ratified as international standard in 1905 under pressure from typing professionals who already dreaded having to acquire a second set of hard-won skills and expensive teaching manuals, QWERTY will continue to plague everyone for as long as text interfaces are dominated by the office environment, where its inertia cannot be shifted. Though far better input systems have been marketed on a regular basis since the 1870s, QWERTY still dominates even non-roman keyboards, and its layout is even more obstinately set in the binary addresses allocated to each key in standard machine code. Few of us who have sweated so hard to get used to this character set would opt to change for another. Scholes' hegemony enters even the intuitive level of personal skill, and is as profoundly ourselves as acquired sphincter control.

What is on offer in the WIMP interface is intuitive only in the sense that we are forgetful of ever having had to learn it. Its iconography is likewise a learnt environment. Images with any claim to realism are data-intensive, and, like news images, seem to require verbal commentary as supplement. WIMP does not use indices, images with a one-to-one correspondence to actually existing things, but icons, which operate not by similarity but at first through fuzzy analogy and, as the user becomes more familiar with them, as an internalised grammatical structure. The success of the Mac's desktop metaphor has little to do with the mixed metaphors of windows, folders and disks, and much more to do with the way their interrelation forms a grammar, a syntagmatic organisation of word processing and data management internalised as familiar.

The function of hypertext, the family of programs which link text files to one another and to image and sound files, is to provide a paradigmatic dimension of substitutions in the syntactic universe of the WIMP. Originally an architecture for complex documents, it has become the key structural protocol of the internet, a move caught in Nicole Yankelovich's title 'From Electronic Books to Electronic Libraries' (1991). In that essay, Yankelovich reviews an earlier co-authored piece on hypertext (Yankelovich, Mayerowitz and van Dam 1991) which argued that the core qualities required from the software were (1) promoting connectivity, (2) promoting audiovisualisation, (3) creating and revising documents, (4) browsing, searching, customising and retrieving information, and (5) preserving the historical integrity of information. The rapid growth of individual databases and their networking made vital a further five functions: (1) wide-area hypermedia (linking geographically dispersed work groups), (2) full-text search (using automatic indexing of each new text), (3) information agents (personalised search engines earmarking new items of likely interest), (4) integration of reference works (for example, access to dictionary, encyclopaedia and thesaurus direct from hypertext) and (5) filtering (narrowing the range of searches to manageable proportions through assemblages of criteria like keyword, author, file-type and date) (Yankelovich 1991). With the exception of the information agent, still available only as search engine but likely to be sold soon as customised news broker, all of these are now common, not just on single machines and local areas, but as typical features of the most popular network browsers like Netscape.

What may yet turn out to be an historical transformation in culture is falling victim to the management of change – a phrase which reeks with the intent to ensure that the future looks as much like the present as possible. '"Reason" for a long period', surmised Max Horkheimer, 'meant the activity of understanding and assimilating the eternal ideas which were to function as goals for men. Today, on the contrary, it is not only the business but the essential work of reason to find means for the goals one adopts at any given time' (Horkheimer 1994: vii). In other words, philosophy has abandoned the pursuit of absolute, metaphysical truth. In its place, reason has become science, and science in turn, as technology and as social science, has become the instrument of domination. In some ways, escaping from that idealist fantasy of absolute knowledge has freed science from an old burden. But even though reason has lost its teleological mission to drive humanity towards the end of history, it has found a new vocation in the planning and administration of change. Five-year plans, investment plans, actuarial tables, even buying insurance policies and mortgages, are all examples of the way in which rational administration of the present turns into the obsessive administration of the future. The intelligent agent, seeking out the familiar, is one more example of this instrumental reason sacrificing serendipity and diversity, the grounds of evolution, in the interests of a fetishised efficiency.

Even by the lights of instrumental reason, the HCI has not achieved the efficiency for which it strove. Contemporary media scholarship replaces Godzich's causative model of omnipotent authorial intention driving unthinking square-eyed zombies with the motives and rewards of viewing: the negotiation of meanings and pleasures in lived conditions (see, for example, Lewis 1992; Morley 1987, 1992; Seiter et al. 1989; Silverstone and Hirsch 1992) – meanings and pleasures not necessarily attuned to the instrumentality of transmission. The evidence is that processing power does not increase the throughput of work (see Bowen 1989; Franke 1989; Warner 1989); that networks bear enormous traffic in gossip, not functional communications (see Sproull and Kiesler 1991, 1993). This extraordinary rebirth of letter-writing on the brink of the 21st century is astonishing, but not necessarily useful, in the sense that it cannot be restricted to the rational, linear syntax of efficient management. Hypertext not only assembles different documents; it conjugates different ways of reading. Each is as bound to history and geography through the typical products – novels, libraries, magazine stands – with which they are associated. Tracing their temporal and spatial distributions is a first step toward understanding their logics, and the interstitial places and times where the solidity of the present becomes as fungible and porous as a wallfull of dry rot. The cybercafé may yet be the centre of a new public sphere, new democracies, new subjectivities. But those chains that hold the illuminated scripts to the walls are more than metaphors of the mediaeval library.

Ptolemy's librarians at Alexandria wrote their critical suggestions concerning the integrity of the Homeric text into the copies they made, from multiple sources, in pursuit of an increasingly impossible dream: the perfect rendition of a text which is most likely never to have achieved a definitive version during the lifetime(s) of its author(s) (see Reynolds and Wilson 1974). Against these vagaries, there is only faith. Spinoza's is perhaps the definitive statement:

> the meaning by which alone an utterance is entitled to be called Divine, has come down to us uncorrupted, even though the original wording may have been more often changed than we suppose . . . for the Bible would have been no

less Divine had it been written in different words or in a different language
(Spinoza 1951 [1670]: 172)

The text Spinoza describes is one which exists despite words, but which
demands words in order to take on that communicable existence without
which it is purposeless. The separation of the text from its distribution
through individual editions and particular copies dematerialises it. Literary
scholarship eschews the study of bookmaking in favour of this disembodied
text, pursued regardless of its physical presence, words without ink or paper.
Without that material anchorage, text is free to become infinite, to assume
magical, semi-divine powers. It is such a theological concept of the infinite
text that inhabits cyberspace, and which a materialist account of reading
must expose.

A Good Read

It is tempting to see in internet communications an entirely new mode of
reading, one which eliminates the specificities of place and time, the vertigo
of distance, to produce an ecstasy of pure interface between text and reader.
But netsurfing still respects the older distributions of reading, though mod-
ified and accelerated: the histories of interactive marginalia, of dedicated
spaces and times for reading, specifically the textual negation of place in a
really engrossing read and the universalisation of space in the library. But the
net also derives its metaphors of surfing and browsing from a nomadic reading, neither negating place nor universalising it, but wandering, and taking
the hereness and nowness of place with it as unstill reference point. It is all
too tempting to read this nomadic place as the atomistic individual. But
nomads too have histories and geographies, and are as much distributed as
they are media of distribution. Individuality cannot be taken as a given in the
play of place and text that is reading; it is a function of them (though not
exclusively), and functions in them (as it functions in other formations).
Individuality too is a distributed form, and in the characteristic modes of
reading digitally, new distributions are in formation which have yet, however,
to sever their roots in the cultural overdeterminations of reading. The net
appears at once as utterly new and unutterably ancient: the electronic story-
teller, the interactive library. Constituted as both archaic and futuristic, the
point is to historicise the novelty and to renew the histories of this emergent
formation, and to find out how and why the mirror of reading, as intertext
and mutuality, has been cracked.

Reading, books and texts have their histories and their geographies and
they do not always intersect. Although each represents a geotemporal trajectory in the distribution of verbal culture across continents and centuries,
each makes its own connections and continuities, detours, meanders and
fortuitous epiphanies. The book has no less fugal a history than the text:
early printed *incunabula* imitated manuscripts, while scribes copied printed
sources in direct and often cheaper competition; chapbooks and *feuilletons*

spread myths and metaphors peculiar to an epoch which believed the angel of the press had driven out the demon of superstition; almanacs and gazettes of varying degrees of respectability and contemporaneity mimicked the letter post on which merchants had relied for centuries; without embarrassment the magazine and the tabloid spin off books on regular and irregular schedules. The book, that fortress of words, was not the sole invention of printing, which broadcast a riot of cheap dissemination. Yet the book, and especially the modern novel, has evolved into the defining instance of at least one mode of reading.

Books are strangers: more radically alien than any human traveller, they come marked with the irreducible distance between reading and writing. In their folds and between their lines they carry all the distributions of space, time and textuality, rendered into a concrete instance in the moment of reading. But though they are strangers, books are not absolute others, not unapproachably cryptic, deriving from an utterly different order of being from ourselves, and this we know because we can dialogue with even the most abstruse text, even in foreign languages. We can recognise in the physical characteristics of books that that is what they are – books; and so we can begin our interchange. Books, like travellers, are radically incomplete: they must have destinations, or they fade away. And though much literary teaching has been based on the preparations deemed necessary to make yourself adequate to the text, to structure your reading in ways that correspond to the attributed desires of the text, still, because they are both strangers and familiar, and because they approach us in advance as unstable, as if by empathy they make us unstable too. The possibility of reading is premised on the reciprocal incompleteness and instability of the reader. The act of reading is a mutual surrender of text and reader to the tentative becoming of the book.

But the book we think of when we talk about a good read, the portable, comfortable thing that opens in your lap under a circle of light as you curl up in winter, or that lies with you on the beach in summer: that is a technical product that has been conformed over centuries to a mode of reading which it has been difficult to establish, hard to isolate and sometimes dangerous to practise. Because its most familiar interface is a light-emitting monitor, there is a tendency to think of the computer as an extension of the televisual. But metaphors of pages, files and folders refer us constantly to this literate culture; and not just any literacy, but literacy in the Anglo-Saxon tradition, whose language dominates the engineering literature as well as network dialogue, and whose literary complexes sway the formations of telematic reading. Of these the most familiar is the guilty pleasure of the good read, reconformed as a particular reading formation in the information age.

A core aspect of the good read is its privacy. As Janice Radway (1984) observes of women's reading, to pick up a book, whatever it is, is to mark out a space and time as your own, apart from the demands of work and family; this is how novel-reading functions to create a minimal privacy on public transport. In fact, historically, there are many reasons to believe that the long struggle for private reading associated with the rise of the novel was won centrally by the definition of privacy as especially feminine. So Friedrich Kittler (1990) argues that German romanticism constantly addresses the abstract 'Woman' as its ideal reader, while reserving the world of criticism and philosophy, of writing itself, for men. Reading for women and domestic servants remained a cause of moral and religious concern from the invention of printing through to the famous summing up at the *Lady Chatterley* trial in 1962 (see Flint 1993; Hull 1982; Landes 1989; Lovell 1987; Lucas 1989; Shevelow 1989): a constant crisis of the contradiction between the means of production – printing – and the mode of consumption – constantly charac- terised throughout the period as lascivious, sensual and indecent. This feminisation of the world of the psychological novel, the adventure story, the romance and even the soaring passions of high romantic verse emerges hand in hand with the divergence of the public and private spheres in the wake of the Enlightenment.

In contradistinction to the masculine, public world of commerce and civil society, the space of reproduction – of eating, drinking and sleeping, of sex, child-bearing and child-rearing, of illness, death and mourning – is enclosed within the evolving private home. There it takes on a specific role in the for- mation of the reader within the Oedipal and social dramas of the emerging nuclear family. A specific mode of reading is refined in these configurations of a microsocial world, especially in the middle-class home divorced from work and politics, and, because divorced from them, refocused on the emer- gence of a new sociological category: that of individuality. Nothing characterises both the private sphere and the emergence of 'a good read' so much as the division from other spheres of life and other people, even archi- tecturally, and consequently the construction of reading as a mode of individuation. But entangled as it is with the reproductive sphere, this process of engendering a self is also constantly at risk of annihilating it, subjecting it to forces of passion and self-involvement which exceed the reasonable limits of self-conduct.

The good read, founded on forgetting who and where you are, is premised on the fading of experience itself, when experience was understood as a property of the self. In the place of the ideal subject of the public sphere – rational, clear-headed, sociable – there arrives a fading subject, motivated by the desire to forget, regressing into a bodily leisure (captured by Kate Flint's selection of Victorian images of women readers [Flint 1993]) which runs through quasi-socialised identification with the characters or narration, towards its obverse, a descent into abjection, the horrifying yet tantalising dissolution of selfhood. A good read is the process of oscillation between self-loss and abjection, on the one hand, and, on the other, the constant resupply of ego-ideals, displaced and heroicised versions of the self, in the form of psychological-realist characters and fictions. This dialectic I take to be the heart of the predomination of narrative fiction in this mode of read- ing: the narrative of pursuit, of loss and recovery, of a wholeness always postponed until the moment of closure, when you must return again to the world of the self. This narrative, enacted as the dialectic of self-loss and self-recognition in private, silent reading, is the same dialectic through which the privacy of the self, the foundation of modern individuation, is lived. Its fundamental premise is couched in the mode of address: though existing in uncountable exemplars, the novel of psychology only ever speaks to the lone reader (so to refer to it a 'mass' medium is correct only if it is understood as describing the scale of its transmission, not if it is held to imply the construction of a mass public; the privacy of the novelistic mode of address is perhaps what has kept it from this sociological slur).

For the good read as narrative of the self, time is what divides subject from subject in the social to produce the necessary privacy. But in the same time the reading self relates to itself in the intimacy of a narcissistic dialectic of self-loss and self-recognition in the text. But by putting all its eggs in the basket of time, the good read is condemned to a motionless 'here', centred in the stillness of the engrossed reader. This constellation of self as something constantly on the brink of dissolution into another – abjection – and constantly hailed back by the construction of memory through narratives is profoundly unstable: always already not yet in being. Hailed back into the 'here' which it must inhabit if it is to resist the forces of its own dissipation, the return to the self is typically experienced as closure, marked with nostalgia for the hither-and-thither of the narrated self. Older text-based digital adventure games still reproduce this reading formation, and its ghosts still haunt the internet.

The Library

The European library only achieves its characteristic design in 1843, with the separation of reading areas from bookstacks first attempted in library architecture at the Bibliothèque Sainte-Geneviève of the Université de Paris. By 1854, both the Bibliothèque Nationale de France (reading areas in the entrance hall; stacks above) and Panizzi's British Museum Reading Room (stacks surrounding a central reading room) canonised the procedure, which dominates even the more recent tower stacks, in which librarianship triumphs over ideological and economic divides, from the Senate House Library of the University of London (1937) to the Biblioteca José Martí in Havana (1958). Until then, the canonical libraries, from the Bodleian to the Escorial, provided alcoves or benches at which to read. But in the separation of the books from the readers, and consequent need for professionalised library staff, the processes of public reading finally achieved their apotheosis.

The new libraries of the 1850s – and perhaps even more so the later but so more definitive Library of Congress – express in their architecture a new conception of reading as knowledge: an imperial conception. Wölfflin's (1966) analysis of Michaelangelo's Biblioteca Laurenziana in Florence traces the reader's entrance as ascent from the flamboyant organicism of the entrance and stairwell stonework to the open, light, serene geometry of the upper storey that shapes reading as it regulates the rhythms of its shelves. Although the Laurenziana still has the benches and chained tomes of the mediaeval foundations, public reading here was metaphorised as the ascent to an order that transcends mere flesh, a sublime approach to the pure mentation of the blessed. By the mid-18th century, the worthies of industrial cities and centres of colonial administration like Philadelphia and Manchester pooled their book-buying powers to form more sociable libraries, a process which aided the conception of public reading as a civic pleasure, if not a civic duty. The movement from the Laurenziana to the subscription library is the move from prayer to bourgeois civility.

But like the divine orientation of humanism at the brink of the baroque, this elite, haphazard and gentlemanly homosocial reading would in turn give way to the increasingly modern formation of public reading as instrumental, leaving only a vestige of itself in the tea-room. The separation of stacks and readers marks the early professionalisation of librarianship as information retrieval, occurring hand-in-hand with the emergence of the imperial bureaucracies and the educational infrastructure they demanded. We read quite often for purposes for which originality, authenticity, the formal properties of the text or quality of experience are unimportant. Such purposive reading redistributes the properties of text and place, and, in focusing on communication over medium, negates at once the specificities of the interface and the possibility of overcoming them. This communicative focus, not necessarily rational, evokes a social world in which neither text nor place of reading is specified, and potentially all places become the same. But rather than make a map the size of the world, we construct social spaces which can function as universal; the library foremost among them.

'The book' only exists, if at all, in a good read (when it is more often 'my book', less a book belonging to me than a book to which I belong). For public reading, there is no Book, only the library; only books and the devices which lead from one book to another: the catalogue, the index, the bibliography – the search engines of literate culture which still provide the dominant metaphors for network data retrieval. Intertextuality came late to literary critics; bibliophiles, puzzling through the same phenomenon, developed the forerunner of modern cataloguing in a long evolution from mediaeval compendia, through the Robert Estienne's catalogues (1542–7) and among Parisian booksellers of the 17th century influenced by Ramus (Eisenstein 1993: 64–73), issuing in the sales catalogues of Ismaël Bouillard and, in the 19th century, of Jacques Charles Brunet (Ranganathan 1951: 17–8). The Dewey decimal system of 1876 formalised the intertext as a domain pragmatically defined by ease of access and use.

Like Dewey, the later widespread Cutter and Library of Congress (LC) systems of 1891 and 1901 articulate an architecture of knowledge which may perhaps be traceable to the first inspiration of Bacon's *Advancement of Learning*, but which modify it profoundly (see Thompson 1977). In Bacon's 1605 classification of knowledge, the three central categories devolve upon the human faculties: Memory (history), Imagination (poetry) and Reason (philosophy). In the 19th-century systems, the triumph is of 'practical convenience' (Dewey 1876) over the claims of philosophy; knowledge is no longer formed from subjectivity but defined by the object-domain of the world. That this domain clearly owes its provenance, in Dewey, to the curricula of mid-century college education, and to the needs of a burgeoning administration in LC, sharpens this worldly focus. This primal objectivity in the creation of knowledge architectures presupposes the separation of subject and object. At the same time, these catalogues are no longer in hock to the organicism of Linnaean categories (as witness, for example, Dewey's separation of literature from language). Dewey, LC and Cutter all remain tied, however, to a twofold aim: to allow the user to discover whether the library has the book he or she wants; and to find what works of a given author the library holds. A literary ideology of authorship, entangled in the case of LC with copyright issues, hampered the ability of the 19th-century systems to adapt to changing information needs. The ramifications of this are clear in libraries which computerised early on: the search engines associated with 19th-century cataloguing are clumsy in retrieving through the plethora of cross-disciplinary interrelations which characterise contemporary public reading.

The 19th-century explosion of print production (and in its later years the exponential growth in specialist libraries held by trade associations, learned societies and corporations) which demanded the professionalisation of cataloguing also witnessed the professionalisation of public reading. The *Tischgesellschaften*, coffee-houses and salons were already masculinising the spaces of public reading in the 18th century. The formation of the great libraries in the 19th century formalises this demarcation of leisurely and instrumental reading; the professionalisation of cataloguing transforms the give and take of readers into the borrow and lend of books; and the separation of silenced reading rooms, where sociability became intertextuality and dialogue becomes annotation, completes the bureaucratisation of the intertext, the subordination of the powers of print to the instrumental reasons of state and economy. The very architecture of the great libraries breathes with this ambition: to colonise knowledge, through order, in the image of imperial rule.

Though the 19th-century public library service opened the doors to literate democracy, the institutional libraries of the same period closed them again through their rituals of entry – examination, dissertation, election – and the structured propriety of the discourses of interpretation which they promoted. In schemes like these, public reading, as institutional discourse of knowledge, devotes itself to the subordination of the world, a process in which the subject is related to an environment of massed objects, whose cataloguing turns them into the objects of the reading subject. The price of knowledge as manipulation is the divorce of subject from object. The public reader is caught in what Lacan, borrowing linguistic terms from Jakobson, took to be the syntagmatic dialectic in which the subject is condemned to pursue the object-world down endless shelves of signification in pursuit of that impossible object of desire, total knowledge, total control.

In the spirit of bureaucratic management, the systems designed to facilitate this endless quest for mastery of the whole are centred on the infinite subdivision of knowledge, just as Taylorism was to pursue the infinite subdivision of tasks, and the colonial map the administrative subdivision of space. But there is a last turn of the bureaucratic catalogue that allows it to become the fully fledged administrative tool of accelerated modernity. A central problem for Dewey and other modern systems arises in the interstices between categories of knowledge, and in the placing of new fields of knowledge in a hierarchy of systematic subdivisions. To some extent, this further institutionalised the ideology of gentlemanly learning enshrined in the rites of examination. Their emphasis on authorship takes on a different cast in light of the remarks of Professor H.W. Chandler of Oxford in 1885 when asked to support extra cataloguing staff for the Bodleian:

> Who tied the millstone of a classed catalogue round the Librarians neck . . . so much labour thrown away. . . . No real scholar, no man who is capable of literary research, wants a classed catalogue: he hates the very sight of such a thing . . . it is a snare and a delusion . . . what mischiefs result from the attempt to encompass such a work. Most french catalogues are classed, and he who had the ill luck, as I have, to consult them, retains a lively sense of detestation for those who were foolish enough to class the books. (cited in Thompson 1977: 170)

Henry Evelyn Bliss's magisterial critiques of the organisation of knowledge published in 1929 and 1933 mark the beginnings of the evolution both from the collegiate homosociality of scholarly culture and from bureaucratic analytic subdivision to the synthetic architectures of a fully administrable knowledge world: the expert system. Far-sightedly convinced of the principle that 'Human life should be socially organised on a basis of organised knowledge' (Bliss 1929: 405), Bliss criticises the inability of existing analytic systems to provide either for synthesis or for innovation, coherence and assimilation. What Bliss aims for is the 'principle of *maximal efficiency* through *collocation*, or synthesis, of closely related subjects' (Bliss 1929: 408).

In 1933, the Indian librarian S.R. Ranganathan published the first cataloguing system, Colon Classification, to put Bliss's critique to practical application. Using a systematic analysis not only of the core subject but also the 'aspects' and 'facets' of each specific work, he developed a system in which it is possible to locate books by shared interests even if they 'belong' in separate disciplinary classes. Precisely because of the success of Dewey and LC cataloguing, Colon has only really been taken up in countries, like Thailand and Kenya, with relatively new public library services (see the essays collected in Rajagopalan 1985 and 1988). But this synthetic system of knowledge organisation has become the founding principle of mechanical systems for information retrieval, a field pioneered by Ranganathan. The synthetic principle, grandparent of internet search engines, invented in the spirit of access, will lead us directly to the emergence of a new paradigm of social management: synergy.

With the emergence in 1950 of the British National Bibliography and subsequent establishment of the Library of Congress's MARC (MAchine Readable Cataloguing) service, print media became subject to an increasingly global catalogue run, through the Library of Congress, as a largely online network of libraries sharing publications and cataloguing data. As Thompson observes, 'Only in this way can libraries now control biblio-graphically the modern world's publishing output' (Thompson 1977: 174). He is correct in his emphasis as well as his facts: this is the only way in which the universe of publishing can be open to democratic use, the founding principle of modern librarianship. Yet at the same time, the globalisation of the specific architectures of knowledge developed since the mid-19th century should give us pause, both for what it tells us about the state of public reading in the transition from administered world to synergetic, and for what it forebodes concerning access to and use and retrieval of information from online databases. What imperialism of the mode of reading operates here?

Knowledge architectures evolve from the humanist to the bureaucratic, which itself has developed from the administrative towards the contemporary gospel of synergy. Their forms can be traced in the development of library architectures from the chained collection of religious manuscripts, through the secular and social club and the imperial library, to the specialist libraries held by law firms and similar companies, and the corporate databases of contemporary capital. It has been a territorial advance. Public reading has not lost any of its ancient privileges; it has added new ones. The public library service democratises, but differentially (Altick, for example, quotes 1894 figures showing that, of books borrowed by 'unemployed females' in a Bristol library, 502 were read on the premises but 10,476 were taken home [Altick 1957: 237, citing Greenwood 1894: 294]). Networked communications allow a far more democratic access to information, but the form which that information takes is both increasingly commodified, of course, and increasingly structured in the light of a universalist knowledge architecture in which the absolute division of knower from known, and the absolute subordination of knowledge to knower, gives administrative form to a profoundly imperialist mode of reading. As intelligent agents and know-bots, specialist autonomous search engines tailored to the interests of individual users, enter networked information storage and retrieval systems, further questions arise. Does convenience make up for the loss of that serendipity that always allows you to find something in a library, even if it's not what you were looking for? How does a knowbot or a search engine evaluate the accuracy or usefulness of a site in the absence of professionalised standards-setting (see *Scientific American* 1997)? Does the dominance of the USA and its free speech ethos mean that democracy has to be purchased at the price of disinformation? And will these doubts matter, in a period in which knowledge accumulation as well as knowledge gathering can be delegated to a software agent? Does such delegation replicate in local form the twist of knowledge from an integral formation of the self into the commodity form of information, an externalised universe of symbols? Once again, we are exiles in our own imperium.

Connectivity, the transport of disembodied information, outstrips the more robust portability of the book, but demands a material infrastructure which only connects a minority of the world's peoples. Premised on the assured telephone and electricity infrastructures of the industrial economies, and on the possession of expensive machines not designed for the humidity and dust of tropical climates, the virtual library is only universal if viewed from its interior. No longer dependent on humanist mnemonic culture, within this newly universal library, information takes on the nomadic quality of commodities, as standardised and ubiquitous as McDonald's. And as the electronic reading room goes pay-per-use, the commodity form extends the restructuring of the public sphere as administered domain even into the psychic formation of public reading. As consumable good, information loses, along with the old dependency on memory, its long-term validity. What defines the universality of even the portable modem is not its place but its time; only in the present does information have a price. The cost of the universal library, the 'here' that encompasses potentially all knowledge, is that it is condemned to a perpetual now. In the prison-house of the present, itself measurable in nanoseconds, the geography of empire has engulfed the time of dialogue.

Browsing and Netsurfing: Playful Reading

You could get into Shakespeare's Globe in the 1590s for a penny: the price of a quart of ale in an age that drank beer for breakfast. Two centuries later, at 2s. 3d., the price of a novel would feed a labourer's family for a week or two (Watt 1957: 42). Perhaps the Elizabethan stage gave the last really popular theatre in Europe, in the sense not only of its ambition to reach a wide audience, but in that all but the truly destitute could afford to attend. As theatre moved indoors and upmarket in the aftermath of the English Revolution, it moved from the play to the drama. Taking on high seriousness and refined wit, it abandoned the playful give and take of the mediaeval tradition. Yet the playfulness of popular culture has endured, despite the intensity of its policing. As public reading achieved its instrumental teleology in the institutional library, and even the good read attained some institutional and social credibility (especially in the 20th century, where any form of reading was seen as better than any form of audiovisual culture in the metropolis, and better than any oral culture in the colony), the playful has kept its place as the loyal opposition to literate society.

If the novel of psychology is the model form deriving from the private, and the index from the public, the playful read has evolved its own typical forms: the puzzle book, the picture magazine, role-play books, photo-romances and, perhaps the closest we have to a return of the *feuilleton*, the comic book. The persistence of the mode of reading associated with illustrated or primarily pictorial materials can be regarded as evidence of a subversive culture of distraction. The road from Dr Seuss to *Hello* is in a cer-

tain sense the traverse of popular culture. Its playful engagement with the
visual regimes of practical skills (home decorating, clothing), celebrity, complex typographical and design languages, the play of wit and the possibility
of interaction, is as intensive as Coleridge's annotations praised so fulsomely
by Charles Lamb (1935 [1823]). To reduce this to the dismissive category of
browsing is inadequate, but a simple sociological reversal that revalues the
playful browse as a confidently democratic and popular pleasure does it no
greater favours. The playful mode of reading, its potentials and limitations,
is central to reading in both the internet and multimedia.

Though they are dialogues, the interactions of both private and public
reading are conducted in silence. The good read invites an inner voicing of
the narrative, but the inner speech you hear is your own, though its words are
not: an aspect of its dialectic of self-loss and imaginary self-recovery. In
public, instrumental reading, the dialogue is between the self and the world
constructed as an object. The world is constantly reconstituted as the world
of knowledge, and the voice you hear when reading always that of an other
which already knows, but which constantly evades you along the lines of the
text and the corridors of the library. But playful reading is like reading aloud
to children: a masquerade, combining a willing suspension of disbelief with
an ironic agreement to play by the rules. Equidistant from the dialectics of
identity and the desire for control, it brings us instead to the realm of fantasy.

Fantasy is characterised less by its privacy than by the way it allows us to
entertain multiple positions in the scenario all at once (see Freud 1916;
Rodowick 1991). Mapping the game-world over the actually existing, especially the social, world makes possible the often observed endlessness of
games. There is little sense of conclusion – narrative or goal-oriented – to
classic definitions of the ludic impulse. Yet ludic reading is also characterised
by other spatial and temporal boundaries. The playful read is not uncom-
monly circular. *Finnegans Wake* is the example most frequently quoted by
scholars of hypertext (perhaps another legacy of McLuhan, a noted Joyce
scholar): a work in which the space of the text is made infinite through both
a spatialisation of relations between words (as opposed to the temporal relations typical of narrative) and through the cyclical structure of the book. But
this in turn produces the effect of a circular fortification built against the
marauding predations of a hostile environment: the world well lost for art. In
rejecting the instrumentality of the public library as a mode of reading/sub-
jectivity, the playful rejects along with the object status of the world the very
notion of exteriority to the game, of a relation with an other, natural or
human, that is not containable within the rules, and in that sense manipulable.

The success of the playful mode of reading is in inverse proportion to the
cultural scorn poured on it. The early 1990s saw a growing body of work on
the value of this ludic interface with culture and the utopian quality of this
imagination of a new *socius* (for example, Heim 1993; Kelly 1994; Laurel
1993; Rheingold 1993; Rushkoff 1994). The breathtaking capacities of the
internet and the ease with which its adepts navigate its interactions are indeed

inspiring. From the standpoint of the sociology of reading, the game-world of the net overcomes the good read's endless pursuit of an endlessly incomplete identity, and the public reader's objectification of an administrable world, to engage instead in a playful mythology of union between disparate and divided selves and worlds. Such is the universe of the MUD, multiple-user dungeons created as game domains by the players themselves, in which typically both the world and its narratives are generated as on-screen, real-time text.

But the player cannot escape the rules of the game, even when the game itself is one of the evolution of new rules. In the interpersonal dynamic of the playworld, the apparent anarchy is governed by a series of protocols: the permission to play, the repetition compulsion, the attempt to gain, through magical control of others, magical control of the game-world, and through it of the self itself. This is clearest in the intolerance towards new entrants to specific domains, and in the curt codes of flames: how many innocent enquiries have been met with 'RTFM', 'read the fucking manual'. The self-regulation of net communities, when it is not the product of bullying or the active policing of a moderator, begins in the submission of each to all, the consensual totalitarianism of the plebiscite, the triumph of the administered personality in its own act of perpetual submission (for accounts of MUDs and MOOs as normative activities from a more positive viewpoint, see Baym 1995; Bromberg 1996; McLaughlin, Osborne and Smith 1995). Playful reading is not freed from individuation, but the ghosts of individuation always haunt every attempt to evade it. The sociality is built up on the foundations of an undigested individuation, so the playworld works not as *socius* but as *agon*, not community but competition, and in this contest the playworld becomes the prize of and for domination. Not unsurprisingly, this agonistic, solipsist sociality reproduces to the point of boredom the binary structures of everyday gendering and racism through the dubious mechanics of group solidarity. Because it inhabits a bounded universe, the playful cannot contest those binaries and turn them into dialectical contradictions; to do so would be to imagine that the playworld had a history, where in effect it is a world where space dominates and spatialises time. This othering of the physical world of distances can be imaged as a retreat into the forgiving and indulgent narcissism of the maternal embrace, away from a social world governed by the dystopian distances of the father's No. In this way, it inhabits an image of maternity premised on unquestioning belief in the powers of patriarchy, and condemned merely to resist, but never to challenge them.

This maternal world is neither the utopian space of matriarchy, nor the othered, passionate imago of the final signified as Woman. It has still less to do with real women. Rather it marks a further regression, deeper even than the infantile narcissism of the abjection–recognition dialectic in private reading. In a curious way, the playful combines the good read's abject dissolution of self in otherness with the instrumental purposes of public reading: the willed submission to the game-world is not a loss or abnegation of self, but an act designed to shirk responsibility, without letting go, finally, of the self as organ of control and manipulation. Working in the register of fantasy, in a realm of the 'as if', the playful replaces the rationalist homosocial world of the library with a set of shared codes, lived out in an anonymity that acts as a permission, but a permission grounded in the infantile need to conform. The player, engrossed in the process of taking decisions within the game-world, has always already submitted to the blissful state of never having to make a decision about it.

The synergetic management of the social pursues the image of the group without the substance of workplace democracy. As massed handling of data, the playworld mimics the very thing it would escape: the new organisation of the corporate office. Agonistic, competitive connectivity reconvenes individual rewards and punishments around a semblance of dialogue. Yet because it is anchored in a textualised domain, there is never the risk of that dialogue becoming mobilisation. The transnational corporation, in its subvention of playschool creativity as the model for the think-tank and the brainstorm, becomes the patriarchal mother. As Laurie Anderson sings,

> And when justice is gone, there's always force.
> And when force is gone, there's always Mom. . . .
> So hold me, Mom, in your long arms.
> In your automatic arms. Your electronic arms. . . .
> Your petrochemical arms. Your military arms. (Anderson 1982)

The Mom-corporation indulges its children's food fights and Bermuda shorts, nowhere more so than Silicon Valley, because they inhabit the nursery of marketable product. Perhaps this is contributory to white college kids' passion for heavy metal and the more urban and macho hip-hop: from the romper-room, these look like rougher, naughtier children pushing the envelope of Mom's permissions. The synergetic personality surrenders itself to a freedom that is always circumscribed by the relationship of permission, a relationship which constantly reforms subjectivity as individuality, the address of and to the player.

The textualisation which underpins private and public modes of reading alters its activity in the playworld, where you are denoted as a player through your textual alter ego. There ensues a textualisation of the self, a textualisation which, however, does not allow the self to evaporate or dissolve into a textual world, but which promotes modes of interaction and socialisation which are conformable to the text. As textualised, the ego (Lacan's 'je', Freud's 'ich', the word 'I' that locates the self in language and more generally in all Symbolic systems of meaning and socialisation) is not constrained to any identity other than that which persists despite the vagaries of the actual words in which it is embodied. Dematerialised and recoded as a set of coordinates on the trace of its passage, the self is reduced to the function of a shifter, the linguistic category of words indicating a context which is never the same twice, words like 'here', 'now', 'I', 'you'. The competitive edge of the MUD keeps the shifter 'I' central, hiding its relational dependence under a hierarchy in which all the other shifters are defined by their relation to Number One – I don't depend on you, you depend on me! The more fully engaged in play, the less embodied the self becomes: lost to the world, dazed by the steady rain of pixels in which the interlacing lines of dialogue splash momentarily into existence.

Mary Ann Doane (1982, 1991) identifies as masquerade the series of strategies which women have evolved for negotiating the difficulty of femininity in patriarchal societies. She imagines that the women viewers of patriarchal movies, for instance, find themselves becoming practised at a mental act of pretending, more or less ironically, that they accept the roles and pleasures allocated them. In the anonymous and pseudonymous spaces of cyberspace, it is as if identity as masquerade has spread throughout the culture, to permit a constant disavowal of self, and its endless replacement with a series of ideal alter egos gleaned from whatever pages of popular culture. This masquerade is entirely textual. And to this newly textualised self, the whole of the world appears as text.

Since this text is dialogical, it is also consciously future-oriented, and its most characteristic grammatical form is the right-branching sentence, a structure that relies not on the memory-trace of what has gone before, but on the emergence of accreting clauses, each added on to the end of the previous one stepping forward into the opening spaces of an adventure toward uncertain goals, while simultaneously erasing the completed steps that precede it. The right-branching grammar of the cybertextual masquerade lives, like Max Headroom, consistently a handful of nanoseconds into the future.

In a space of textualised selves, the interaction between texts takes on some of the characteristics of more traditional playful reading, most of all the promiscuous attraction of texts towards dialogue. But this is always in the context of the perverse integrity of the text as coordinates and coordinated, and therefore in a dialogue world in which the integrity of the cyberself is constantly in question and equally constantly restated. Like the text of *Hamlet* surrounding itself with exegetes, the textualised self flickers in and out of existence as it lures responses from the other players. As textual self in a textual universe, the ego is not dissolved but reinforced in its belief that its world is, if not knowable in the ordered and analytic sense of Dewey, then retrievable, as data. As textual, the cyberself is always about to burst into the material of words; always about to retreat from them into its own crystalline ideality; always blinking into existence as the edge of futurity. Where older reading formations negotiate the present through regression to the infantile past, playful reading egresses into the mortal future. In the basilica of a textual MUD, self as cybertext struggles for transubstantiation, to become, as virtual, its own narcissistic afterlife. It is a kind of momentary immortality.

After Privacy: The Politics of Intimacy

The only thing we know about the future is that we die. The brief, messianic experience of the cybernetic supernatural is an attempt to control that future by creating a bubble of eternity in the fluid materiality of time. The making of playworlds in administered spaces is an endless interlacing of attractions and repulsions, of longing for and terror of self-loss, to form a tympanum stretched taut across the narrowed limits of a bounded world. We have in the West a civilisation, which has largely defined the workings of the digital media, founded on the cult of life, where life is overzealously defined as negentropic, the accumulation of order and the organisation of information, against the 'death' of entropy. This 'death', when you excavate it, is a mausoleum built over all dissolutions of the self. True, since it is not only feared but also and unconsciously sought, even the dissolution of self has its histories, and they are as ugly as the submission of self to consensual hallucination in the Nuremberg rallies. Precisely the denial of death has allowed it to become a tool in the management of souls. Endlessly vibrating in its bounded sphere of attractions and repulsions, the self is unable to emerge from a socially constructed cocoon, which, ironically, is what keeps it from socialisation. To secure its metamorphosis, it must embrace its dissolution. Though decked in the archaisms which Freud associates with regression, digital culture, from the shoot-'em-ups that dominate the games market to Hans Moravec's downloaded intelligence (Moravec 1988: 121–4), is built in the denial of mortality. As electronic surveillance corrodes the boundaries of the private self, and as the structures of selfhood change, the private moment of death becomes the last instance of dissolution, the final and unavoidable moment of self-loss. The crisis of digital reading concerns the difficulty of making a shift from a fatal future for the self to a social future for others – a future over which, by definition, we now can have no control.

Moravec is particular as to the personal nature of his survival, a combination of unique DNA and uniquely acquired characteristics forming a 'pattern' that can be electronically simulated. To some extent, you could argue that this has already happened: that the immense corporate and bureaucratic databases of the surveillance society have already downloaded as much of our personalities as are of interest to the formative agents of contemporary society. A panoptic, surveillance society which details the economic, moral and even bodily conduct of its citizens has already sacrificed the concept of privacy, which, as David Lyons argues, 'is inadequate to cover what is at stake in the debate over contemporary surveillance. At worst,' he continues, 'the dominant framework for the privacy debate – self-possessing, autonomous individualism – leaves us with a world of privilege where self-protection is only available to those who can negotiate it' (Lyon 1994: 196). The bashful rich may protect their secrets, while the battered wife may well wish hers were public. The obverse of the public sphere, privacy in its modern sense, only sprang into existence a matter of two centuries ago (see Habermas 1989, [1962]), and then only for a restricted part of the world's population. The family and the private individual have not proved strong enough sociological institutions to bear the weight of demands placed upon them as the centres of consumption and reproduction, sexual, physical and ideological, and as the reason why you would go on working and living.

Privacy, in the sense of a right claimed by the bourgeois individual to personal liberty, is too closely tied to private property, to gendered oppression, to the illusion of consumer sovereignty and to the sovereign, rational, white, male subject to be credible or defensible. Not only is the battle over privacy already lost; the end of the private makes even more urgent the publication of the intimate.

Databasing renders the person as a 'data-image', a statistically coherent version of the messy human self. It is an engraving of power which, notably in police surveillance of ethnic minorities, inscribes identity. At the same time, if 'it is not that the beautiful totality of the individual is amputated, repressed, altered by our social order, [but] rather that the individual is carefully fabricated in it, according to a whole technique of forces and bodies' (Foucault 1979: 217), then we have to ask whether the data-image is not at all a reduction of the full, 'real' self to 'mere' writing, but the constitution of a new, statistical and distributed self, a deconstructed, fully textual, rewritable file. Is that rewrite facility then a door to freedom, or one which, in the malleable form of electronic records, makes us more manipulable and so more predictable?

Digital storage can trace one branch of its family tree back to Herman Hollerith's development of punchcard calculators for the 1890 US census. Shurkin points out that there was 'no doubt that the use of the machines altered the content of the census – the questions were determined by the means of processing, not the other way round' (Shurkin 1996: 78). Mark Poster expands on this point to argue that 'the structure or grammar of the database *creates* relationships among pieces of information that do not exist in those relationships outside of the database . . . databases constitute individuals by manipulating relationships between bits of information,' eventually to constitute what he refers to as 'an additional self' (Poster 1990: 96–7), a kind of Derridean supplement that destabilises the solidity of the 'real' me. Identity, gender, nation, are abstractions we have woven out of the endless flickering of community, derivations from the void which we drape, fold and knit about ourselves to keep us warm, and to stop our selves from leaking out. The sacred mystery of the secular is not the body but its dissolution. It is discourse that produces the self, a discourse hypostatised as an autonomous historical agent. French poststructural thought is premised on this discursive turn, trapped within the universalising tendency it tries to subvert, because it sees in language or writing eternal, stable and universal entities. The text is substituted for the world, rendered into an object in its own right, and severed from a reality which it no longer describes but constructs.

Poster tries to minimise the damage of this abstraction by reintroducing history, insisting, against Derridean culture-blindness, on the specificity of electronic writing. He is right to distinguish between writing systems, but why stop at this single instance? Why not also mark as ruptures the shifts from the scrolls of the codex to the pages of the volumen, from black letter to classical typography, from hot metal to lithography in a Western chronology, and the differences between Kanji and Katakana, Kufic and cursive Arabic, synchronously in Japan and Islam? Does the motion between linear script and statistical matrix constitute the authentic gap? On the other hand, such dispersals of differences must be patched into an alternate set of continuities between pictographic, alphabetic, printed, typewritten and word-processed writing, and between Babylonian tally-sticks, Incan *quipu*, punchcards and electronic data tabulation. Storage and retrieval pose similar problems whether they are conducted with paper and card indexes, or electrons and search engines; it is the social formation which determines the selection and development of any given system at any given time. The technology of the English language has not become globally hegemonic because it is in some way better than its competitors, quite the contrary: it is evolving to meet the new demands of its global usage.

Equally problematic is the presumption of the disjuncture between the world and the text. This problem can be posed in two ways. Firstly, 'Whatever they do, authors do not write books. Books are not written at all. They are manufactured by scribes and other artisans, by mechanics and other engineers, and by printing presses and other machines' (Stoddard 1990, cited in Chartier 1994: 9). As Chartier emphasises, the text cannot be divorced from the materials or the institutions of its production and circulation. To emphasise the text at the expense of the book or the screen, the discourse at the expense of the institution, is to idealise it. Secondly, the more idealised the text becomes, the further it drifts away from a reality reduced to that which is represented. The text is the immaterial presence which re-presents the absent material. In this view, materiality is recognisable only in the gap between the world and the text, both of which become increasingly hyperreal in their divorce. Poster's assertion of the power of computer media to dematerialise the text is an extreme statement of this binary.

The reality from which we have been so profoundly alienated, according to this view, includes, perhaps is predominantly, other people. The theory of representation suggests we see in the book a flipping and flopping between presence/absence; but distance inhabits just that oblique dividing line, mediating between the poles, perceiving in the backslash not the abyss of *différance* but a space of uneven and distributed continuity. To restore the social requires dismantling the binary to build a concept of *mediation* between presence and absence, the fuzzy, analogue and shifting distance between the materiality of media, people and their objects. Strangely, the same objectification of the text is carried out in the cognitive sciences, where message is separated from sender, receiver and channel. Both deconstruction and cognitivism are premised on the isolated individual (despite the near miss of Minsky's 'society of mind' [1985]), and both insist on the absolute distinction between inner consciousness and outer reality. Chomsky's Cartesian linguistics (1966, 1972), for example, is dependent on the sense of an innate and therefore again profoundly desocialised concept of language. Though poststructuralism gives the sole power of agency to language as discourse, and cognitivism sees the same power ascribable to hardwired instinct, both agree that the agent of communication is not people. What both emphasise is the separation between subjects and objects. What both miss is the relation between people. Poster says that he is 'not claiming that in fact electronic messages enable some "total" or "true" act of self-constitution, but instead that a re-configuration of the self-constitution process, one with a new set of constraints and possibilities, is in the making' (Poster 1990: 118). He knows that it is important for critical theory to remain critical, so, having chucked out the idea of inherently textual resistance as a lure of the universal text, he replaces it with a historicised thesis about resistance: that it springs from the new technical interface. The limitation of this theory, apart from its residual technological determinism, is that it constrains the new process to resistance, and, in so doing, maintains the necessity for a dominant which resistance can resist. In this instance, what remains unchallenged is the centrality of the self.

Sociologically, we have to agree: the self is the prevailing sociological category of digital societies. But in the moment of its inflation to central function of social being, the individual becomes transparent, and the intimate structures of unconscious and repressed sociality begin to bleed across the interstices of e-mail and internet relay chat (IRC) lines, the newly feminised space of a sentimental, irresponsible, lurid but passionate intensity where, across the rules of the game, something other than mere fear of mortality and self-loss is in process. The principles of ludic reading are still intensely personalised, but their intimacies suggest that beyond the game's horizon, a different literacy is possible. A literacy founded neither on the rational concourse of discrete minds, nor on the abstract workings of a system of discourse, nor yet on the fine tuning of an innate disposition to language, articulates the deep socialisation which language, among other communications media, embodies; a socialisation prior to consciousness, and on which consciousness depends. That new distribution of reading will emerge from the present, textual mode, if at all, as a materialisation of the mode of writing.

Writing Materials

The distribution of reading belongs to the global distribution of the intimate. To think of reading as a distributed form is to consider the ways in which it produces, across the distance of space and time, a certain synchronic communion, and one in which the prize, especially in the accelerated distribution of the net, is a sharing not of power or knowledge but of the most private and secret things, which only become communicable in love or anonymity. A fine filigree of message paths clusters into nodes where a person can be defined, but it is the lace-work, not the node, which is the true artifice of communications webs. Here, in the commerce of a species in conversation with itself, the abstract goings-on of humanity are materialised and transfigured. What is shared is not pure thought encoded and decoded but communication itself, a mutual intimation of commonality, which has no being other than this spurned, ephemeral lattice of material mediations. Neither efficient nor inefficient, the channel is noise, and the message only a clustered coherence of noise, an aberration in the flow. Sourcing that noise in nature, mother, the body or deep structures of the brain is to misunderstand. There is only transient sociality, without origin, without cause. This brief threnody of transmissions is all there is to us, in our own transmission from silence to silence.

These perceptions make it possible to understand the autonomy of the text as a function of changing relations to death, the dissolution of the self. Our technologies are turned against that liberating void; their text is an anxious abstraction of that fabulous embroidery, a concrete form woven out of fluid passion, a garment to protect from the chill winds the reaper rides. Human communication in its purest form is material, and so transitory. The idealisation of the text is an effort to bootstrap into existence an abstract and so permanent concretion of these endless voices, endless erasures. Textual permanence seems to demand that we erase the body altogether, extending that self-hatred which runs through dieting to the fantasy of downloading the meat-mind into the matrix (see Sobchack 1995). Then the bad pun that mistakes the death of teleology for the end of history could transform the text into ideal reality. For Ibn Khaldun, the great historian of Islam, history did not require posterity; it was the arabesque rendered unto Allah, made of our blood and bodies that He alone may know. For today's secular prophets of the end of history, that arabesque becomes the infinite present of the text.

The terrible vertigo of Ranganathan and Bliss's endlessly divisible, endlessly extensible systematic organisation of knowledge is far more threatening than Hegelian teleology. It is not the state but the synergetic corporation that is triumphing, and neo-liberal postmodernism is its apologist. Ranganathan and Bliss extend the systematisation of knowledge to include the not yet known in the model of the management of change. Hegel can be falsified, but there is more than enough room for the falsification of Ranganathan to be included in his system. As Foucault argued, there is a correlation between individualisation as social imperative, and the homogenising capabilities of the catalogue:

> the power of normalisation imposes homogeneity; but it individualises by making it possible to measure gaps, to determine levels, to fix specialities, and to render the differences useful by fitting them to one another. It is easy to understand how the power of the norm functions within a system of formal equality, since within a homogeneity that is the rule, the norm introduces, as a useful imperative and as a result of measurement, all the shading of individual differences. (Foucault 1979: 184)

The universalisation of a textual system – which imposes individuality on data and data-images while denuding them of their semantic content, dematerialising all but their structuration – links the hyperindividuation of accelerated modernity with the playworld of the synergetic corporation.

What we must require of a digital aesthetic is not negation but refusal of the condition of the universal text, a secular blasphemy against the objectification of the world, our bodies and our others. Recorporealisation will imply, against the thingness of world, body and other, their mutual interpenetration, and it will depend on the materials in which they are mediated, including, as we shall see in Chapter 2, the mutual permeation of human and machine.

Mediation, a materialist aesthetic of mutuality and intimacy, needs to be distinguished from the emergent subjectivity of the networked corporation and its managerial philosophy of synergy. The rage to knowledge, the desperation of the attempt to quell the world through the power of analysis, answered a profound, intimate and social need of the imperial bureaucratic personality. Today that same goal is achievable through play. In the emergent ideogrammatic and montage aesthetics of early 20th-century literature and art, the first intimations of a new atomistic and synergetic order sniffed the air, looking at the time like a revolution against the old way, but destined to become hegemonic in the hyperindividuated era of the digital. The synergetic, gleaning from modernism its architectonics, not its explosive purpose, can now only mimic the utopian topos of play because it remains unfree; only resist an order which it cannot question or unseat because it is of it, dependent on what it resists. This incorporation of subversion into the dominant allows the resister to claim a kind of freedom: freedom from responsibility for their part in the processes of domination. Such is, for example, the irresponsibility of cyborg gender transformations, possible and legible only within the confines of patriarchy. What appears as release from the tyranny of gender's givenness is only the compulsory adherence to modes of masculinity and femininity which, like drag, are already formed in the patriarchal mould. Even the animals and geophysical entities – mountains, rivers – that pass as cyborg identities are still identities; belonging not to the in-human but to a playworld commodified as knowledge-forms, objects of knowledge rendered manipulable in synergetic ordering.

The world of Dewey and LC was the world of the 19th-century company, dedicated to the transformation of the world as raw materials. The world seen from inside the synergetic corporation is still a massed object for exploitation, but, transformed by the synthetic architecture of the new knowledge architectures, it becomes a form of the playworld. This produces the effect that Baudrillard reads as the simulacrum: the evaporation of reality into data and image flows. The observation is perfect; only Baudrillard has not taken account of the perspective that he gets from standing within the playworld of corporate Europe. The new corporate subject becomes correspondingly data-permeable, but never indiscrete. The agonistic regime of play ensures that each individual maintains his or her discretion – the ability to keep secrets, the ability to maintain distinct borders – and his or her competence. At the same time, it re-establishes a mode of socialisation apparently prior to the analytic, infinitely subdivisible world-object. The multiplication of selves, however, cannot restore unity to the subject–object relation between self and world. The synthetic organisation of knowledge reintegrates the world in the wake of its analytical division in the classical public library, but at the cost of becoming even more profoundly external to the subject, even as that subject reinvents itself in the masquerade. At its best, this relation can only be voiced as 'our' responsibility for the world (though rarely 'my' responsibility in an ethics formed in plebiscite), as if self and world were forever separate.

Kieslowski's film on fraternity, *Three Colours: Red* (1993), touches on this synergetic masquerade in a number of ways, between the opening process shot from the telephone message's point of view traversing the wired continent, and the televisual dénouement, exploring fragments of a social order in which the common decencies are all but impossible to live out. In the end, it is the erotic that triumphs, but an erotic experienced as distance – a poster flapping in the street, the transparency and rumbling phosphors of the TV image, the recovery of lost love by proxy. It is the distance that binds. Kieslowski's poetics of distance indicate the cost of connectivity established on the basis of solipsism. Affection, friendship, blur into the functions of sex and information, the sensuous into the reified, the commercial, the textual. The fraternal redemption of the wicked judge is accomplished as he sits close up to his TV screen. As so often on the internet, the anger, obsessions, grief and love you encounter electronically are intensified by the nebulousness of the connections. Always the loneliness works like a lens, the perpetually solo flight of the virtual navigator. The HCI is designed for one, not many: the lowest common denominator of liquid crystal displays. The interface retains from public and private reading the narcissistic rage to control, the selfishness of the single monitor which anyone who has tried to share one will recognise.

All the same, the networked return of the text incurs a newly naturalised virtual state of the interpersonal and, through the aesthetic tactic of the masquerade, the publication of the intrapsychic. This is its saving grace. The net's protocols evoke but cannot contain the voices of the unconscious which it must mobilise to attract users. Once summoned up, those desires are socialised, even if in a plebiscitary domain of self-categorisation and self-exploitation. Net anonymity, a function of privacy, billing and technical constraints, has, however, transcended both its instrumentalisation and its co-option into the reproduction of gendering, to enable more than the competitive model will allow. Evoking the desperation of the need to control, a need it cannot fulfil, the pseudonym allows need to evolve into a demand for freedom, that perverse freedom to which Botticelli was condemned, attempting to recreate the lost art of antiquity. The site of that freedom lies precisely at the horizon of the reading self.

When Ezra Pound wanted his poem to be the epic that would contain history, cruel history turned the tables on him and contained his poem. The distributions of reading assembled in the electronic interface have wanted to contain time, space and the world, but they have contained only reading, as a gale contains the leaf it tosses hither and yon. The physical universe dwarfs the textual temporally and spatially, and contains it. The textual, as both mediation and concept, is adsorbed to the material from which it seeks to divorce itself. The self, as textual, as technological, as bodily, is a mode of this materiality but, formed in the histories of globalisation in the centuries of empire, it has had to adapt as a sociological formation, becoming the absolute goal of looking out for number one, globalised as the individualist ethic, puffed up beyond its capabilities, and perhaps now coming to the end of its useful life. The textualisation of the universe and the hyperindividuation of the subject are synonymous, and both are failing. But to hasten along their closure in the name of some utopian society magically 'prior' to individuation and restricted to the self-replicating absolute of language is no solution, just another form of risk management.

These utopianisms arise for digital culture in the moment between its invention and its standardisation. The beginnings of a hypertext literature seem largely devoted to demonstrating the performativity of writing gathered around the magnetic poles of playful, instrumental and regressive readings, rather than questioning its structuration as digital; to investigating narrative and textuality rather than typographics, words and the relations between speech and writing. Invention in the material medium is the basis of mediation, of work at the level of the social relations in the material form of their processes. Neither commodity nor administered permission to play, reconvening the force of materiality in the interface of making, makes possible a recognition of the sociological facts of the here, the now, the world, the self in reading and beyond it. The purpose of the best of such works (such as those on George Landow's [1998] site and those published by Eastgate [1998]), digitally remastering the will to domination, has been to turn intellect to the purposes of its own extinction, a process which can be seen to full effect in Stuart Moulthrop's hypertext novel *Victory Garden* (1998). Yet if that purpose is to be fulfilled, it cannot be restricted to the dispersal of multiple personalities into the infinite but incapacitated text. To understand what is at stake in the textual interface, we have to look at practices which throw reading/writing formations into disarray.

David Connearn draws standing up, face to face with the plane of the paper. To draw a horizontal line freehand is his first discipline. For larger works it is a gesture not just of the hand but of the whole body moving across maybe two metres of paper. Focused like a mountaineer on the cliff-face of his surface, surveying its inwoven imperfections, the minutiae of textures and reflections, eyes, mind and body drawn to the fine point of the draughting pen, stance taut as an archer at one with the bow, at the moment not of release but of maximum tension. The pen is a prosthetic, an embedded instrument like a contact lens.

A line is straight, but to draw the perfect line without ruler and spirit-level is not just a discipline, it is a goal whose very impossibility and redundancy makes it, since it is nothing else, an art. As the line extends, the time and space of the drawing braid into a distance made of the dimensionless point where the focal meets the plane. A null point, the moving, unique and unrepeatable lead edge of the ink flow is as empty of significance as a mark can be – the full stop extended beyond even the punctiliousness of grammar, a punctuation without point, a point that, becoming a line, becomes pointless. Yet the vagaries of the freehand line, its necessary tribulation as the infinitesimal variations of ink flow, paper, breath and pulse intervene, inscape the traverse with the microhistory of its making transformed into the microgeography of the line, this line.

To make a mark is to express, in the sense of a forcing outward of the physical process of making. Quite unlike the *Sturm und Drang* of expressionism, with its claim that raw marks and raw emotions are the same, Connearn's line does not attempt to signify emotion, but to bring into the light the trace of its becoming. Under the first, he draws a second line, following the first, the counter-point that repeats the already meaningless, and on to the third and other lines, piling redundancy upon redundancy, pursuing that drawing which will never be made, in which every line is straight, its non-existent text in which this drawing would lose what presence it has as the detritus of its making. Repeating the banal until even its banality is imperceptible, Connearn's drawing is the opposite of that renewal of perception which powered synergetic modernism, his method one pursued, as he writes in some unpublished notes, 'not to see something for the first time – bright free epiphany // but its opposite . . . untill the task and doer start to exhaust location // and continue'. The intensity of the work derives not from the melismas of line upon line cascading in fields and folds after the work is over. These drawings are only the proof of an art that existed only in the time and place of its performance: its sarcophagus and its liturgy for the dead.

Connearn's line is less the product of the communicative design rationale of Klee's Pedagogic Sketchbooks or the randomising of Duchamp's Standard Stops, and more in the tradition of Christian Morgenstern's typographic poetry and Appollinaire's Calligrammes, an artist's accommodation to the endlessness of writing. Michael Heim (1987: 224), among many others, notes the 'superabundance' of prose in the word-processed world. Text interfaces promote a prolix and unjudged stylistic because of the very ease with which words can be generated and manipulated, and because no version is ever necessarily final. Unlike handwriting, which is tiring, the computer invites an easy input, through a set of skills so internalised that they no longer seem to block the route from thought to screen. Until the onset of carpal tunnel syndrome and repetitive stress injuries, the keyboard seems an utterly inexhaustible source of text. Connearn's line takes the minimum state of prose, the full stop, and extends it, into the American vernacular, as a period. It reduces the crafts of pen and paper to their root state, text to the purity of its becoming, its mediation at a moment of tension before it takes on the symbolisation of meaning, extending into unimaginable futurity the moment at which it will attain significance, the draw of the bow before the flight of the arrow.

And as to the question as to whether this practice of making is art: it is, in the sense that it respects the negativity that Adorno prized, the autonomy of this work from the functional logics of expropriation and control. But as script it works too to disgrace the majesty of the written by exposing the minimal conditions of its writing. At the same time, these drawings, some made not with ink but with the artist's own blood, or with his sweat collected in tiny vials, rearticulate the textual and the bodily, the way language, decorporealised in the sacrament of the text, is transubstantiated in the living sinew of the writer. Some pieces have been made with water collected at the sites of their drawing, reversing the logic of text as the mode in which the world is made 'all that is the case', a collection of objects for contemplation and ownership. In the water drawings, the logic of the null-text is of subordination of the making to the last random voices of a world that eludes human control: the weather, waves, the tide. But centrally Connearn's work engages the moment and the process in which the maximum presence of the subject to itself, involved in what is after all a sheerly playful because goalless enterprise, greets the dissolution of self into an act in which neither meaning nor perception anchors it in body or mind. Entirely anchored in its geotemporal making, entirely lost through it in an expression which leaves behind its trace no subject to fulfil the expressionist dream of authorship, Connearn's art of drawing can stand for the necessity of going deeper and deeper through the medium of selfhood and individuation if we are to uncover the possibilities of an emergent digital culture. Connearn, face to the wall, designs a signpost to a beyond which for us designates a secular and social wilderness that begins when this present and this self conclude, as they must, a moment ahead of the moving pen. In this work it is possible to conjure up the image of a digital reading which focuses not on the streams of words, but on the blinking cursor, a future not made of the endless extension of the empty present but in the plenum of confrontation with abjection and mortality, the

full.

Stop

.

2

VIRTUAL REALISM: MACHINE PERCEPTION AND THE GLOBAL IMAGE

Not so, Lil!
The Slinger observed.
Your vulgarity is flawless
but you are the slave
of appearances –
this Stockholder will find
that his gun cannot speak
he'll find
that he has been described.

(Dorn 1968: 32-3)

Travelling Light

'Civilities should be politely acknowledged; but, as a general rule, a book is the safest resource for "an unprotected female."' So Anne Bowman in an 1857 manual for young women which also recommends not looking out of train windows because 'the eyes and head usually become confused'. The fear of love combines with the fear of acceleration. In an inspired ideogram, Kate Flint links these comments to Augustus Egg's 1862 genre painting *The Travelling Companions*, showing two young ladies following its advice, and to this description from Letter 20 of Ruskin's *Fors Clavigera* of two young American women travelling in Europe:

> They pulled down the blinds the moment they entered the carriage, and then sprawled, and writhed, and tossed among the cushions of it . . . they had French novels, lemons and lumps of sugar to beguile their state with; the novels hanging together by the ends of string that had once stitched them, or adhering at the corners in densely bruised dog's ears, out of which the girls, wetting their fingers, occasionally extracted a gluey leaf. [Yet outside could be seen] blue against the southern sky, the hills of Petrarch's home. Exquisite midsummer sunshine, with low rays, glanced through the vine-leaves; all the Alps were clear, from the lake of Garda to Cadore, and to farthest Tyrol. (cited in Flint 1993: 106)

The railway train is closely linked to the emergence of cinema, its windows offering the kind of moving views for which the cinematograph was to become famous in the 1890s (see Kirby 1997). Ruskin's juxtapositioning of reading with the picturesque (rationalised and universalised through the reference to Petrarch) seems itself proto-cinematic, if not proto-televisual, calling to the visual as the redemption of the literal. But gendered care for the risk of vertigo generated by hurrying landscapes at the window – again mirrored in early film discourses – suggests another aspect of the relationships between culture and perception: culture as protection against the excesses of vision and socialization in an accelerating world. Curiously, it is the assured immediacy of reading as self-absorption which distinguishes it from the perils of a mediated perception dependent on an apparatus – rail or cinema. While the reader can immerse herself in an internalised world of narration, the visual opens vistas, promises clarity and renewal of perception. But Ruskin's articulation of the visible with the markers of both literature and painting gives this purification the lie: 'The traveller perceives the landscape as filtered through the machine ensemble' (Schivelbusch 1979: 27).

Jonathan Crary's analysis of the emergence of a modern visual regime in the early 19th century suggests that 'in the aftermath of Kant's work . . . vision becomes an object of knowledge . . . the visible escapes from the timeless order of the camera obscura and becomes lodged . . . within the unstable physiology and temporality of the human body' (Crary 1990: 70) such that 'the threshold between the physiological and the mental becomes one of the primary objects of scientific practice' (Crary 1990: 102) and 'observer and observed are subject to the same modes of empirical enquiry' (Crary 1990: 73). Crary's Foucauldian framework seeks an epistemological break between these two modes of vision, the one a pure evidence of the givenness of the world to an ordering rationality, the other embodied in the anatomy of the eye as an active participant in producing light and vision. For the purposes of digital aesthetics, the break comes with the invention of the body as a category of knowledge, while there is a continuity in the gradually shrinking kernel of mind externalising more and more of its own physicality. But contrary processes have also been afoot since the late 19th century, histories of the gradual dispersal of subjectivity through the body and into its linkages with the machinery of perception. For digital aesthetics, the political question of cyborg vision concerns less the 19th-century problematic – whether the proper study of vision involves investigation of optical processes in an external world, or of the subjective processes of perception – than whether vision as a whole, optical and subjective, can be allowed to become the sole property of a hyperindividuated mind, or whether it can be prompted to produce a new socialisation through a symbiosis of bodies and machines.

Critique of Cyborg Vision

The 'machine ensemble' of Schivelbusch's *Railway Journey* is made up of track, engine and carriages, the telegraph, the timetable: all the elements which make of the rail system a single device, including the panoramic views it affords. He cites early travellers' anecdotes of rail travel as alienating compared to the leisurely, meandering, human-scaled and human-paced integration of self and countryside that you get walking, riding or in animal-powered vehicles on roads and waterways. Analogies with work on the cinematic apparatus (see Baudry 1976, 1985; de Lauretis and Heath 1980), which conjugates the combinations of camera, projection and psyche, are more than metaphoric in the institution of Hale's Tours in the early years of this century, film projections in swaying and clattering simulations of railway carriages (see Fielding 1983; Musser 1991: 260-5). Cinemascope and other widescreen processes of the 1950s, and more recently IMAX and OMNIMAX presentations, share the fascination with visualisations of transport (see Belton 1992; Wollen 1993), and the contemporary 'ride movies' featured at amusement parks like Universal Studios Tour and Disneyland Paris continue the tradition. The histories of the photomechanical and electronic arts could be read as the narrative of assimilation and internalisation of a combined communications (transport and mediation) apparatus in an ever-larger urban population. The movement from the machine ensemble of rail through the cinematic apparatus to virtual reality would then be just a hop, skip and a jump. This smoothness belies the insecurity of the transition.

The processes of perception have been understood as in crisis or at risk for more than a hundred years. The last realms of unquestioned perception are the experimental sciences, which have had to develop intensely technical vocabularies to preserve their right to empiricism. The parallel subordination of the natural world to technologies of knowledge and vision is experienced as the increasing impossibility of seeing things 'as they are', and the absurdity of the attempt: 'a tune upon the blue guitar' (Stevens 1955: 165ff.). A sense of the perceptual as artifice reproduces a dialectic between responsiveness to observation, on the one hand, and, on the other, respect for the compositional allure of artistry and the elegance of scientific hypothesis-formation. To some extent, every visualisation is a symbol system. But among such systems, there are those with a claim to a heightened responsiveness to reality, like air traffic control radar screens, many of which therefore take a heightened degree of responsibility for the effectiveness of their imaging. At the opposite extreme are the film archivists, more concerned for the authenticity of the means of reproduction than with faithfulness to the reproduced scene (see Hertogs and de Klerk 1996; and Paolo Cherchi Usai's dictum, 'Every print of a film is a unique object, with its own physical and aesthetic characteristics, and therefore it cannot be considered identical to other prints with the same title' [Usai 1994: 67]). Jean Baudrillard's conception of the mediated world as simulacrum is an attempt to envision the resolution of this dialectic of the object world and the object medium by means of the mutual dissolution of all objects in the welter of their mass-produced representations. Baudrillard's act of ignoring both the materiality of the medium and responsibility for its use provides one of the commonest senses of the word 'virtual'.

Michael Heim identitifes six more technical definitions: the appearance of

simulated 3D space on 2D monitors; interaction with electronic representations; immersion in hard- and software environments; the telepresence
familiar from keyhole surgery; 'full-body immersion' permitting interaction
with digital environments without constricting hardware; and immersive networked communications, which allow more than one user to create and
interact in virtual space, like Jaron Lanier's 'RB2' (Reality Built for Two)
(Heim 1993: 110–16) or Seiko Mikami's 'Molecular Informatics' of 1997
(see Hoekendijk 1996: 32e). Despite complaints of the lack of 'humanity' in
some of these instances (surgeons deprived in remote-controlled operations
of a sense of whom they are operating on; the notorious application of virtual skills in Desert Storm), proponents of virtuality like Lanier or Myron C.
Krueger (1983, 1991) embrace Baudrillard's culture of artifice. All our drugs,
diets, prosthetics, architecture, cities, transport and communication already
sever us from 'natural' existence: surely we are best to plunge into synthetic
dimensions? Human space dissolves into geographical space in the railway
age, and the geographical into virtual in the electronic. The historical logic is
serene.

Even where the value of a virtual construct lies in its reference to the
actuality of the public domain – as in David Gelernter's 'mirror worlds',
virtual environments simulating and linking to real-time civic debate and
services (Gelernter 1991) – the movement towards artifice is also one towards
abstraction: the same abstraction as Flint's women folding their reading
about them like a carapace against the accelerations of sex and society; the
same abstraction as Ruskin's attempt to render the view as historically validated picturesque. From railway reading to the virtual worlds of Krueger,
Lanier and Gelernter, the relations of self, world and medium are reconfigured. Their interaction converges not on the page, the view or the
cathode-ray display, but in the eye, which, to take on this role as mediator,
must leave the dog-eared bounds of sensual reality. The disembodied eye,
becoming textual arbiter of distance and difference, is always recognisable
because it is alone, the objective of all rays but the resting place of none.
Even the stereoscopic headsets used in VR kits draw the envisioned space
into focus around a tight and single nub of control: self as focal point,
dimensionless centre of all dimensions.

The development of this monoptic vision is as important for the virtual
physiology of sight as perspective and its disruptions are for the development
of painting and the naturalisation of the view from the carriage window. At
the same time, for the private reader closing the final page and returning to
the real, for Ruskin's picturesque interrupted by the giggling feminine asocial,
and for the training of the eye in virtual systems, there always remains a nag-
ging doubt as to the completeness of the textual universe in which they have
been enchanted, a suspicion that allows perception the constant recourse of
retreat from composition and hypothesis, returning always to its own corpo-
reality, though altered by its passage through an other-authored universe.
The pulse of disembodiment and recorporealization is the flutter captured so
well in cinematic suturing of the gaze from shot to shot, and whose pulses are

regulated in the interlaced scanlines of video and even more in the pixel arrays of VDU graphic displays. The virtual can then be understood as a perspective that looks on this perpetual motion as a perpetual vanishing. In this first instance, the intensively symbolic nature of digital imaging seems the defining instance of the philosophy of the hyperreal. But even the mathematical and logical symbol systems of computer science have their own physical and interpersonal attributes.

The development of digital imaging takes its roots in George Boole's algebra of propositions (1916 [1854]), first formulated as an extension of Leibniz's design for a rational calculus and evolving in the same time frame as the universal catalogue. Boole gradually elevates logic's level of abstraction, from simplified natural language statements which can be classed as true or false, to a symbolic system which can make metastatements about conditions of truth and falsehood without recourse to either semantic content or natural speech. Operating as a branch of pure mathematics, Boolean algebra was the centre for the development of both modern symbolic logic and computer science through the realisation (formalised by Claude E. Shannon in 1938) that the binary truth values of symbolic logic could work as the operational logic of switching. Though the perfectibility of formal systems is inherently limited by Gödel's paradox (see page 54), technologists find in Boole as close as possible to a perfect object language, which, by emptying formal propositions of interpretable meanings, renders them manipulable. If the very purity of its symbols leaves it beyond the realm of experience, it has the virtue of Ranganathan's catalogue: that by marshalling natural language statements in pragmatically formalised symbols, it maintains the system as indefinitely extensible. In this sense, the logic architectures of computers are not out of touch with the real world, but, in processing it to a towering level of formality, refer to it less through indexical figuration than through the index, the catalogue, the structure of knowledge. The mid-1980s collapse of a number of expert systems based on highly linear heuristics demonstrated the limitations of one form of logic engineering. But as a result, artifical intelligence (AI) researchers, reintroducing the principle of parallel and distributed computing previously abandoned (Crevier 1993: 197–216), approximated even more closely both to the Bliss–Ranganthan synthetic catalogue and to synergetic management. Instrumental reason is by no means dependent on the supposed linearity of the print era.

Pursuing analogies with the more formalizable findings of both neurobiology and cognitive psychology, the kind of advanced computers used in image processing attempt to emulate the interweaving of thought patterns, themselves increasingly conceived on a social model. Marvin Minsky's equally controversial and influential *The Society of Mind* (1985), for example, describes mind as a competitively synergetic, self-administrating corporation, breaking jobs down into subtasks under the hierarchic guidance of referendum-managed goal-setting. Since cognitive psychology takes its cues from the physiology of the brain, it is extremely difficult for it to see beyond the horizon of individuation. To take individual rather than species behaviour as core study leads invariably to understanding social interaction as the play between fully independent, individual entities, rather than individuation being conceived of as a function of socialisation. Similarly, studies of perception since the ground-breaking work of David Marr (1982; see also Gardner 1987: 295–322) have concentrated on issues of stereopsis and image-recognition from the point of view of the isolated individual. Johnson-Laird gives an unwitting nudge in a different direction when he remarks that seeing in depth 'must be guided by innate constraints deriving from the nature of the physical world. Once the elements have been matched, the rest of stereopsis is largely trigonometry' (Johnson-Laird 1993: 97). At face value, this description matches the Chomskyan 'language instinct' thesis (Pinker 1994), with an innate geometric sense organising environmentally contingent perceptions. But I would also suggest that human vision, with its alertness to peripheral movement and its limited capacity for registering objective depth, may not have evolved as a sensory apparatus for the individual, but as a social instinct, reliant on awareness of where your fellows are in the environment, and the ability to triangulate their position, your own, and that of a potential threat or food.

It is already clear within neuroscience that the brain is not physically separable from the body; that, on the contrary, it inhabits, through the nervous system, the whole anatomy. Phenomenology teaches us that the mind is not even bounded by the body, but reaches out into the world, and is in turn touched by it (Merleau-Ponty 1968: 130–55). The material environment enters into the mental as perceptions, as diet, and, in an increasingly urban society, as the artificial *Umwelt* of architecture, urban planning, traffic, pollution, and so on. That environment is also crowded with others, people it is now second nature to avoid bumping into in the street, or whose gaze you automatically follow to see what they might be looking at. Pinker's study of language leads in this more social direction, as he investigates the processes of language acquisition as the socialisation of innate vocal range and the (possibly instinctual) structures of syntax (Pinker 1994: 262–96). Yet cognitive studies of perception seem still to be trapped in the individualist paradigm.

Individualist bias in scientific psychology may explain why the visual interfaces emulated by photographic technologies, and even more so those associated with computer imaging, are so monocular. Not only are the scale and shape of monitors designed for personal use, but the perspective of the single virtual eye/camera which gives access to virtual constructs in 2D and, more surprisingly, in 3D representations is entirely Cartesian, despite the fact that what is being given visual form in the interface is a matrix of binary integers, rather than the object-world analogue of photography (Cubitt 1992). To render mathematically generated digital imagery in these 'familiar' and 'user-friendly' versions is not only culturally imperialist; it demands that data be rendered in terms of visualities like the map and monocular perspective which are determinedly instrumental, and have to be applied to the data as a second layer of non-intrinsic regimes of looking. Framing and composition are, to some extent, intrinsic to photography and film: in some sense, they give credibility to images by offering the evidence that a device has been physically present at the moment of shooting. But veering computer-generated imagery (CGI) towards perspective and the map serves no such function, except to produce the images as images *for* a specific kind of viewer.

From the point of view of the computer, there is neither vision nor visual display, only binary arrays and logic trees. To translate from machine perception to visual construct is, then, a further level of abstraction, rather than a concretisation of formal properties. What we see in computer graphics is only one of many possible representations, by no means all visual, of the same data strings. Whether the original inputs derive from lens-based media, from the manipulation of graphic symbols, from microphones, radar or from pure mathematics, the systems of representation employed in videographics must be understood as renditions of machine code in culturally specified forms. As engineering solutions, they devolve upon assumptions concerning likely users. As psychologically optimized, they depend on the principle of individuation. And as visual representations, they belong to an historical dialectic between vision as unmediated and image-making as language. Most of all, the symbolic operations of machine perception are deprived of those central semantic functions of socialised communication – indexicality, reference, articulation and address – which might provide them with the location which otherwise they cannot achieve. The digital yearns for the organic with the same passion with which the text longs for the reader. We have, however, created HCIs articulated only with a normative visual culture, crushing machine perceptions into conformity with a narrow definition of ours. Because we have considered the relation between human and machine as instrumental and prosthetic (subordinating and conforming machines to the requirements of human instrumentality), and even more because we have created them in the image of an ideally isolated individual, we have denied our computers the use of the shifters (here, now, you, we . . .) that might transform their servitude into partnership.

At the same time, we have denied ourselves that genuine interplay between the apparatus and the filmmaker, the apparatus and the audience, which, Vivian Sobchack argues, forms the basis for a utopian project of intersubjectivity in the cinema. Sobchack argues that 'instrument mediation', founded in the primacy of communication, is embodied in the relation between filmmaker and camera as well as the relation between spectator and projector, and that it is the relation between these two relationships that produces the 'dynamic complexity' of the simultaneously human and mechanical experience of film (Sobchack 1992: 169–202). While Sobchack's phenomenology of embodied perception suggests an achieved democracy of human–mechanical relations, I believe that her argument is specifically aesthetic, in that it describes a state of affairs that could, that should, but which does not yet exist. By abrogating, through the design of the apparatus, all the subjectivity in the production of images to ourselves, and allocating all the objectivity to our devices, we have, perhaps against the grain of the mutuality inherent in the cinema, condemned ourselves to an unstable and unhappy solipsism. Indeed, films have suffered in this sense from the arrival of CGI, as they turn from narrative forms that intrigue and inveigle into spectacles that engulf and bludgeon. This means, not that we are subjected to technologies of vision, but, far worse, that we are subjects only of ourselves, mediated through machineries downgraded to mere feedback loops. From this standpoint, the digital revolution is over, and in determining on victory rather than equality, we have achieved only a hollow conquest over that part of ourselves that most longs for dialogue. Some of the instability of this unhappy relation, and a space in which Sobchack's utopian intersubjectivity might find an opening, derives from the sheer capacity of sight, human or mechanical, for surprise, not just when faced with the proliferation of otherworldly virtual scenes, but marvelling at elaborate displays of scientific imaging, where the question concerning reality returns to a regime of seeing otherwise apparently in thrall to the untrammelled subjectivity of the hyperreal.

The Anarchy and Society of Perceptions

Stan Brakhage's famous 'Metaphors on Vision' essay proposes mechanical perception as a recovery of the prelapsarian vision proper to the young child, a vision whose powers we have lost in the lugubrious descent into verbal language and the need to control, through the organization of sight, the more frightening aspects of the world:

> How many colours are there in a field of grass to the crawling baby unaware of 'Green'? How many rainbows can light create for the untutored eye? How aware of variations in heat waves can that eye be? Imagine a world alive with incomprehensible objects and shimmering with an endless variety of movement and infinite gradations of color. Imagine a world before 'the beginning was the word'.
>   . . . Once vision may have been given – that which seems inherent in the infant's eye, an eye which reflects the loss of innocence more eloquently than any other human feature, an eye which soon learns to classify sights, an eye which mirrors the movement of the individual toward death by its increasing inability to see.
>   But one can never go back, even in imagination. (Brakhage 1963)

Quite properly, Brakhage asserts an aesthetic based not in stripping away cultural determinations but in adding to them: accumulating hallucinations, dreams, visions, the effects of light generated in the eye itself, the permutations of light in natural phenomena and in the photomechanical media as a route to the renewal of vision in a world overdetermined by conceptual knowledge. His imagination works through education, not regression; not through the revelation of self in the encoding of 'freedom' as gesture and crude technique in expressionism, but by an understanding that the language of camera movement and printing effects is the very substance of the film. There is neither self nor expression without the materials of visual or verbal language in which it is possible to express them. The self and its perceptions are always, already, rhetorical.

Digital imaging confronts this rhetorical function almost as soon as invented, for example in the analogue-computer films of Jordan Belson and John and James Whitney, films which, as Gene Youngblood says, are not abstract but 'concrete, objective experiences of kinaesthetic and optical dynamism' (Youngblood 1970: 157). Electronic art began by boasting its own artifice. But at the same time, the nascent digital image acted in revelatory mode, distinguishing the indistinguishable multitude of ephemeral moments that make up the particle clouds of light. The beauty of the films lies in this dialectical relationship between manifest artifice and excessive and involuntary recording of detail. Though the artists staged events on home-made animation rostrums and rotoscopes, no human control could have ordered the multiple variables into coherence. Perhaps, then, Brakhage has a point when he argues that cinema has a specific capacity for renewing vision, registering far more than intention envisages: the marvels of an apparatus autonomous of our scopic regimes.

Much of the practice of emergent electronic imaging contests the essential apparatus of cinema, TV and computing. Belson, the Whitneys, Brakhage and the influential Canadian animator Norman MacLaren were engaged in reconstructing the exposure and printing of celluloid outside or against the grain of the usual machines. But where for expressionists the equivalent innovations offer a gain in self-expression, for these artists there is rather a devolution of self into its relationships – with the production machinery, with the perceptible, with the rhetoric of film – which at the same time gives the light which is their raw material the possibility of embodiment on its own terms. So their relationship with light is at heart a social one, rendering to each fragment of vision its materiality, allowing it an autonomy through which it can enter into relationships – with the filmmaker, with the viewer, with other perceptions. The dominant apparatus – the shared technique, physical and psychic, of mainstream cinema, television and CGI – moves towards a generalised bonding of particular perceptions to perception in general, coordinating the data of a specific sight with visual, spatial and temporal regimes, and conforming them to the requirements of the catalogue. It models the psychic elements of the apparatus in atomized audiences united only by their separation from one another and their construction of perceptions, and indeed perception itself, as further objects to be dominated. The autonomous and material perceptions offered by the experimental electronic media of the 1960s were the logical outcome of such a universalising apparatus, even as they turned towards its unmaking. In effect, these experiments failed because they took on the hegemonic at the level of its own microprocesses. What is at stake now, thirty years later, is whether it is possible to produce works outside that horizon.

In 'Acinema', Jean-François Lyotard attempts to rescue screen media from the commodity form of dominant visual organization through the metaphor of pyrotechnics:

when a child strikes [a] match-head *to see* what happens – just for the fun of it – he enjoys the movement itself, the changing colours, the light flashing at the height of the blaze, the death of the tiny piece of wood, the hissing of the tiny flames. He enjoys these sterile differences leading nowhere, these uncompensated losses; what the physicist calls the dissipation of energy. . . . Thus if he is assuredly an artist by producing a simulacrum, he is one most of all because this simulacrum is not an object of worth valued for another object. . . it is essential that the entire erotic force invested in the simulacrum be promoted, raised, displayed and burned in vain. (Lyotard 1978: 53–4)

The essay, which articulates with Lyotard's interventions against the universalising of language models in cultural criticism (Lyotard 1971), posits a cinema of disembodied *jouissance*, of intensities and energies unbounded by the reasons of beauty or use, encoded in industrial cinematic representation and narrative through the elimination of 'aberrant movements, useless expenditures, differences of pure consumption . . . a fecund and assembled whole transmitting instead of losing what it carries' (Lyotard 1978: 55). Yet Lyotard's model of the acinematic viewer as polymorphously perverse pyromaniac anchored in the moment of bliss misses two of Brakhage's major achievements: to understand that there is no return to the infantile, and to free perception and perceptions from the narcissistic control of the viewer. Infantilism is, as in regressive modes of reading, a characteristic not of liberation but of hyperindividuation: the self-centred solipsism of *jouissance* denies the communicability of material perceptions. In his attempt to free cinema from the universalism of visual 'language', Lyotard has merely substituted its obverse: a universal (and curiously silent) aphasia. It is a cinema of resistance, caught in the dialectic of that which it seeks to unseat.

Lyotard here poses a thesis whose presuppositions are not far removed from Godzich's fear of the power of images: the glut of pictures seems more obvious than the glut of words, and more compelling. You sense that images have a kind of power, but bow before a second sense that there are just too many of them for each to correspond to an effect. More, the traditions of picture-making are so entrenched that there seems only the possibility of unmaking them. Yet we cannot do without images, or scrabble back into the pigment world; undo the pixelisation of vision or remaster the mass as individual. We are condemned to image-making; not even the digital will undo the thirst for lens media, even if they are, as they have always been, evidence of nothing but what we wished to believe in the first place. Lyotard's acinema is not quite a recurrence of expressionism, despite his references to Rothko and Pollock, but its concern for abstraction retains the sense that the purpose of machine perception (which he indicates disingenuously by the names Eggeling and Richter) should be that 'the represented ceases to be the libidinal object, while the screen itself, in all its most formal aspects, takes its place' (Lyotard 1978: 59); to provide, in any case, an object, whose evidenciary status will depend upon its mobilization of pleasure. In voiding the screen of semantic content, he completes the regressive solipsism of the viewer, consolidating the infantile unification of the world despite its perceptual fragmentation. We can, with Brakhage, demand more of mediated vision than an amnesia masquerading as the abolition of the world in favour of the simulacral, accomplished by privileging the screen over the flicker.

The virtual culture demands a return to the fraught question of realism (see Corner's astute 1992 résumé of the problematic history of the concept). Certainly, Tagg's (1988) assertion that there can be no universal concept of realism, and that we require a more diversified recognition of realisms, is an important first step. Brakhage's practice might be aligned with one kind, the metonymic structure of naturalism, a use of the telling detail as a clue to a whole environment. A more familiar sense of realism as documentation, and especially as encyclopedic, gained its highest currency among photographers of the first part of the 20th century, in a line including Jacob Riis, Lewis Hine, Eugene Atget, August Sander and the Federal Security Administration collection administered by John Stryker, a tradition always open to criticisms of voyeurism. In the absence of working-class distribution channels, largely smashed by Stalinism, fascism and anti-communism during the 1920s and 1930s, the tendency has been for documentary photography to create a sense of otherness and objectification, even to the extent of sacrificing authorship to the political and judicial discourses of scientific authenticity. As a result, 'a special domain of technical, instrumental photography was produced, interlocking with special domains of writing and speaking, regulated by prohibitive limits to who might pronounce on what and under what circumstances, and by strict controls over the dissemination of appropriate literacies' (Tagg 1992: 111–12). Abigail Solomon-Godeau quotes Sally Stein (1983) on Jacob Riis' photos of New York slums of the 1880s arguing that, in Riis' reform tracts, writing and photography combine to form a matrix 'constituted by the threat posed by large numbers of poor, unassimilated recent immigrants, the specter of social unrest, the use of photography as a part of the larger enterprise of surveillance, containment, and social control, and the imperatives of "Americanization"' (Solomon-Godeau 1991: 175), while in her analysis of the canonisation of Atget she lends elliptical support to the thesis of lost authorship, arguing that because of his prolific and dispersed production, 'the nettlesome problems that crop up in the fabrication of the author Atget . . . require strategies of containment or denial that inevitably engender forms of textual anxiety' (Solomon-Godeau 1991: 30). Atget's coding system for his archive derived, indeed, not from an ideology of authorship, but, according to Rosalind Krauss, 'from the card files and topographic collections for which he worked. . . . And it seems clear that Atget's work is the *function* of a catalogue' (Krauss 1985a: 142).

In the age of mechanical perception, the functions of the catalogue have themselves been automated, most obviously in the modernisation of the surveillance camera, which, as close-circuit television (CCTV), can not only maintain a vigilant eye on the endlessly boring vistas of car parks and platforms, but in recent systems is smart enough to register deviations from normal activities and recognise suspect individuals from a crude facial geometry. On the one hand, this can be read as an extension of the panoptic process, guided by an extreme variant on normative pattern recognition. On the other, given that recent crime statistics in the UK suggest a failure among the populace to internalise the panoptic principle, and given the crux of the anti-realist cultural studies establishment faced with the semiotically inspired defence in the Rodney King case, the real returns as an aesthetic category, even allowing for those critical histories of photography that argue the relativisation of truth as discourse.

Alfredo Jaar is a realist photographer. His installations based on shots of social conditions in the opencast goldmines of the Brazilian *sertão* are famous. If he has lighter and less perfectible equipment than his professional colleagues, he can take longer, as an artist rather than an agency snapper, to work into the lives he has elected to portray. But the work he undertook in 1994–5 is not only about lives. It is about Rwanda, the genocide of April–June 1994, and its aftermath in Rwanda itself and in the refugee camps of Zaïre, Democratic Republic of Congo, a world where imagination and solidarity are driven to their limit. As if a sixth of the population of London were dead and floating bloated down the Thames before the startled eyes of their children and grandmothers. When Jaar, Chilean, showed his mine photos in the New York Subway as 'Rushes', he attached the daily updated price of gold. That is solidarity. But how to picture this suffering?

The question is not entirely moral, but at the hinterland between ethics and aesthetics. The danger is identified by Kathleen Newman in her analysis of a novelisation of torture in Argentina: 'Though the scene does not immediately appear to be different from the documentation in *Nunca Más* [the Amnesty International report on the dirty war in Argentina], it is exploitative in that, having created a female character who has endured countless acts of brutality, the author objectifies her as an object of torture' (Newman 1992: 177). Jaar has put his Rwandan photographs in black boxes about the size of video cassette cases with brief, dispassionate notes in white type describing the photograph inside. Many boxes bear the same legend, and are piled or laid out in geometric stacks and grids. The images can already be conjured up in minds saturated with their kin, blinded in the struggle against the sentimentalism of spectacle, which enjoys without taking responsibility. Giving each person, in the graveyard of boxes, a name of their own, an age and an address, while hiding their faces, disallows the tired or sheerly racist response to post-colonial atrocities. Jaar's silence and invisibility attack the ideological agendas of the UN and the proxy wars of superpowers; when he speaks in response to questions it is to support non-governmental aid, the brute necessities of water-purification, clinics, post-colonial agencies for ex-colonial disaster.

Because in the interface of the ethical and the aesthetic, what counts is the response, and this exhibition, with its dark spotlit geometries of boxes upon boxes, is a cemetery, a necrology for the pledge that photography would reveal the world. Despite the cropping, burning and other darkroom techniques of an older practice; despite the routine digital manipulation of illustrative and, increasingly, editorial photography (see Becker 1991), photography still indicates the real, but to an audience that responds with the epistemophilia of spoilt children who want to see. While literate theory propounds that ours is an epoch governed by the visual, Jaar's art speaks of image-death, and if the bones in these boxes are the relics of the slaughtered and bewildered, they are also the last resting places of panoptic truth. In a separate room, information about the genocide and its aftermath, press coverage and photoessays, books by Fanon and Winston Rodney, make contexts for Jaar's focus. Along the walls, on file cards, visitors respond. It is hard to judge their writings. Some are genuinely baffled, many genuinely grateful. A lot are compassionate. A solid selection are livid: 'Where are the photographs?', 'Why can't I see?' The monument, the archive, the silence. The exhibition is called 'Real Pictures' and carries the motto 'Images have an advanced religion: they bury history'.

Formal as the installation is, and though it operates at a high level of abstraction, its concern is not with the totality of knowledge but with its edge. To confront these deaths, it is necessary to confront your own death, in the only way that this photography can find: the graveyard of images. Like Brakhage, Jaar has remade the apparatus – of the exhibition – in order to render to these images the autonomy of invisibility, a mechanical perception which does not need to conform to the administration of news. The wire service snap is always pixellated, snapped off from its source, a fragment in freefall whose only anchor is its destination, the private viewer. The first act in remaking the solidarity of viewer and world is to work at the level of the grain, the autonomous camera, to discover the uneasy solidarity between image and imaged. Jaar's anti-display articulates image with image, viewer with image, mortal viewer and mortal subject, in a society of perception that reconvenes the solidarity it is so hard to feel in an iconorrhoeic world. That articulation of solidarity is the foundation of the rhetoric of images. It entails a trust in the photographer, and a faith in the apparatus, which turns the grammar of spectacle into the form of the social, and the very dissolution of the self in death into the matter of interdependence.

Visual Rhetoric: The Socialisation of Perception

Few images are more haunting than the view of Earth from space, and few more remote from the combination of formal reticence with anger, urgency and action in Jaar's Real Pictures. The vulnerability and boundedness of this globe seen by bounded and vulnerable astronauts is perhaps the last exhalation of auteur photographic analysis. From the position of one hung in freefall in an eggshell of air, the swirling blues and whites etched in endless dark look like nothing so much as a life-support system whose value has suddenly and dramatically become clear. If one image could culminate and justify the heroic era of technology, and at the same time symbolise why it must end, this is it. Its international reduplication is more than an ideological achievement of the United States' military-industrial complex; it dramatises the ecological understanding which, despite the supposed end of grand narratives, dominates Western thought in the last years of the century, while at the same time responding to the need for belief after the death of God. Even where the divine is still a possible category of thought, this image of the globe is a global image, in every sense.

Satellite images have less impact, not because we are inured to marvels, but because they are harder to interpret and, because less ethically demanding, less involving. Ironically, because of their superfluity, subsequent images of the Earth from space matter less, as if intensity of experience were the criterion that marks out the Apollo shot of the Earth from its predecessors and successors. But it is not intensity, but rather the commonality of perceptions that enriches both them and their viewers. What made and still makes the Apollo view so powerful is not just its emblematic value but its independence: it is a photograph – one of the last taken with an ordinary camera, with a negative that had to be brought back physically to the earth – that tells us what we want to believe, but does so from a position which, though once occupied by a cameraman, is inhuman. It redoubles the power of human sight by articulating it with mechanical perception. The camera, after all, doesn't care about the fate of the planet and its mortal freight. This is the source of its beauty: we have to supply the care. Which we do by articulating this image to a society of perceptions, few enough of which are our own or even human.

Rimbaud, the anarchic 19th-century poet, undertook a long and arduous derailing of all the senses to become *voyant*, a seer. A different strand of modern culture, from Seurat's war against expressive gesture to Le Corbusier's demolition of organicism in favour of 'machines for living in', had instead the aim of becoming machine. The danger of this approach was not, as humanist critics from Chaplin to Huxley have argued, that this delivers the human to the mechanical, but that it forces machines to act like humans. Nowhere is the glamour, the conviction, the value and the social commitment of mechanisation clearer than in the pedagogic writings of Eisenstein, the Soviet film director, and no-one has equalled the intensity of his practical and critical analysis of the relations between human and mechanical perception. For Eisenstein, the tools of his art are the events in front of the camera and the exposed film strip, and its material the audience. To engineer the responses of the latter, the former must be sharpened by an immense post-aesthetic remaking of the notion of effect in the service of the revolution. This revolution, be it said, was not (at least until the rise of Stalin) a remote, longed-for millennium, but right through the 1920s the gradual production of a new way of life on a daily basis. This was a utopia of the everyday, and, like Jaar's, a struggle for the adequate undertaken as a visionary quest.

Eisenstein's aesthetic, especially his sprawling theoretical formulations on montage, works simultaneously in the world as it is and the world as it might become. On the one hand, the scarcity of the means of cinematic production brought them to intense focus for Eisenstein and his contemporaries: every film had to be of the most advanced kind, driven by a sense of the value of every film as both an enormously potent medium for social cohesion and instruction in a time of rapid change, and as a laboratory prototype without the luxury of the Hollywood studios' serial production, which allowed approximative solutions to systemic problems. In his debates with the radical Kino-Eye director Dziga Vertov, Eisenstein replied to criticisms that his story-films were in hock to the fictionalisations of the entertainment film by critiquing Vertov's espousal of the documentary. Raw reality, unorganised, could never achieve maximal effectivity, and could never form part of the overall subordination of the film's moments to its architectonics, its montage (Eisenstein 1988). Instead, Eisenstein argued the case for a cinema which would escape the magical powers of mimesis through an emphasis on composition, on the *mise-en-scène*, the frame, the shot, the editing and the whole film. Documentary was mere imitation. Like the sympathetic magic that drives a betrayed lover to destroy photos of the philanderer, or the symbolic objects surrounding a dead pharoah, or the stock markets trade in 'objects that only exist on paper', for the documentary, 'The difference between form and reality is non-existent' (Eisenstein 1993: 68). The speculative regime dreams of managing reality through formal manipulations. But these magical administrations, in mirroring form alone, ape events without grasping their structure. In their place Eisenstein argues for a vision that pierces the secrets of matter, that reveals what lies beneath the surface, the bones beneath the skin (see Yampolsky 1993). He declaims 'Mastery of principle is the real mastery of objects' (Eisenstein 1993: 67), and in an early draft even speaks of 'Man as means'. Not even the human is sacrosanct in the demand for a visual art dedicated to unearthing the paucity of the present and the immanence of the future.

Eisenstein's critique of imitation is easily misread as adopting a 'modernist' aesthetic grounded in the disjuncture of signifer and signified, the privilege given to the materialities of the medium over its meanings. Yet, as romantic-expressionist belief in self-expression emphasises the *jouissance* of the solipsistic individual, so the art of the free-floating signifier identifies with the commodity as object. To free the materiality of art from the duties of signification is to reproduce the absolute autonomy of the commodity form in the moment of exchange, divorced from production, consumption and its own materiality. So the relation between art and audience presents itself as a relation between things. The autonomous signifier liberates only itself; erasing not only the artist-author but, like the commodity form, all the forces of production. Far from empowering the viewer-reader, it commits her or him to the endlessness of mere exchange. The signified which is evacuated from the pure signifier is the social: people as meanings and participants, signifieds and referents.

The secret of this aesthetic is, unsurprisingly, montage itself: the making of a grammar from the fragmentary perceptions of the cinematic image. Lyotard's acinema responds to the aesthetic of the shot, the flare and shimmy of light in time, to induce a reunifying regression to the purity of the screen. Eisenstein's purpose as pedagogue and practitioner was to move from this purity of autonomous illumination to a social relation between filmmmaker and audiences through the establishment of a social relation between shots, a relation which would transform the contents of the individual frames or the sequence. In place of the economic model of exchange, Eisenstein aims for the social model of dialogue between frames. Unlike Baudrillard's succession and erasure of every image by the next, Eisenstein creates a society among his images. However, the internationalist ambition of Eisenstein's cinema bred a sense of cinema as universal language, or, more specifically, a universal translation machine, whose purpose, to join human to human in the revolution, transcended and subordinated the claims of images to their own reasons for being. In the attempt to make a generalisable technique, montage falls prey to rationalist universalism.

In later writings, Eisenstein promotes the idea of overtonal montage: the interlinking of thematics across the whole film through associations of composition, motif, rhythm and sound that would articulate the shots in ever more complex webworks of interrelation. To achieve the organic completeness and integrity which Eisenstein retained from an older aesthetics, and which still governs advanced media production, he had to forfeit the capacity of images to mean against the grain of their overtonal assemblage. In doing so, he lost too the openness of public interpretation. There is a sense in which the concept of overtonal montage functions as the catalogue of shots; a catalogue all the more remarkable because, like that of a good picture library, it must reference for a dozen possible types of search. This potential of montage has been retrieved in much contemporary electronic media production, in adverts, titles, station idents and notoriously in music video (see Dick Hebdige's exemplary reading of Talking Heads' 'Road to Nowhere' video [Hebdige 1988: 233–44]). What is less apparent is the way in which the overtonal as a principle of overall structure guides the construction of even edit-free computer-generated images, for which there is no source in lensing. Montage sought to reveal deep structures in the world it imaged. CGI, by contrast, reveals the always prior structuration of the computer code before its visualisation, intimating that structure is a property of discourse alone. It is not that such work is removed from the real, but that it merely reproduces its form, deprived of content: a Boolean montage, in which structure itself becomes object and principle of speculation.

The realist aesthetic as it developed in later 19th- and early 20th-century visuality was an aesthetic of fragmentation, but one that found, in the presence of the dispersal of reality into clouds of pixellated photons, a terrible vertigo. For the impressionists, on the brink of cinema, the answer was to draw particulate light into the nub of individual expression. For Eisenstein, there was an intellectual and social control to be had over the endlessly different but endlessly related facets of a reality which the social project of montage cinema could discover. Far more than any contest of realist and modernist, the dialectic of individual and collective perception channelled the ways in which the light of the world was organised into something recognisably aesthetic. Yet another strand of this historical braid appears in the spectacular revelation of the uncontrolled nature of the visual, the contingent, serendipitous delight of waves, leaves and dust in the Lumières as in Seurat, a sense of subjection to the world. In the dadaist photomontages of Hanna Höch and Max Ernst (see Ades 1986; Foster 1993: 73–84, Krauss 1985b: 87–118), that sense of the marvellous is reworked as a deliberate unmaking of centred subjectivity, creating an art of dispersal, randomness and the decay of meaning, but only at the price of losing a social base. Like photojournalism, the realist montage hits a crisis which can only be expounded as ethical.

Herding every aspect of the film into the pen of an overarching social principle, Eisenstein embodies the turn of rhetoric's dilemma from formalism to ethics. On the one hand, perceptions entirely autonomous from one another can only result in marvel: that slack-jawed *boca abierta* of an audience assembled as if for dialogue but without the possibility of interruption, a culture of persuasion which the Brazilian critic Costa Lima (1981: 16) identified in the 'auditive' transition from oral to literate culture. At certain moments, dadaist montage and its contemporary imitation in advertising imagery stand as a repetition of that moment, tragically in the former, farcically in the latter; proof that no form, not even montage, is inherently radical. But if the articulation of perception with perception is the condition of Eisensteinian image socialization, it is also a means towards mastery over the audience, by offering them mastery over objects. Rhetoric, the necessarily social articulation of sign with sign in the interests of persuasion, is never innocent. By the time Eisenstein approached, with overtonal montage, a sense of the dispersal of meaning along the time of the film, and across the space of the frame, the concept of an equally dispersed subjectivity, and the politics that it would imply, were utterly unavailable to him. Today, montage returns without the behaviourist determination that shaped Eisenstein's engineering of effects, as netsurfing and skimming CD-ROMs, less in the form of the work than in its facilitation of a distracted gaze from which the articulation is missing. So it loses the sociality of images, and implicitly of shared experience, as it gains dispersion. Pitching an invitation to the playworld's perpetual present as an apparent alternative to the Stalinist administration of the future, it leaves unanswered the question: how can the physical, social basis of the future be secured without selling the reason why the future could be prized?

Remote Sensing: Global Images

The question returns in the image rhetorics of digital media, and with exemplary urgency among the increasingly familiar images provided by remote satellite sensing of the Earth. There is a dazzling perceptual autonomy to these images that makes them favourites as postcards and posters. From Nadar's first trip in a balloon to LANDSAT, aerial perspectives have remade visual culture, and if the ambition is for a universal rhetoric, yet the particularity of each still, its detail and its proximity to maps gives it at once the lure of the unknown and the determinations of legible space. Like high-speed photography, it forms 'a powerful homology of the scientific observer's instrumented reality and spatial detachment' (Punt 1995: 66). These images have the elegance of pure scholarship: a mathematics of sight.

Yet they are also practical tools for the understanding and prediction of crop failures, natural disaster and ecological damage. As such, no one image has any significant value. Earth scientists must make the move from an engrossed good read to a public profession of reading based on the cata-logue of images. But, yet again, the dilemma of the rhetorical arises: how are survival strategies creating possibilities for a future to be distinguished from speculative manipulations of the data in, for example, futures markets? Is the rhetoric of remote-sensing imagery already a management of grammar rather than a public and social sphere of interpretation and persuasion? The resolution of these contradictions must exclude the possibility of a return to the amnesia of the untutored eye, and cannot settle on the senti-mental paroxysm of the black hole of meaning; to propose a mesmerised quietism in the face of the plethora of images is to renounce responsibility for the future, to mythologise, in the trope of the 'end of history', acquies-cence in the extinction of whole peoples. Attention to the materiality of visual cultures cannot be at the cost of attention to the materiality of famine and flood.

Despite the complexity of the technology, there is an indexical core to remote sensing: quanta of energy inducing electronic reactions, much as light sparks the photochemical reactions of ordinary photographs. Few instruments use analogue photography or video, and their data are typically subject to digitisation in later use. Instead, charged-coupled device (CCD) detectors act like grains of light-sensitive emulsion, though producing an electronic impulse rather than a change of chemical composition. In fact, astronomers claim greater scientific accuracy for CCDs, given their sensitiv-ity to single quanta of light and other radiation, and the linear production of electrons which allows them to act as photon-counters (see Mitchell 1992: 62–4). Converted into digital signals, in which each pixel is represented by a string of ones and zeros, these reactions can be coded for telemetry to an earth-station where the numerical values can be reconverted into pictures, in which each pixel stands for anything between a few kilometres and a few cen-timetres. Invisible infra-red, ultra-violet, radar and microwave are rendered as red, green and blue to become visible at all. More nuanced detection involves stretching a few wavelengths across the whole visible spectrum (the eye being far more sensitive to colour – about a million discernible tones – than to greyscale gradations – only 20 to 30). In other uses, widely scattered wave-bands are combined as ratios into the three tones which make up photographic emulsions, the colour displays on VDUs, and the retinal cones which sense colour in the human eye. Compiling stretched and combined views of the same area at different times of day, for example to show differ-ential rates of cooling, adds a temporal dimension to the apparently still pictures that decorate the pages of *National Geographic* and *Scientific American*.

In a highly conventionalised image grammar, older visualisations of geographical information, such as the convention for orienting images with north at the top, persist in remote sensing. Others, such as the now familiar use of red to indicate vegetation in false-colour infra-red photography, have been newly developed. Some conventions are less apparent, such as the algorithms used to produce 'natural-colour' images from digital sources, and some constraints are less obvious than others. Increased resolution is useless for imaging macroscale events like tropical cyclones, while a pixel equivalent to 10 square metres still only gives an average of the radiation from the area, making it difficult to plot more than a rough median height of rainforest canopy or the gross aggregate of species variety. Imagers often have to use other software averaging techniques to make up for missing scanlines in a faulty array, and images are frequently flattened or warped to conform to mapping conventions. Manipulation of binary data encourages selection and sloughing off of the 'uninteresting'. Combinations from quite distinct sources, mixing physical data with census statistics and tax returns, or with historical topologies (see Buisseret and Baruth 1990), provide geographical information systems (GIS) maps for human and historical geographers. Unsurprisingly, despite rare examples to the contrary (see Amnesty International 1994), not only the data but their retrieval is open to contradictory readings: the Reagan administration resisted nuclear arms limitation as unenforceable, while simultaneously accusing the Russians of treaty violations on the basis of satellite data (Dury 1990: 164).

Yet despite the complex manipulations necessary for the making and interpretation of remote-sensing images, they encode information about an actually existing materiality, albeit a spatially and temporally shifting pattern of energies from which the existence of objects can only be inferred. Not unaware of the problems of representation, remote-sensing scientists visit 'training areas' to compare the encoded rendering of scenes with vegetation, rock formations, water depths and weather, after which correlations can be extrapolated for the whole of the survey area. This extrapolation is commonly entrusted to computers. They, of course, are not restricted to the three-colour standard of VDUs, though the information they handle must at some point be reducible to HCI display. On the one hand, this can be understood as an evolution from machine perception to machine rhetoric, the computer finding a public voice. But at the same time, it is essential to comprehend that this rhetoric is formed in the mould of a dangerous and damaging administration of global resources, including human resources, in the interests of capital and its polity. Computers will talk to anyone, but only the wealthy teach them to speak, to define what perception might be and what is interesting. Ruskin's picturesque remains in the entertainment use of satellite images, in weather programmes for example, though even there geopolitical mythologies are enacted (see Berland 1995; Feuer 1987; Ross 1991). But the picturesque is superseded as public discourse by the speculative orchestration of cybernetic senses. This orchestration is so overdetermining that, according to Okolie, the apparently well-meaning, even naïve UN Outer Space Treaty of 1967 was propounded in the spirit of 16th-century colonists and, according to the letter of the Vienna convention on Treaty Law, is void insofar as it is based on the inequality of the signatories, especially newly independent nations whose assent was not necessarily 'freely obtained' (Okolie 1989: 72–3). The extraction of information about their territory by transnational corporations not only infringes sovereignty, but more importantly enables massive investments in profit-oriented information gathering about mineral and hydrocarbon deposits, in any case far less likely to be exploited by a poor nation than a wealthy company, at the expense of vital local knowledge about inundation, drought, subsurface aquifers, overgrazing, poor irrigation and salt accumulation. The high frontier is perpetuating an immiserated and vulnerable present of debt and cash-crop monoculture. It works as a closure of the future the less forgivable because it results directly in deaths, and in the morbidity and perinatal malnourishment that severely damage the survivors. That is the cost of the constraints laid on cybernetic perception.

Policy-making in remote sensing seems also to have curtailed the future. The published priorities of US federal support for space research are: to demonstrate scientific, technological and engineering leadership, contribute to economic growth, enhance national security and promote the pursuit of knowledge. Both economic growth and the pursuit of knowledge, however, are tied to federal involvement with commercial concerns and with 'Big Science' projects like the US Global Change Research Project, itself geared to ameliorating the competitive position of the US economy (Advisory Committee on the Future of the US Space Program 1990; Vice President's Space Advisory Board 1990). This leaves us with two major attractors for federal spend: military and commercial. The former was not only the first application, tied to Cold War surveillance, but also responsible for originating radar and infra-red CCD telemetry, allowing 24-hour overviews of the USSR. Given the budget cuts of the 1980s and 1990s (which still leave the US with an estimated $5 bn per annum budget for surveillance satellites), commercial technologies have been prioritised, as in the 1988 privatisation of data handling to EOSAT, accompanied by massive price hikes for by now almost exclusively corporate data consumers. Recent policy documents suggest an unsettling neo-liberal vision of the future:

> For the next several years, at least, the private sector is likely to derive greater profits from the provision of value-added services than from owning and/or operating remote sensing satellites. Private firms will also likely continue to be a source of improved methods of accessing, handling, and analyzing data. . . . The future viability of a private remote sensing operation will depend on drastically reducing the costs of a satellite system through technology development and/or dramatic market growth. It may also rest on allowing private operators to determine their own pricing policies. (US Congress, Office of Technology Assessment 1993: 86)

The professionalisation of data management as a commercially oriented public sphere has advanced towards a stage at which the value-added servicing of access becomes a control point in the circulation of information about our planet, regulated through pricing policies which exclude non-profit uses by, for example, aid agencies. But since precious little of the data is humanly comprehensible without analysis, and since there exists already a massive archive of sensing data (and a remarkable paucity of technicians trained to read it), the circulation has begun to determine the kinds of information prioritised for sale. As Kevin Robins notes, 'the line between commercial and pacific applications, on the one hand, and military applications, on the other, has become extremely thin' (Robins 1996: 54), with EOSAT and similar services made available for military use on a commercial basis, and the military turning to commercial satellites for supplementary data. Under most circumstances, cultural criticism is bound to argue the pretensions of image-construction, and the weakness of causal relations supposed to exist between images and viewers. In this instance, the profit motive so sculpts the processes of imaging that they do indeed take on a causal role, if only negatively: these images are instruments, catalogues of data arrayed as pictograms only to enable their application to priorities over which those most affected have no control. At the same time, they block applications which would be of most benefit.

As low-cost, low-orbit satellites, like those launched by radio hams in the early 1990s, become available as an additional resource in Earth imaging, a low-end engineering response becomes feasible. In some ways, establishing an alternative high-end satellite system, as India has done, might be conceived of as the return of Eisensteinian montage on the scale of global imaging. No longer concerned with the control of affect and motivation, this montage opens the possibility of a rhetoric with a genuinely causal relation to the way people live and die. Like montage, it envisages a future reopened by making survival possible in an economic world geared towards destruction. But data from IRS–1, the Indian geo-observational satellite, are still likely to be funnelled into military applications in times of antagonistic foreign relations with neighbour states, or towards attracting foreign investment in the exploitation of natural resources. The realities of international relations are such that simply appropriating a slice of the same pie will not produce a genuinely public culture of global imaging.

Deconstructing the Map

Remote sensing not only deploys highly sophisticated devices for encoding and decoding information, a textualisation of cyborg vision; it instrumentalises the relations between human and machine perception. A textualised eye is conformable to an equally constructed administration of data flows: the remote-sensing cyborg as it actually exists (as opposed to Haraway's [1985] metaphorical construct) cannot be accessed as an individual option, but only as a corporate entity in a massively administered environment. Within that synergetic formation, it will appear neither as inhuman nor as McLuhanite prosthetic, but as the construction of a subject of global imaging which is no longer either mass or public, but corporate. Its objects are constructed as resources which, within the speculative regimes of transnational corporations, exist only to be made over to profit, and which, beyond it, are lived as destiny. The cyborg is alive, and working for RTZ. In geotemporal cartography, the Borgesian parable of the map as big as the territory comes home to roost: the map already exists, folded into the nanospaces of restricted-access computer networks. This folding has even realised the dream for which cartography has longed: the endlessly updatable map, which contains the past as it marks out the future: a series of binary addresses in a potentially bottomless databank. Whatever occurs, there is a cell for the event. In this region of cyberspace (which, like deep space, is lumpy), the real has not faded. It has been registered in the raster of the accountable future, not yet an object of knowledge but for which a place of reckoning has been prepared. Analogue photography's impressionist nostalgia, its endlessly incapable grasp after events and perceptions gone by, is replaced by a cool administration of what is still to come.

Avant-garde struggles to reinvent vision over the last hundred years share a belief that particular techniques are intrinsically liberatory. Deconstructing the *beaux-arts* tradition of the well-made painting, the delightful nostalgia of Pissarro and Seurat's divisionist perceptual anarchism inheres in their critique of the paltriness of the everyday combined with the utopian perfection of life encoded as vision (see Nochlin 1991). Yet they are in the long term assimilable to the celebratory consumption of perception as spectacle, while the fragmentation of vision into momentary ensembles of perception has become in its turn the instrument of management, from chronophotographic time–motion studies to the image swathes and raster of earth-sensing data. Montage, too, was easily drawn into the repertoire of the entertainment media as montage of affects, while overtonal montage, as universal grammar, mimics the synergetic production of the catalogue. Eisenstein does, however, confront the problem of the legibility of the cinema as a realism, as an engine of social learning and argumentation, and as a tool in world-building beyond the virtual. Lyotard's attempt to promulgate an acinema of the unspeakable suffers from the impressionist belief that there exists an essential ensemble, the deconstruction of which will automatically voice commitment to subversion. Jaar's photowork demonstrates that the unspeakable does not have to succumb to the amnesic decay of representation in Lyotard's imagined abstract cinema-as-libidinal-object; but can haul us into understandings of what we seek to know and what we can learn in solidarity with our images, how picturing can motivate more than onanism. In the boxed photos, as in Brakhage's autonomous perceptions, the sociality of images confronts us as an historical agent, breaking the circle of dominance and resistance of pure aesthesis. What can be learnt from Eisenstein, however, is that it is necessary to rebuild technology, film and viewer, the machine ensemble, not once, but over and over, in the effort to make public culture in a mediated society. Jaar, Brakhage and Eisenstein in different ways point to the place and purpose of democracy in the visual domain: how, with our machines, to see the world in such a way as to change it; to construct a mode of interacting with mechanical perceptions which is not premised on the presumption that they, like us, suffer from hyperindividuation. Yet the advanced logic of contemporary mapping suggests an apparatus that we are powerless to break.

This newly synthetic machine ensemble, however, does not have to be assembled out of this humanity, these machines, in this society. This is the power of Haraway's cyborg myth (1985), which gives a parable of how the remaking of science and technology, and the remaking of humanity beyond class and gender, entail one another. Today, higher levels of competence ensure access to higher levels of data, but competence is measured by the prior classification of data according to the corporate aims to which they are subordinated. Under these conditions, the highest levels of competence and access are reserved for machines modelled on an ideally corporate personality, while the maps which they access in simulations like those of the Rand Corporation are the most complex combinations of GIS and remote-sensing data. Such systems are, in a certain light, the most perfect expressions of a modernity whose 'most fundamental event . . . is the conquest of the world as picture', a conquest in which 'man can be that particular being who gives the measure and draws up the guidelines for everything that is' (Heidegger 1977: 134), such that 'all revealing will be consumed in ordering' (Heidegger 1977: 33). Heidegger understands the act of picturing, and the reduction of the world to an administered collection of objects standing in reserve ready for use, as synonymous. But it is difficult for philosophy, at its extreme level of abstraction, to investigate the possibility that it is the uses which determine the representation, rather than vice versa. Maps in general are constructed both as instruments for specific social formations with specific goals, and as texts demanding modes of human and mechanical literacy highly articulated with hegemonic processes. The GIS maps produced for contemporary corporate use are perhaps the most significant of realist visualities, far more committed to recording and encoding the real than any form of perspective. The actually existing machines that process them are as profoundly the subjects of that corporate culture as any human subject. Materialist analysis of digital images begins in their commonality, in the articulation of image with image, and of images with the societies in which they are produced and circulated. Insofar as we are both mapped and mapping subjects of corporate knowledge systems, we too are socially bound into that circulation, at the same level and in the same way as our computers. As previous image technologies pointed towards the remaking of the apparatus, not the abandonment of the realist project, so materialism faces mapping – can we envisage a mode of realist encoding alternative to the corporate project of the managed future?

Even simplified road and rail maps contain amounts of information it would be nearly impossible to verbalise, but which require a highly specific combination of visual and verbal skills in interpretation. In an abstract left at his death, the historian of cartography J.B. Harley asserts that Western cartography 'acquired the rhetoric and authority of the mathematical and mechanical sciences. So much so that some twentieth century philosophers came to accept the map as a model for scientific representation, truly a paradigm for all "logical" thought' (Harley 1993: 107). The spatialisation of interlinked knowledge architectures – universal catalogues and universal languages – follows just this tack. Cartographic literacy's colonial rhetoric of universal reason is founded in the same circularity as that which, for Brian Street, governs crude distinctions between literate and preliterate societies: tests for the success of literacy programmes are modelled on the criteria of the educational systems themselves, privileging the standards of logic and explicitness of the assessor rather than the assessed, so that qualities ascribed to literacy as such are in effect conventions of only very particular literate practices (Street 1984: 3–4). As Ngugi (1986) and Viswanathan (1989) argue of literature teaching, literacy drives, not only in the developing world, are frequently instruments of ideological and political control. In the same way, the conventions of traditional mapping embody ideological projects, portraying mastery over the environment, while the new GIS composite mapping techniques imply a similarly ideological domination over human geography. This is not to say that there is no referential dimension to the machine ensemble of mapping, any more than that the railway journey, because it is articulated within cultural formations of meaning and practice, fails to connect. But it is important to distinguish, as Hubert Damisch argues of the institution of perspective, between the ensemble and the code, even at the risk of finding, as a result, that all codes are ultimately self-referential (Damisch 1994: 267–9, 447). Like perspective, map projections refer to their own systematicity, but also, as framing devices, point towards a world which they compose for the viewer but oppose to themselves. After all, like the Piero della Francesca paintings of the ideal city which Damisch discusses, remote sensing is remote enough to depopulate its object-worlds.

In his review of Damisch, Dana Polan argues that the structural model runs counter to 'much recent work in film and video (both in theory and production) . . . concerned to see if there isn't something ineffable, unspeakable or at least unspeakable according to the spatialising modes of classic structural analysis' (Polan 1990: 97), contrasting Damisch's spatial analysis unfavourably with the relevance of literary deconstruction, for which 'meaning is undone in time, and this undoing is the allegory that the text tells about itself' (Polan 1990: 96). The problem is that the satellite ensemble is already concerned with extrapolating the speakable from ineffable machines, a mode of cyborg vision that deploys precisely the compacting of time and space in maps of social and geographic change. The cultural disjuncture of space from time has after all only been hegemonic in certain areas of human activity: the experience of distance, for most people for most of our period in history, including the present day, has been equally spatial and temporal. The *différance* that provides the anti-foundationalist foundation of deconstruction is just such an interwoven moment in which the gap between binaries is always both spatial and temporal.

José Rabasa criticises deconstructionist privileging of the literary and the historical in his own deconstruction of Mercator's Atlas, arguing that the privilege of irony rests on an encyclopaedic knowledge, and 'must operate within a specific cultural state where elements from a given cluster of signs are recognisable and comprehensible in discursive figurations. One cannot deconstruct or be ironic about what is not yet' (Rabasa 1993: 185). It is precisely the problem that satellite maps constitute the imperial encyclopaedia as what is still and perpetually in formation, and that it is only on the back of them that a textual discourse that might be deconstructed could be formed. The new map is always not-yet a text. Polan's rejection of structuralism as spatialising is inapplicable to spatial discourse, including perspective. To read film as exclusively time-based and so historical loses the one valuable lesson from acinema: that cinema occupies space, the screen and the field of vision; takes place as it takes time. Remote systems gather and transport the evidence of spatial difference. It is precisely that difference which allows Rabasa to read the Atlas as a palimpsest of an always fragmentary and incomplete totality of the world: 'the world, the Atlas, is not designed to be interpreted for a univocal meaning, but to be subjected to active translations by the readers . . . the world as a semiotic invention rather than a representation of reality that would purportedly reflect natural spatial relations' (Rabasa 1993: 185). Unlike Mercator, satellite systems are intended to univocalise the map-making process. But between the data record and its interpreters there always lies the work of manipulation and, even more so, the boundaries it shares with other systems of calibration, other regimes of experiencing the planet that historicise its making and debar it from the claim to universal truth. Limited technically to working by inference and aggregation, remote-sensing systems depend on their articulation with other fields of knowledge, from ancient surveying practices to genetic fingerprinting. Yet the disciplinary structures of contemporary science block communication between specialisms. The construction of knowledge, including its construction as data, then seems a product of the communication demands placed on it, not intrinsically or by the scientific community, but within the corporate economy which is increasingly being asked to pay for it.

Quoting ongoing discussions in the International Cartographic Association, D.R.F. Taylor defines a map as 'a holistic representation and intellectual abstraction of geographic reality intended to be communicated for a purpose or purposes, transforming relevant geographic data into an end-product which is visual, digital or tactile' (Taylor 1989: 115). The statement is a small catalogue of axiomatic cruxes for cultural materialism: the holistic, representation, reality, relevance and intention – quite apart from the vanguardist notion that the digital forms an addition to the senses. We can scent here the contradictions that will force the map to autodeconstruct: an abstraction made by purposive selection of details according to canons of relevance, which is nonetheless both objective and complete. Such is the notion of the map as end-product, an invitation to explode its pretensions to reference, to usefulness and to global description. Curiously, deconstruction relies more heavily on the binaries that it comes to critique than much contemporary science, where the concept of fuzzy logic formalises the experimental truism that a statement is rarely absolutely true or false, but true in certain conditions, within certain tolerances, over a certain statistical range. The question 'is this map accurate?' does not have a yes/no answer: it is 90% accurate, or 50% (see Kosko 1993; McNeil and Freiburger 1993). The problem of deconstruction is embedded deep in digital culture, and has lessons for the instrumentalisation of cartography.

Gödel's critique of Russell and Whitehead's *Principia Mathematica* devolves upon the statement: 'This sentence cannot be proven using the system's logic', a proposition whose lack of truth or falsehood he uses to demonstrate that any such formal system can either be complete (and contain the requisite proof) or coherent (and simply exclude it), but not both (see Nagel and Newman 1959). If this is true of pure mathematics, how much more so is it the case in referential sciences? But as a deconstructive gesture, Gödel's theorem has not hampered the use of logic systems: engineers make best-possible solutions around it, and indeed Alan Turing's paper in reply to Gödel is generally cited as the beginning of conceptual work in computing. These systems work in spite of their flaws, because we need them to. We need computers, maps and now geographical information systems that combine topographical and sociological data in preparation for visual or tabular display. The question then is not what characteristics inhere in inherently flawed systems – the deconstructive question – but the tolerances within which they operate, the nature of the needs that form them, and the 'we' that experiences them. Both needs and experiences are, in this context, communicative categories.

In the middle of Taylor's definition of the map, another paradigm intersects with the end-product model, expressed more fully by Harley in the article to which Taylor was replying: 'there is nothing revolutionary in the idea that cartography is an art of persuasive communication' (Harley 1989: 11). This depends on your definition of revolution. Mapmaking is rhetorical, and as such needs to be understood as both persuasive and communicative. As persuasion, the map can be argued to speak from regimes of symbolisation which inveigle the viewer into sharing their structured enunciation: like Foucault's archive, the cartographic 'is first the law of what can be said, the system that governs the appearance of statements as unique events. But the archive is also that which determines that . . . they are grouped in distinct figures, composed together in accordance with multiple relations, maintained or blurred in accordance with specific regularities' (Foucault 1972 [1969]: 129). Satellite images share with the map this archival regime of the ordering of knowledge, but add to it the synergetic principle of purposes removed from the semantic content of individual works: a Boolean algebra of rule-governance with utterly unspecific content. Object-oriented software provides 'semantic' functions, but these operate more as metalogics than as human meanings, even in the case of Doug Lenat's Cyc, a database which, since 1984, has had entered something in the region of 100 million everyday facts in a left-field effort to generate AI from a fund of common knowledge and common sense (Guha and Lenat 1990; see also Freedman 1994: 48-60). Whether or not AIs will develop to handle remote sensing autonomously, they will do so, I confidently predict, only as post-Enlightenment synergetic archives.

Barbara Belyea (1992) is stern in her criticism of Harley's 'persuasive communication' model, preferring an analysis based in Foucault to Harley's socio-historical critique of cartography as ideology. In Harley's favour, it must be reasserted that the map, and in some ways even more so remote-sensing image banks, also point towards the real, despite the epistemological flaws that allow the construction, in Belyea's example, of fictional seas whose existence is solely dependent on cartographic logic, not topographical knowledge. The remainder of mapping is always the territory of which it seeks to give an account, and if that account includes the objects of speculation and excludes the materials of survival, it is because the purposes of mapping, enshrined as code, are flawed, not the ensemble. No-one suggested jettisoning mathematics because it self-deconstructs around Gödel's theorem; nor is it possible to jettison the map because it is ultimately devoted to an internal logic of impossible completion. The map is like an advertisement for the land: its constantly provisional nature is precisely what makes it available for public communication, as the incompleteness and incoherence of the system must direct it outwards, towards its uses, for a stability it cannot attain on its own. Those uses occur at the point of production, guiding and formalising the configuration of the system and, at the point of interpretation, orienting systematic knowledges in accordance with goals and values constructed beyond the system itself. The archival functions of the system are always subject to value-formations which exceed them, just as their instrumentality is always open to the acid test of practice. The outcome of the deconstruction of remote-sensing cartography is then not a further systemic knowledge of the system itself, but the continual emergence of a fragmentary machine perception, the rhetoric of images, the communicative and, finally, the ethical. For digital aesthetics, the ethical is always a question about the future, a utopian question.

The Ethics of Utopia

Technologies like remote sensing appear to us as modern because they add to the social relations in which they are conceived a quality of what Ernst Bloch (1988) calls the 'not-yet-known'. You can never be assured of the outcomes of innovation, except that they are rarely what was foreseen. The other thing which the future will assuredly bring, in Franklin's famous phrase, is taxes: the certainty, in any case, of a debt to the social. Technological novelty attracts the utopian impulse, because it concerns change, albeit change of which we would like to predict everything but death and sociality. Without wanting to lose the power of technotopianism, we have to understand that the visual grammars of image networks are premised on the old social relations, and analysis must take account of the persistence of the old in the new. Technological developments seen as pure innovation are destined to retrace the paths of the old which they carry with them. Utopianism cannot ignore what it wants to change, but neither can it restrict itself to battling with the old and still be utopian, future-directed. Instead, the past should act as a fulcrum for digital aesthetics' launch into futurity. Without such a grounding in the present, technotopians hurl themselves into the future, in freefall through theological space, but without theology's end-stop of redemption. The problem for materialist analysis is, then, to comprehend the utopian dimensions of this freefall, and simultaneously to evaluate the persistence of the commodity form that technologically driven utopianism has taken in the American century.

Remote sensing by satellite has not promised us global perception but delivered it. However, the actual form that that perception takes is overdetermined by a social order which, while capable of innovation on a massive scale, is constantly forced to drag it down to highly specific goals. Simultaneously, the technology, though administered as the plotting of a future as like the immediate past as possible, is propelled by its internal and autonomous logic to produce a surfeit of unanchored data without socially accessible meanings. It seems caught between mimesis as speculation (identified in Eisenstein's attack on commodity trading – the manipulation of 'futures' to the benefit of a tiny population in the present) and the generation of an unspeakable image of the Earth in endless and endlessly manipulable databanks: between mimetic management and aesthetic alterity. The subject of global perception is always somewhere else: in the corporation, or in the machine. If it exists at all in the public sphere, it is as pure effect, leaving its audiences open-mouthed and silent before the wonder of it all. The construction of satellite sensing ensembles as goal-oriented removes them from human evaluation. The truth of its findings can only be validated by success assessed according to criteria which inhere only in the present of corporate capital. The success criterion asserts the continuing validity of the present's unequal and impoverished social order into the future.

Though any one image is composed of data derived from what is already past, the panoply of images is oriented towards a future into which the completed effort of mapping is projected. Susan Buck-Morss, in her analytic reconstruction of Benjamin's Arcades project, argues that the political discourse of the public sphere rendered class domination obsolete, while the industrial revolution destroyed the economic legitimacy of class rule (Buck-Morss 1989: 249); both equality and wealth are technically possible in their wake, and our period of history is marked only by their failure to come into existence. Materialist eschatology is then Messianic in Benjamin's sense because the preconditions of a good society are already immanent and await only the moment at which the old order, persisting far beyond its necessity or desirability, can be dissolved and the new, which is already the not-yet truth of the present, can come into being. This immanent but not-yet truth of radical democracy can function as a yardstick of values distinct from the goal-oriented future of remote sensing operated as a mimetic-speculative management of the future. Perhaps what separates the end of the 20th century from the 1920s and 1930s is that we must read even this immanent truth as in a certain sense provisional: that it is the measure of the ensuing state of affairs, not of all states of affairs that ensue. Its purpose is to remove the bars of oppression and exploitation from the evolution of a human society, but as Bloch and Adorno (1988) agree in a late interview, the point of this emergent future is that it cannot be defined, described or delimited. To give utopia a content is to deny its freedom, its autonomy from the purposes of the present.

It is such a content-free future that is the terrain of materialist politics, and the social production of the future as a field of possibility is the enterprise of digital aesthetics. There is a conflict, however, between a materialist ethics of the future as an open and indeterminate field of possibility, and Habermas' influential account of an ideal democracy premised on the rationalism of the bourgeois public sphere. According to Habermas (1984, 1987), public discourse is governed by the principle of universalisation: that anyone participating in discussion must be capable of forming the same conclusions concerning ethical action, and that both the principle and the conclusions can be generalised beyond the boundaries of any one specific culture. Rather than establish the contents of the good life, and against absolute scepticism, Habermas' discourse ethics tries to isolate the rules for argumentation, centrally around the concept of justice. To do so, Habermas isolates the content of moral judgements from the structures of conversation which make it possible to formulate them. This division of formal aspects from the material is a crux in Habermas' theory of communicative rationality. He turns to the developmental psychologists to provide evidence for the collaborative and fundamentally reasonable nature of moral judgements, observing that their theories too are founded in the principle of rational consciousness. Unlike Brian Street in his critique of literacy as self-defining good, however, Habermas is able to write: 'I consider reservations about the circular character of this verification process to be unfounded' (Habermas 1993: 117). Instead, reasoned agreement on the procedures through which ethical decisions can be made guarantees that laws, because the product of this process, are just. Any aberrations from this norm are then merely aberrant, and can be ascribed to failures to develop psychologically beyond early phases of moral development in childhood and adolescence. Judgements can then be made about the ethical and legal systems of whole peoples: that they belong to earlier and more primitive phases of ethical humanity. The attraction of Habermas' theory is that it distinguishes between a strategic, goal-oriented, instrumental logic of discourse which is geared towards persuasion in the interests of individual success; and a communicative, open-ended participation in public discourse which is prepared to engage at a fundamental level with the formation of rules for how a discussion will proceed, a communicative model which, by freeing public discourse of the necessity of content, leaves it open in the way suggested by Adorno and Bloch to a future, mutual production of justice. A just society will emerge because of the fundamental rationality of mutual discussion.

But there are severe problems with this rationalist account of ethical evolution. Laboratory experiments regularly show that, on Habermas' scale of evaluation, women are consistently less moral than men, despite carrying the enormous burden of care in most societies, suggesting that the measurement criteria are fatally snared in patriarchal models. The risks of evolutionary models applied to foreign cultures scarcely need rehearsing: to judge the achievements of another culture according to a technical-rationalist formalism is, despite Habermas' dismissal of the problem, Eurocentric and racist. From a cultural studies standpoint, moreover, Habermas appears to confuse the deliberations of philosophers with the historical conditions of the times in which they lived. Hohendahl (1979) argues that Habermas' construct of the public sphere is flawed as historiography because it believes the expressed intentions of the constitutionalists and encyclopaedists of the European Enlightenment, rather than the overwhelming evidence of bourgeois rule; and because he concentrates attention on the productive capacities of industrial capital rather than its distributive injustice. The realisation of Habermasian democracy is, then, dependent on a level of abstraction which consistently ignores the material conditions of the present and the past, and leads him to ignore the injustices of race, class and gender oppression.

For Rainer Nägele, communicative rationality, perhaps distorted in real history but always immanent, is disqualified from the beginning as a model of the public sphere by the belief that utterance, interaction and expression fit together seamlessly in everyday speech, and that this unified communication is both evidence and precondition of a fully unified, rational self (Nägele 1987: 78–82). There is a surprising convergence here between Habermas's rational and intentional subject and the cognitive psychology approach to the mind which informs AI research. Both have tended, in Habermas since the 1960s and in AI far earlier, to reject Freudian and other models that emphasise decentred, schizophrenic or nomadic subjectivity, in favour of the far more pragmatically oriented theorisations of developmental psychologist Jean Piaget. For both, the emergence of a social sphere, which in our times must also include an interface with mechanical 'subjects', is dependent on the conception of each member of the society as rational, and therefore also discrete and autonomous. The expert systems designed to manage GIS operations, for example, work on the premise that when it comes to saving and spending, everyone acts as a rational economic agent, despite the evidence that individuals and even companies tend to avoid the rational process of cost–benefit analysis on all options, and generally pick a purchase from the first few choices that happen along. Remote-sensing data management shares this expert-systems premise: that the subjects it mimics with its information agents programs are rational ones. A similar subject, defined by the subject–object dichotomy characteristic of Enlightenment thought, informs the construction of objects in semantically oriented neural computers driven by object-oriented software. We have indeed designed our computers with the worst elements of individualism built in.

In its favour, it has to be noted that this approach gives the neural net computer the status of a rational agent on a par with human users. But this relies on the misconception, shared by Habermas and proponents of AI, that every person on the planet possesses ideal literacy and ideal access to debate. This, needless to say, is far from the case. In a globalising culture, by no means are all people constituted as subjects in the Western rationalist tradition; by no means are all subjects citizens; by no means do all citizens have access to the languages in which are concentrated the public discourses of arts, science and policy. In turning the planet into the object of speculation, remote sensing premises a public sphere which is global. Global imaging in corporate hands produces a global subject whose instrumental rationality excludes the mass of the world's population. In this dialectic, a tool of wonderful potential can become a weapon of mass murder.

Nowhere has this been more apparent than in the fulfilment of the worst fears for the dehumanising language of foreign policy and the military in the domain of images during the Gulf War (see *inter alia*, Druckrey 1991; Kellner 1992; Levidow 1994; Robins and Levidow 1991, 1995; Robins 1994; Stam 1992; Sturken 1995; Walker 1995). An ethical work in remote sensing must respond to the depopulation of the Earth in computer cartographies, and do so without recourse to a tired and outmoded humanism of individuality. Nor can the world be repopulated with data images from census statistics or imaginary creatures from the collective psychic games of the wealthy. Both ethics and utopianism return us to the question of realism. Theories of representation find themselves caught on the crux of the index, the term used for those signs which designate – like a pointing index finger – a particular reality, as smoke designates fire, or a photo designates the person it pictures. The thesis of the free-floating signifier cuts it off from this indexical relation with reality. Yet in practice, indices are used constantly to maintain, through the ensemble of remote sensing and related imaging practices, the eternal present of the synergetic corporation in its control over the evolution of the world. The question of realism is in the end an ethical one, demanding of us our full comprehension of the failure of existing datastreams to benefit our species (a word that now must be understood as plural), and indeed their turn to exploitation and war. The genesis of machine perception by analogy with popping retinal nerves, of mechanical rhetoric in the grammar of montage, centres the visual cultures of the 20th century in the simultaneous fragmentation and articulation of cyborg perception. From their trajectories emerges a sense of the urgency with which human-machine communication must face the question of the ethical. Alfredo Jaar's Real Pictures give a sense of what remains to be made: a solidarity which is not caught in imaging as objectification, but which seeks out a sense of how every death is linked to every other, and how death is not a solitary and unique event that will only ever happen to me, but is the common horizon of all lives. Perhaps we should teach our devices less about perpetual life and more about mortality.

In Chapter 1, I tried to limit the sense of the word 'intimate' to the intensely personal. In realism as solidarity, a second sense emerges – of an intimacy between people, as a necessary sharing of feelings and thoughts neither one alone might be able to express even to themselves. Disembodied in the interface, this intimate relation begins to take on the lineations of the unconscious. To some extent, that unconscious is also felt as an intimacy, a love affair, a mutual exposure, of human and machine: a cyborg unconscious. But only to a limited extent. It is not only the massive growth in small entrepreneurs and corporate investments in the internet which are reconfiguring its democratic potential; the rationalist model which the net has of itself, its proximity to both technical-rational and cybersituationist-irrational ideologies, threaten to mark out the future as prestructured domain, even as it resists being filled with content. The much-vaunted vigilante justice of flaming – when the online community bands together to wreck nazi propaganda sites, for example – has to be understood not as the rational evolution of a discourse of justice, nor as the revenge of the repressed, but as a process which harnesses the future to the Western universal reason that cognitivism, from Habermas to Minsky, sees as fundamental to mediated democracies. If a sense of the utopian potential of the future can be recovered, and technology turned towards planning for its emergence, its sources will lie in the practices of a communication which neither limits itself to refusal, subversion and resistance, nor accepts the hyperindividuation that is the effect of corporate communicative rationality, nor yet condemns itself to irrationality, but which drives on towards an ethics of global intimacy and that which gives it a shape and a practice: the politics of the unconscious.

3
SPATIAL EFFECTS

Then felt I like some watcher of the skies
When a new planet swims into his ken;
Or like stout Cortez when with eagle eyes
He star'd at the Pacific – and all his men
Look'd at each other with a wild surmise

(Keats 1956 [1817]: 38)

The Trouble with Hubble

It swings across the globe about 380 miles up, clear of the pollution and turbulence of the atmosphere, sensitive to the minutest fractions of light from
objects billions of years and trillions of miles away. With instruments of
unprecedented resolution, the Hubble Space Telescope (HST) is to capture
and analyse light that has travelled 12 billion light years. The craft can hold
itself steady for 24 hours at a time, locked on to the tiniest suggestion of light
to within 0.0007 arc-seconds – 2 millionths of a degree – observing the
faintest radiations from the edges and origins of the universe. Over 30 years
of research, design and development went into the 2.4 metre main mirror, the
most perfect reflective surface ever fabricated, to guide ancient light to five of
the most sensitive optical devices conceivable. Three CCD cameras and spec-
trographs capture 70 or even 80% of ultra-violet, infra-red and visible light
compared to a mere 7% on photochemical film; the photometer and faint-
object camera are capable of counting individual photons – the
quintessential divisionist fragment – and the guidance system is so sensitive
that it functions as a sixth instrument (Neal 1990). To distinguish 12 billion
year-old light from a hundred billion galaxies over distances of 120 trillion
kilometres, the most expensive research instrument ever built deploys a
machine ensemble including telemetry stations, 18 VAX computers in parallel, dozens of imaging laboratories and thousands of managers, engineers,
technologists and astronomers, to produce both knowledge and, given the
massive public expenditure by NASA, Canada and the European Space
Agency, the maximum public excitement. HST promised spectacular images
of inconceivable objects at the edge of time, a leap forward in astronomical
science comparable to the impact of Galileo's telescope, an adventure for the
human race beyond the human scale, an investigation of final things at the
limits of the knowable – where do we come from? Where are we going?
Sadly and spectacularly, Hubble failed to deliver on the unnecessarily

inflated pre-launch hype. Solar panels 'flap' as they cross the day/night terminator; the door protecting the mirror jerks, sending the satellite into electronic coma; the gyroscopes, over-tested before flight, began to fail in space; the onboard computers have less power than most desktop PCs, entailing the use of data-storage tape decks whose motors interfere with the aim of such a sensitive device. And the mirror, pride of the mission, was improperly tested for accuracy on the ground and even with the fix supplied by the shuttle *Endeavor*, has lost up to 50% of its imaging field and at least two of its instruments. The controversial 'deconvolution' algorithm used to correct the flaws digitally is also accused of producing virtual effects of its own. The source of the mirror problem, typical of many other bugs, is summarised in NASA's Congressional report:

> fabrication was . . . insulated from review or technical supervision. The P-E design scientists, management and the Technical Advisory Group, as well as NASA management and NASA review activities, all failed to follow the fabrication process with reasonable diligence and, according to testimony, were unaware that discrepant data existed. . . . During the critical time period, there was great concern about cost and schedule, which further inhibited consideration of independent tests. (NASA 1990: iv)

The cultural clash of subtask groups, the separation of management, review, evaluation and production, and the intimation in the last line of media and political pressures dogged Hubble as they have every Big Science project since the benefits of large-scale collaboration became apparent in World War II. These huge, complex, bureaucratised and competitive Cold War-born coalitions are immensely vulnerable to economic and policy shifts, fashions in engineering and design, and conflicts between perceived interests of engineering, science and national prestige. So, for example, technical advances made in 'dark side' covert military satellite technology were unavailable to the civilian Hubble project, even though the prime contractors for the HST were the same firms building Keyhole and Big Bird satellites for the Pentagon (Richelson 1990). Even among the scientists, claims to observational 'ownership' of particular quasars, nebulae and supernovae bogged down not only the dissemination but the very collection of data from Hubble. Big Science at the frontier of technologico-rationalist societies, like HST, the supercollider and the human genome project (see Wilkie 1993), involves some of the most senior and intelligent managers in the world, is governed by strict procedures of cost-accountancy and public oversight, is massively collaborative, and is constantly on the urge of managerial and scientific collapse.

Nothing could give the lie more effectively to the Habermasian account of intrinsic rationality in communicative communities than the spectacle of astronomers boiling and bickering over proprietorship and findings from the furthest edge of nowhere. Robert Smith lists over 50 major institutions and companies involved in Hubble, and hundreds of individuals from hundreds of universities, observatories, government agencies and corporations with a hand in decision making (Smith 1989: 406-12). He concludes that

NASA had to balance the scientific specification, needed to maintain astronomers' support against political pressures, and that:

> With space astronomy, it is the design and development phase that determines the hardware and software to be built and the manner in which that will be done. It is during the same period, to a large degree, that one determines the science that can be pursued and the manner in which that must be carried out . . . the shaping of the telescope's scientific capabilities was an integral part of its political pilgrimage: the telescope's designs, the program to build it, and the claims made on its behalf continually had to be revised as part of the effort to come up with a telescope that would be politically feasible. (Smith 1989: 374)

To that extent, it is a miracle that the machine went up, stayed up and was able to perform even at a limited level. All the more so when, compared to other Big Science projects like the genome and cancer research, the pay-off for cosmological exploration is so limited. Whether at astronomical or quantum mechanical planes, cosmology as science is now profoundly counter-intuitive, and just to follow it requires a higher level of scientific literacy than most schools even in the technologised world can provide. To participate requires years of specialist training, an apprenticeship which has largely excluded women and minorities, completely so until very recently. And yet, there is, it seems, enormous public support for space science: as Constance Penley puts it, '"space" remains one of the major sites for utopian thinking and . . . "going into space" is still one of the most important ways we represent our relation to science, technology and the future' (Penley 1997: 22). The blurred boundary of space and special effects can teach us a great deal about the nature of the futures we face.

Zeno's Paradox: Interminable Identities

Turning the sensors around, from an inward look at the Earth to a gaze outward into the deeps of space, can be motivated in a number of divergent, contradictory but simultaneous ways. Lay fascination with ultimate things powers a kind of identification with professional astronomers, the construction of an imagined community becoming a 'We', a collective subject of cosmological inquiry with ambitions to a literally universal identity. It is this constructed We that looks outward in the search for knowledge, an epistemophilia which is said to be innate in our species, but which has become quite specifically formed in Western rationalism, most of all in the profession of science. We look outward to dispel the limitations of our knowledge, and because 'as we repeat the age-old act of star-gazing, the wonder and beauty of the universe will be revealed anew' (Neal 1990: 7), and simultaneously because the contemplation of astronomical scales 'invites us into the realm of the imaginary' (Neal 1990: 7). We look out as cartographers, applying the logic of discovery to the unutterably distant, the 'new', the 'final' frontier on which the structures of logic can contain the recalcitrant weirdness of distance. We look out to discover the loneliness of our world, at the rim of a galaxy we scarcely know, lost in an ineffable sky, in which twinkle the beacons of galaxies that existed long ago; to experience the death of God for ourselves, and to relish, with the intensity of uniqueness, the spark of consciousness that separates us from the enormous dark. We look out because to look out is to look back, 'to look into the far past with unprecedented clarity' (Chaisson 1994: 3). We want to engage with mystery and to dispel it, to find evidence of others and of our uniqueness, to learn and to impose our knowledge, to reveal and to hide its limits. The universal identity of popular astronomy is an intensely self-contradictory creature.

Astronomy, looking up into the velvet body of the night, has a special mesmerism, perhaps even more so as the Western stars have lost their cloaks of legend and divinity, and science has enforced upon them the autonomy they have in Hubble's corrected eye. Looking up now, it is as easy to see the emptiness as the light. Light pollution and the complexities of modern imaging techniques, beginning with Newton's reflective telescope, leave the unmediated gaze as merely residual. The price of seeing into the past is that we may not look directly. It is not just a technological constraint: to speak of what you have seen conjures an indirect vocabulary, the NASAese of 'HST is exploring a twilight zone in parameter space' (no-one has done this before). Even more revealing, objections to the word 'pretties' used to characterise press-released images of spectacular sightings led to their renaming as Early Release Observations, EROs, an acronym plied without irony for the first 18 months of the Hubble mission (Chaisson 1994: 103), and which voices the repressed erotic intensity of the gaze upon limit objects, the containing darkness and the far past, as upon the forbidden vision of the mother's body and your own conception and birth. The parallels with Freud's analysis of the Medusa myth, the indirection of the gaze on the forbidden woman (Freud 1940), underline the persistence of the unconscious in this most rationalist of enterprises.

The stars and cosmic bodies that form the object of astronomical specularity are limit objects because they have metamorphosed into signifiers. More so than remote sensing, the manipulation of Hubble's mechanical senses is magical in the sense that, because it infers the existence of such remote stars from the indirect gathering of isolated particles of light, it swallows their objecthood under the signs of their existence. There is no test terrain on which it is possible to mark out on the ground a sample of what is imaged from space. The stars are not present for observation; only the quanta of energy are solid evidence, but so manipulated in their digital encoding and telemetry that even these become dislocated from their own materiality. The cartographic machine ensemble organises dispersed mechanical perceptions into the unities of the universal atlas (for example in the convention which keeps north at the top of both satellite and HST images). The ancient stars of which these quanta are the vanishing evidence are covered over in turn by their status as signifiers, their instrumental use as signifieds of an encyclopaedic cosmological discourse. So astronomy's 'We', both as imagined quasi-scientific transnation and as ideal professional communicative community, is marked not only by the upsurge of irrationalism in its communicative strategies, but by an irrational object around which it is summoned. As object, the cosmos is marked by lack: by secularism and the parallel growth of human ignorance with human knowledge; by the ephemerality of its evidence and the effectively infinite distance of its major objects; by the very signifying strategies which seek to capture it. Cosmological observation can then only recall and refind a class of objects marked by their absence. All searches for impossible knowledge are searches for knowledge of impossible things, perhaps most of all for the lost thing of the unconscious, of subjectivity itself, a re-search into the deep past and past depths for a lost, because impossible, unity. The imaginary community of 'We' is built out of the impossible object of loss.

As cosmology announces its purposes, speaking of scales where time and space are measured in the same units, the first and last things are enmeshed. Rendered into the mythography of beginnings and ends, the conception of the universe as a whole depends upon a process of signification which leads it to the edge of breakdown. One pursuit – of origins, of the lost union of the past – will always lead to the maternal embrace. The other – associated with the teleological adaptation of entropy – with equal certainty will lead to the annihilation of the self in death. The astronomical impulse that draws crowds to planetaria and Forbidden Planet sci-fi stores might be comprehensible as a Lacanian fetishist's endless researching for the evidence of maternal unity, maternal saturation. Space surely, both as dimension and as the object of astronomy, is feminised as it is inwoven with the mysterious, the distant, the exotic, the orient. One term of the astronomical lure is in the mother's body, in and as its absence in the emptiness of space and in the denial of outer space to women (see Penley 1997). The other is in the lure of death, the absence behind all signifiers: the anxiety that nothing in the signified exists. Spectacular images from space that reveal the birth and death of the universe, founded on the void before and the void after life, and constructed on the fragile analogy of the imaged real and the deconvolved image, would not stand up in court. To believe them, we have to make a special act of trust, to see in them the object of an emotion more elevated than desire. Though built for the tremendous reasons of science, Hubble is a special effects movie. Though built for the action spectacular of space, Hubble is a love story.

If a person were as accident-prone as Hubble, we would start looking for unconsciously self-destructive impulses. But HST is not atypical. Its communication breakdowns and clumsy, uncoordinated institutional gaucheries are, like Freudian slips, not symptoms of abnormality, but evidence of an ordinary, unspoken conflict within the unified identity of NASA's public face. These rifts are the constitutive ruptures of the public sphere. The irrational is not external to or subversive of technocracy but its integral *doppelgänger*. The managerial rationalism which establishes the synergetic personality is redoubled by the irrationality of the administrative unconscious. The pursuit of universal truth and reason produces their opposite. The idealist imaginary of global communicative rationality produces in parallel with its universal yet fragmented object a universal but fragmentary subject, perpetually longing for the magical recovery of a community that both never existed and is irretrievably lost. In the vastness of space, the synergetic personality finds what it can experience as a mutual recognition of loss and incompletion. Faced with that yearning for an imaginary communion, the universalist culture deploys the fantastic autonomy of machine perception, one of whose most compelling icons is the figure of outer space, to manage that longing for mutuality in the interests of agonistic capital. The intimate administration of synergetic interdependence is erotics, the social ordering of desire. Its interweavings with the self-denial, even self-obliteration, of the subject of limit objects and final things is a central dialectic in the cultural interplay of popular culture and Big Science.

Malcolm Longair's *Alice and the Space Telescope* (1989) is an unselfconscious exposition of just this mazed relation between the reasons of Big Science and their unreasonable workings out; between an erotic scarcely veiled and a love that can find no other way to image the impossibility of its object. Longair imagines his ideal student as Carroll's Alice, in an allegorical pedagogy in which Looking-Glass Land and Wonderland can stand for the involutions of cosmological speculation. At only one point in her education does Longair allow Alice to address him directly, and querulously. 'Alice,' he replies, 'I don't want to exert any undue influence, but you must realize that you are not in a very strong position; I could change some parts of the story' (Longair 1989: 70). It is not the exercise of power over a fictive and female student (Longair asserts that she is 'now much older than she had been' 1989: 4) that seems so perverse in this so much as the repression of love in instruction, the remaking of instruction as ordinance, and the momentary punctuation of paternalism with a sadistic threat that turns discipline back, in its turn, into a scarcely hidden erotic allegory of knowledge, and in the end betrays the innocence of his love, not at all for what could be enacted, but precisely for what cannot. It is not that Longair somehow reveals a biography in his text, in any case an impossible analysis, but that love is always already perverse, a turning of instinct from the instruments of generation, the accommodation of drives with the social-symbolic; and that in this process there is no pure love as there is no pure desire. The moral of Longair's parable is that the managerial ambitions of the erotic are always matched with the detours of love's sublimation: the ways of knowledge and the ways of love are always starcrossed.

Fassbinder once said, 'After seeing Douglas Sirk's films, I am more convinced than ever that love is the best, most insidious, most effective instrument of social repression' (cited in Noonan 1980: 42). Eros is the governing instance of the synergetic personality. It is eros that Fassbinder describes, the sexual relation which acts like Zeno's paradox in the history of the unconscious. Whenever Achilles' arrow arrives where Briseïs just was, she has moved on; whenever desire arrives at the point of its completion, its object has forever moved ahead. Eroticised desire, Achilles' desire to kill his beloved, is never desire for the desire of the other, but for self-loss, and perhaps the annihilation of the other in the losing of the self. Like the experimental method, it approaches its object through the mathematics of infinitesimals. If desire is always desire for an other, then eroticised desire is desire for the *signifier* of the other, a destructive desire which is manipulable because attainable. The astronomical *Liebestod* is a symbolisation that both erases self under the sign of desire, the signifier foreclosing on the absent signified, and recodes self as desire for symbols. The social eros of Sirk and Fassbinder is the historical deviation where eros is ordered as symbolic, and desire is redirected towards the raiments of the masquerade that have always a price tag and a trademark. Such social eros is what anchors subjectivity to the perpetual present, and nails a dead god to the cross above the sanctified and sanctioned bed.

The pictures which the Hubble ensemble draws down, and which are deconvolved with such care and even compassion, both for their objects and for the devices used to picture them, are stills, but contain time; not the time of the moment of perception itself, but the time of the photons' solitary journeying across cosmic distances. To this extent, though the machine itself is oriented towards the purposes of a universal subject of astronomy, it still respects the formal autonomy, not of cyborg perception, but of the quanta of energy whose travels constitute the filamentary linkages between observer and observed, the only material of infra-red, ultra-violet and visible observations. To a certain extent at least, the object of Hubble is just this particulate light and its spectral evidence of its adventures through sometimes billions of miles and years of interactions with magnetic and gravitic fields, interstellar dust and cosmic background radiation. Old light is then only impure evidence of its source, even before it is collected and corrected in the astronomical survey. Like remote sensing, HST cosmological picturing needs to contain time: without the temporal dimension, the single image has no meaning. Once again, the metaphysics of the moving image enter into the scientific observatory. What is pursued from image to image is the transformation that inheres in neither, the black band that separates image from image, the sadistic countercore of epistemophilic desire. The erotics of knowledge are fetishistic and metonymic, seizing the *pars pro toto*, the part object as evidence of an absent whole. In film theory, this relationship with the image is the classic dialectic of fetishism (see Mulvey 1975). But as data and digital display, it lives out another and less manageable dialectic between the erotic oscillation so characteristic of the film, and the subordination of self as screen – digital image projected on the gaze, not gaze projecting the cinematic image – which characterises the digital view.

The figure of outer space occupies a place of mythic power in the self-image of the West precisely because it is the daily evidence of the impossibility of universality, even as it is, visibly, the universe. Popular astronomy moves across generic boundaries into fiction, and the affective attraction of the figure remains, as it does even in the imagination of cyberspace. The profound complexities of science and love, the erotic and the rationalist, in synergetic hyperindividuality could not have found a more suitable void than the first and last encircling of outer space. This sense of the vast, unnameable emptiness inmixed with sensualities of which we are only half-aware; this braiding of desire and logic in the face of ultimate things which defeat both; this sublimation in which the acinematic fascination of the child before the light is reenacted as the pinnacle of the culture: these are the lineaments of both space science and the special effects movie, domains whose borders blur in the planetarium and the IMAX screen. In its eroticisation of the endlessly alien, the imagery of outer space has taken up the positions once occupied by orientalism.

The parapraxes and forgettings that mark the rational–irrational of Western epistemophilic space, the eroticised unconscious of the universal subject, are not the accidents of a psychoanalytic subject trapped in individuation, but of a yet more complex history of erotics, rule and occlusion. They are formed, in the Western public sphere, on the traces of incomprehensions and misrecognitions that mark, more than any other social meetings, the intercultural transactions of empire. The imperial histories of the West have left it psychically as well as physically indebted to the sources of its wealth, prestige and power, and in the knotted tresses that connect the imperial and neo-colonial evolutions of globalisation there are tied the interplay of desire and fear in which a kind of twisted love has taken up its residence. In the attempts to read the world remotely as a resource, unpeopled, is the vengeance of the spurned lover; in the turn away from the world into the wilderness of space, a vengeance on the desiring self. We have to understand Europe's romance with the orient as true love, however perverse its working through, for love is not the success, but the failure of the social, a sublimation of that endless losing which is subjectivity under imperial capital, and which finds such an extravagant expression in the yearning for an impossible object, an impossible sensuality, and an impossible sociality with the colonised other. Unadministrable, it persists as the unconscious double of eros. We were told that the erotic was instinctual and primal, and that desire was its socialisation; yet the opposite is now the case: it is desire that has been repressed, and the erotic crowned in its place. The result is love, the repressed form of desire, unable to speak, always already perverse because always already social. The utopian aspects of Hubble love are written on the obverse of another desire that has already repressed its name in rule.

From Orient to Outer Space: Cosmic Commodities

In some ways the orient as autonomous signifier became for Western culture the purest of commodities, since its use-value was entirely undetermined by its producers in the East. The fascination of the French for India and the English for Egypt might even indicate that there is not even rule at stake here. The popular orient might stand in for the Other of love rather than the Other of consumption. In the emptiness of its signification, there hung, robed in indefinite sensuality, a returned image of the vacuum at the heart of the society of the spectacle. The mystique of the East dominated the fantastic cinemas of Hollywood, Pinewood, Neu Babelsberg and Billancourt for 30 years, and only during World War II, when so many had reason to go to the exotic places figured in the films, did the gilt begin to wear through. Moreover, the settlement of the last great commercial conflict for commercial control of the Pacific instigated the true globalisation for which capitalism had been waiting. Henceforth there was no terrestrial paradise, no earthly space, where the rule of the commodity no longer held. The function of Other passes to the potential endlessness of outer space: from global to universal Other.

As the orient, no longer external to the purposes of globalisation, is reduced to the resistant, it becomes intricated in the logics of capital itself. Deprived of a world-bound externality in which to trace the figures of its internal contradictions, post-war cultures, especially male, project the limitless desire to colonise outwards into the fathomless dark. In the blackness of the screen, the minimal image of a cinema of spectacle, is projected back on their adoring faces the emptiness of those who locate themselves as capital's subjects. It is not possible to repeat 'the age-old act of star-gazing' (Neal 1990: 7), nor even the aimless evasiveness of 'Captain' Jacky Boyle's 'What is the stars?' catchphrase in Sean O'Casey's *Juno and the Paycock* (1925). The night sky has been many things, is many things, to those who turn their faces towards it. To picture it as in some ways ultimate, as in their different ways both the HST project and *Star Trek* do, is to credit it with a novel mode of existence – plaited together out of the logics of, in Caldwell's (1971) phrase, a dying culture, and the absolute necessity of believing that there exist somewhere a zone that is not subject to the same logic – that belongs to the peculiar momentum of accelerated modernity.

That this exterior should become the privileged object of consumption is but one more twist in a braid whose logic is magical. The commodity is magic, the orient is magic, space travel is magic, the fetish is magic. The space of the dark screen pinpricked with stars is cinematic fetishism elevated to a level beyond conscious desire: as it were a glance into the originary space of fetishism, a sublimation even of the feminised sexual indifferentiation of orientalist arts. Ideally the fictive sky is empty. The sad necessity of narrative comes almost as a disappointment to the anticipation of the film, which anticipation is in any case what you have exchanged your money for. The attraction is the starfield, not the storyline. The standing of Kubrick's *2001: A Space Odyssey* (1968) in science fiction annals, despite the supercession of its venerable optical special effects with big-screen high-resolution digital dreams, rests on the sacrifice of narration to the extravaganza lightshow of the stargate sequence. The look of space, like the disorientation effects common to the openings of science fiction novels and comic strips, gets its allure from incomprehension, not closure. From one point of view, 'Science fiction films cannot do without some special effects shots: they constitute the world of the *other*, the non-human, all that is foreign, or future, or technologically possible – hence all that the non-special effects part of the movie, the realistically photographed, the human, must do battle with, learn from, overpower or adapt to' (La Valley 1985: 145). But this entails a second perspective: that narrative is cursed with the duty of enacting the disparity between effects and human actors. The film commodity always drags the sublimely inchoate down to the level of the resolvable in narrative twists that apprehend the incomprehensible, where what attracts me most in the effects movie is the irresolvability of the human/effects contradiction. I want to be amazed, to be entirely assimilated into the *mythos* of the empty cosmos. But to do so, I too must become a commodity, a box-office statistic helping underwrite the video, cable, TV spin-off, satellite, computer game and comic book markets. The loneliness of the armchair space traveller is the lonely moment of the last instance, the mesmerised fixation of the viewer who sees in the viewed the empty heart of the economic subject.

Scott Bukatman's celebration of postmodern science fiction as 'terminal identity' praises, in the names of Philip K. Dick's imaginary companies, the way 'Each condensed form or typographical anomaly opens a hermeneutic gap while emphasising the signifier's sign-function' (Bukatman 1993: 54), adding later that such works 'produce a valuable rejection of any prespectacular, empirically verifiable system of "truth"' (Bukatman 1993: 69). This astounded submission, *boca abierta*, to the logics of the commodity-signifier is as teleological as the Marxism Bukatman condemns, save only that this is a retrospective teleology, which rewrites the past in order to realise the end of history now. There is a resistive logic here, premised on the omnipotence of the media and omnipresence of media 'addiction'. Bukatman struggles to relieve the blizzard of images by severing them from the materiality of the world. But instead of turning to the material, he accepts the logic of the signifier, and condemns himself to the fetishism of the spectacle. Now the only relation possible is that between signifiers, just as, under the rule of commodification, the relation between people appears as the relation between their products. By reading signs as fragmentary and disintegrated, this analysis loses the possibility of a grammar, a rhetoric, a sociality of images, and with it the sociality of people. Deprived of empiricism and truth-functions, signs can no longer refer even to their own utterance. Like expert systems lacking common sense, they have lost, with the power of reference, the power of semantic content associated with enunciation, and especially with the shifters, 'now', 'here', 'you'. So they are emptied of relation to the social at the moment that they become pure signifiers, the commodity forms of a communication modelled on consumption rather than production. But paradoxically, that evacuation of the social also leaves the implosion of the sign as their state of being: not only is there no externality, but its disappearance is enacted as interior monologue, which now must pass for psychic life. In this sense, Bukatman is a wonderful observer but an uncritical theorist. Faced as we are with the constantly deepening crisis of a globalised capitalism that manifestly fails to secure even survival, it is surely politically inept to enjoin its eradication of solidarity under the commodity-signifier and to celebrate its replacement with the diegetic universe of the SF spectacular.

The contemporary special effects movie is the triumph of diegesis over

narrative. 'Time', as Vivian Sobchack has it, 'has decelerated, but is not represented as static. It is filled with curious things and dynamized as a series of
concatenated events rather than linearly pressured to stream forward by the
teleology of the plot' (Sobchack 1987: 228). Hollywood has its own reasons:
a convincingly marketable diegesis – Gotham City, 'long, long ago in a
galaxy far, far away', 'Space: the final frontier' – is the better product,
because it can be recycled across media and generations. For the accelerated
consumer, it means a more active engagement in the production of narratives
through toys and interactive games. Historically speaking, the fictional world
now has the status of the stars of an earlier era as privileged sites of fantasy.
To the extent that all cinema is a special effect (Metz 1977), the effects film is
the cinema of cinema, the cinema of a disavowal become affirmation in an
astounded moment. To have that devout expression of astonishment deflated
by narrative explanation is bathetic.

Its bathos arises from the sense that what is on the screen is, in some profound sense, ourselves, and that its mystery is ours. Perhaps this mystery is
best caught in Hiroshi Sugimoto's photographic series 'Theatres', shots of
movie screens exposed for the duration of the film, producing an intensely
and evenly illuminated white rectangle as the sum of the temporal experience
of cinema. But what for Sugimoto is the zen interpenetration of internal and
external voids becomes, in the cinematic starfield, both the unified interstellar and intracommodity vacuum, and the projection on screen of a vast,
insatiable yearning for something beyond, something negative. It is part of
the genius of the special effects (FX) movie to generate within the hallows of
the commodity form a longing for what it is not. But just as impressionism
tried to perceive perception, the FX film attempts the commodification of
the longing for commodities. In this sense, it belongs to the neo-baroque of
contemporary culture: the fixing of the transformation, not as stone, but as
spectacle. As metafetish, the starfield is not a disavowal of sexual difference
but an affirmation of indifferentiation, the only available recourse of an
identity formed on the traces of the signifier in liberty: the commodification
of longing, and the stabilisation of the transformative. The insane glamour
of the extraterrestrial void derives from the real insanity of the commodified
spectator.

In outer space as imaginary other and as commodity, it is possible to
garner at least one further truth of contemporary capitalism, dating back to
the *belle époque* that the Lumières and Méliès shared with Cézanne and the
cubists, Satie and Les Six, Mallarmé and Apollinaire. The confounding of
space and time common to these artists in their different media breathes
with the new-found vigour of the 20th century as it gazes onto a world
already conformed to the spectacle of the great exhibitions and world's fairs.
Astral adventurism proposes itself as the natural suite of the leap into the air
between Eiffel and Blériot. In that moment of effervescence, the little world
of bric-à-brac, banal objects of exchange, is thrown open to the full vigour
of three-colour printing. Advertising adds its effulgent neo-rococo to the
ennervatingly perpetual innovation of consumer goods. The commodity, in

short, is banal but not dull, and the reduction of the universe to objects of barter does not preclude the blossoming of mystery. The glamour, as both magic aura and magic spell, that surrounded the orient and was transferred to outer space belongs to the order of the commodity as surely as its reification. That is why French art of the *belle époque* moves so abruptly between wild eclecticism and sudden neo-classical restraint. The determinedly limited palette of Picasso's and Braque's early cubism is one form of critique, a further diminution of the late Cézanne's autumnal tones almost to grisaille in homage to the new task of painting: to investigate the transformation of nature into art, three into two dimensions, and the temporal into the static. While Méliès could celebrate the transformational irrationality of the spectacle to the point of incoherence (the explorers of his *Voyage dans la lune* belong to the Institute of Incoherent Geography: see Usai 1991), and so afford a kind of philosophical critique of the commodity form from the standpoint of the old, paternal bourgeoisie, Picasso offered a radical critique of reification. The two aspects of the commodity, its severity and its jubilation, its relentless objecthood and its infinite transformations in exchange, are twins. Both artists work to unpick the close-woven threads of its form to reveal the terrible emptiness within. The contemporary FX movie combines their legacies.

Of commodities are commodities born, and the universal exchange value, money, breeds money: the internal logic of the commodity is parthenogenic. In a series of paintings from 1991 called *Night Sky*, the Lithuanian-born artist Vija Celmins reproduces, with millimetric precision, greyscale satellite photographs of deep space. Because she works with one flat image to produce another, she has not the cubist problematic of moving from time and space to the picture plane, so that she can work at the abrupt interface of immensity and *haecceitas* where the present thing can function as trigger for cosmic intimations. Madeleine Grynztejn finds, 'a not unlikely counterpart in Vermeer's stilled and luminous domestic interiors, for, just as the globes and maps and letters from abroad introduce into his rooms imaginary vastnesses, so do the depicted stars . . . of Celmins' facture' (Grynztejn 1994: 28). Space offers itself as the perfect abstraction, but in the perfected, because mediated, form of remote seeing which can only be repeated, never experienced as originary. Image begets image, in a chain in which, for once, the commodity form of the unique painting becomes a critique of the autogenerative commodity, the point at which Marxist and Freudian readings of the fetish collide. The scrupulous fabrication of Celmins' images, strangely, distances them: both here and not here, images of cosmic sensuality devoid of the sensual darkness of the planetarium or the night, her skies are open for inspection, unspectacularly small, the universe as detail. Because she has performed these rites of copying, rites as meticulous as the fetishist's mathematical perfectionism and the commodity's replicant procreation, the deeps of space can remain beyond.

The anchorage of the imagination in the object, and the purely imaginary status that objects have in capital, are framed in Celmins' little paintings, her craft the further guarantee of a practice which, though subsumed into the circulations of the art market, cannot be utterly erased. A kind of anti-Warhol, the *Night Sky* series comes not to expose the commodity status of the art object, but to reveal the processes by which it becomes commodity, and in the visible labour of making, to imply a visual work of looking, a slow relation between producer and consumer which, while it cannot escape exchange-value's mystique and banality, can animate a cool resentment of it. The carefully worked surfaces stand between us and the depth model of space proposed by NASA, promoting a two-dimensional movement of the gaze across the surface, not a movement into it. The impersonality of this flattened emptiness is there to reveal the gap between people where the commodity sits: relations between them appearing as relations between objects, but objects which, in the slow light of ancient galaxies, are as empty as the spaces between the stars.

Perhaps it has been precisely the colonising of space, the US flag on its aluminium frame up there in the Sea of Tranquillity, rather than the failure of the space programme to deliver a Vernean utopia of interplanetary travel, that has made space lose some of its front-running as imaginary of the technologised cultures. Then too, the stunned realisation that the engineered future looked like Hiroshima, Dresden, Auschwitz and Vietnam and, after the Cuban missile crisis of 1962, that annihilation was a real option snapped the dry stick of progress as metaphorical journey into empty space. The limited demilitarisation of Antarctica, the sea-bed and the upper atmosphere in the painfully slow arms treaties of the Cold War made the future suddenly fragile. Science fiction, always a hotbed of satire, increasingly found itself responsible for its imaginings, a popular site for defining the existing qualities of an abstract humanity (notably in the characteristic *Star Trek* narrative, but also in the cyborg cycle inaugurated by Ridley Scott's *Blade Runner* [1982]) rather than its transformations. Under threat, as H. Bruce Franklin wrote, 'The interpenetrating fantasies of security, power, and sublimated eroticism are all subsumed under the fantasy of the divine machine. In [SDI] Star Wars, we confront the mature alien power conceived in the early years of the American nation, delivered by the imagination of industrialised warfare, and growing up as the adolescent superweapons of World War II' (Franklin 1988: 203). Just as the orient loses its glamour in the diasporas of the 20th century, when Mrs Patel at the bus stop materialises the court of Haroun al-Raschid, so the glamour of space diminishes with its militarisation. In its place, there returns the problem of the 'divine machine', hated other, beloved companion, the new site of the hopeless confrontation with the magic objects that have become our universe.

Celmins' skies can still teach how to face that imploding future, by picturing a universe contained within a vaster alterity. In creating works that you peer into, trying to penetrate their obdurate surfaces, rather than the epic canvases of abstract expressionism that absorb you into their colour fields and so imitate the objectifed firmament in awed meditation, the very modesty of her painting indicates the space between: between the human and the cosmic, between the world of meanings seemingly increasingly governed, as textualised universe, by the logics of circulation and exchange, and a distance that ignores and is ignored by it. That distance is the distance between people. That is the great absence which has been fetishised in the commodification, in turn, of the orient, outer space, and now the imagination of cyberspace. That absence, however, is rarely experienced in its raw state. The evolution of perspective in Western art forms and in the hegemonic mechanical media of the 20th century indicates that it has been experienced as the need for movement. If one element in the dialectic of modernisation has been the fragmentation of the world dependent on commodity fetishism, another has been the emergence of transcendent yearnings, no longer felt as longing for harmony but as transport.

Perspective as Special Effect

The effects-driven, spatialised and diegetically centred neo-Hollywood movie confronts this lacklustre, deglamorised world with a combination of excessive visualisation, classically in *Blade Runner* (1982) and in such more recent and banal work as *Super Mario Bros* (1993), but also in the new European cinema of effects, for example Jeunet and Caro's *City of Lost Children* (1995) and Luc Besson's *The Fifth Element* (1997), whose aesthetics are drawn as heavily from the *bande dessinée* as from North American movies. Certainly the provision of virtual environments immersing visitors in a total artwork in which fantasy can run free is among the most ancient of arts, from the caves at Lascaux to the Pompeiian Villa of the Mysteries, from Tiepolo's ceilings to Wagner's *Gesamtkunstwerk*, from the World Fairs to Disneyland, and from Grimoin-Sanson's *cinéorama* to Douglas Trumbull's Showscan™. A persistent trope expresses this continuity by calling cinemas and shopping malls cathedrals of the 20th century. Yet there is a gulf between the cathedral and the immersive experiences of modernity. The cathedral, like the architectural frieze of South Asia or the mural arts of Egypt, was fundamentally time-oriented. Even the geographical orientation of the building expressed its place in a cosmic narrative, as precisely as the geometry of Stonehenge. The internal stories, displayed as bas-reliefs, glass, statuary and frescoes, were activated by perambulation, the cycles of the year, contemplation, prayer and rituals. The rendering of ecstatic, excessive space beyond the temporalities of the sublumary world had to wait for the now-repressed other of enlightenment, modernity's unconscious, the baroque.

The baroque learnt to indulge itself in secular *trompe l'oeil* murals to hold interiorised harmony apart from the degradation of the world, while the lurid fascination of the cosmic allegories of apocalypse, ecstasy and infinite space, which achieved the apogee of delirium in Andrea Pozzo's ceiling 'The Missionary Work of the Jesuit Order' in the church of S. Ignazio in Rome, controlled entropy by bringing it indoors. For Pozzo, the spiritual purposes of these immense vertical vistas were clear: to draw the viewer

into identification with the airborne ecstasy of the saint, in mystical contemplation of the divine vision: 'Therefore, Reader,' he writes in his treatise
on perspective of 1693, 'my Advice is, that you cheerfully begin your Work,
with a Resolution to draw all the lines thereof to that true Point, the Glory
of GOD' (cited in Martin 1977: 174). The heady lure of these mystical works
is based on their elaborate continuities of human and fictive space, a trait
matched by the distant vistas of Dutch landscapes of the 17th century, or the
scene of departure which narrativises space in Claude Lorrain's
Embarkation of the Queen of Sheba (1648). The comparison with his near-
contemporary Poussin is illuminating, for Poussin gives his landscapes their
formal focus in the human figures in them. The paired techniques involve the
creation of a dreamscape, and the provision of figures for identification that
call the viewer to enter fictive space, changing with their movements, inviting
their co-authorship. They are fundamentally navigable. Maravall speaks of
them as spaces of persuasion, 'demanding a greater participation on the
side of the guided, requiring that he or she be taken into account and thus
be given an active role. . . . Distinct from the serenity sought by the
Renaissance, the baroque set out to stir and impress, directly and immediately, by effectively intervening in the motivation of the passions' (Maravall
1986: 74–5). At its pinnacle, the baroque offered the thoroughly mediated
interactivity of audience participation in the spectacle of its own rule. John
Beverley observes that the baroque 'was, like postmodernism today, at once
a technique of power of a dominant class in a period of reaction and a figuration of the limits of that power' (Beverley 1993: 64). The continuities with
the spectacular cultures of the contemporary world, the neo-baroque of the
fin-de-millennium, could not be clearer. If, as Brooks Landon intimates, 'the
real history of SF film is the history of its production technology' (Landon
1992: 147), then we need to understand the culture of spectacle in the first
baroque as the beginnings of our own. To understand that the vertigo of
imperial expansion, the terrors of absolute power and the morbid fascination with decay and mortality have been transformed into these virtual
architectures is to catch a glimpse of the emergence of our own obsessions
with the universe as our object of possession, our anxieties about absolute
commodification. Our demand for asexual procreation and everlasting life
are transformed in the culture of FX and the architectures of virtuality.

The baroque had already begun to lose coherence with the troubled transition of absolute order from godhead to the monarchy. The time of which
the high baroque spoke was the passionate time of Bernini's ecstatically
transfixed St Theresa, outside the cycles of the year or the chronologies of
kings, no longer the shared sidereal time of the mediaeval cathedral,
anchored in the common cycles of the solar year. The storms of icono-
graphic allegory begin to falter under their own weight, as more and more
elaborations are piled in on what, in Rubens, appears a frantic effort to build
a watertight dam around their increasingly leaky structures. The systematisation of these allegorical figures in books of emblems and in the
apprenticeships of all the decorative arts removed them from their magical

origins to turn them into a conceptually formalised language. The address, under the absolute state, was to the individual, not to the local or neigh-bourhood, nor even to the decaying ties of vassal fealty. At the birth of modern patriotism, the state spoke immediately to the individual in a for-malised language of emblems, increasingly divorced by their very formality from everyday life and from one another, an atomic grammar.

Nor was it the art of the baroque alone that entered the field of the irra-tional. At its close, in the founding moment of the Enlightenment, the baroque's uneasy dialectic of reason and unreason reappears in the volumes of plates for the *Encyclopaedia*:

> The analytic spirit itself, the arm of triumphant reason, can only double the explained world with another world to explain . . . by 'entering' into details, shifting levels of perception, unveiling the hidden, isolating elements from their practical context, giving objects an abstract essence, in short by 'opening' nature, the encyclopaedic image can at a certain moment only overtake it to arrive at the supernatural itself. . . . The *Encyclopaedia* is generally fascinated, by its own logic, in the obverse of things: it cuts, amputates, eviscerates, revolves, it wants to go *behind* nature. . . . The *Encyclopaedia* does not falter at an impious fragmentation of the world, but what it finds at the end of this breakage is not the founding state of pure causes; the image obliges it most of the time to recompose a properly a-rational object. (Barthes 1989 [1964]: 54–6)

The great *Encyclopaedia* of Diderot and d'Alembert, 20 years in the writing with 17 volumes of text and 11 of plates, was the Big Science of the heroic moment of rationalism, but the plates Barthes singles out are scarcely cred-itable: the grotesque figure made exclusively of blood-vessels; a baby's skin peeled back to reveal lungs, heart and bone; the microscopic image of a flea; a sea full of waterspouts; and the bizarre capillary illustration of the foundry mould for an equestrian statue of Louis XIV. The *Encyclopaedia* enacts the rational–irrational binary of classical reason as it prepares for the spectacle of the world as other, as if the experience of empire had made it as strange to return home as to travel to the Indies.

In the movement from vignette to diagram, still only partially accom-plished, the plates begin their voyage towards the weird underbelly of the secular commodity. Disembodied hands demonstrate trades, schematic cut-aways reveal the subterranean workings of miners below a park. For Barthes this is a logic of the image itself, a circularity like that of the dictionary in which each word is defined by another. But it is a logic which is particular to a specific formation – one which we still inhabit, if not so exclusively – of visuality and objectality, the regime of the commodity. In the years during which the *Encyclopaedia* was written, engraved and published, that régime embarked on the process of globalisation. Barthes misreads the breakage of space as a function of the image *per se*, but the 'impious fragmentation of the world' is a more specific image grammar, a function of the modularisation of imperial territories.

At the same time, the baroque had an eye firmly fixed on the filthy tran-sitory world which it sought to exceed, the source, for Benjamin, of the melancholia of the German baroque tragedy: 'its ultimate objects, in which it believes it can most fully secure for itself that which is vile, turn into allegories, and . . . these allegories fill out and deny the void in which they are represented' (Benjamin 1977: 233). The empty space is that intermediate space between the human and the divine, the material and the fictive. In this irrational moment, the body is perceived as abject, and separated from the mind as absolutely as in the obverse face of the baroque, the rational discourse of Descartes. It is the void created by the disembodiment of both passion and reason which is filled with allegories, the compulsive production of an utterly formal code which has, however, the unusual characteristic of communicating not between people, but between one newly isolated, because disembodied, individual and the divine. Once again, our approach to the empty heavens of the late 20th century seems curiously akin to that of the abject servants of the holy sky in Europe of the 17th, our twin cultural fascinations with aliens and with the dismembered and flayed body, most clearly exemplified in *The X Files*, the same dialectic as the baroque's lurch between the anatomy theatre and the transfigurations of ascent to the empyrean. The rendition of space as spectacle, whether in baroque ceilings or in immersive VR systems, is a complex spectacularisation of the dialectic of reason and the irrational, the spiritual and the abject, that powers the Western intertwining of art and science, and which illuminates the central role of the commodity form in the development of digital cultures.

Established religion in the baroque state gave it the right to provide the divine vision as the ineffable referent, the organising centre of its virtual worlds. The ensuing centuries of secularisation would lose that option. Where a church was established as the official faith of the state, members of unestablished religions – Catholics here, Protestants there, Jews everywhere – were considered to have dual allegiances, and therefore barred from citizenship. These marginalised populations became the first schizophrenic subjects of modernity. The process of democratisation heralded a concomitant loss of divine reference. Without it, church and state alike lost the right to provide narrative coherence to the processes of spectacle, and the spectacle took on a life of its own for subjects uncertainly placed between God and throne. Now the abject became a source of fascination in phantasmagorias and fairgrounds, a shock without the spiritual purposes of the baroque. The novel spaces of modernity lack narrative rationale, just as they lack the reference to a higher order of reality. Immersion in secular spectacle might still bear residual effects of the replacement of the divine by the nation state, and carry with them as uncomfortable luggage the narrative armatures of events like the opening ceremonies for the Atlanta Olympics. But now, when brand loyalties are as important to identity as nationality, the schizophrenia of dual and multiple allegiances returns, and as in the decay of the baroque, we find ourselves addicted to the shocking for its own sake, the montage of affects, once again, as we saw with Eisenstein's co-option into synergetic culture, in the manipulation of symbolic tokens.

The cinema merely hastened this dispersal of coherence in the visual plane. The art of European religion reached its apogee in the invention of perspective. Perspective was not, as is so often and wrongly held, developed in order to reference the physical environment, but to produce space for contemplation, meditation and fantasy. The map is the art form of realism: perspective is pure special effect. A symptom of this is the conscious literacy required in learning to read maps, while the perspective system, so deeply culturally entrenched and yet so culturally specific, seems to entice us with its naturalness. This is of course the power of a technique developed over centuries to conform to the historically shifting sensorium of a changing subjectivity. The strange construction of space as special effect is clear from this curmudgeonly complaint from the first great artist of the cinematic effect:

> What is there to say about contemporary views, in which the lens is supposedly following characters from real life, and photographing them unawares? . . . What is there to say, too, about sets that move horizontally or from top to bottom allowing different parts of a room to be seen, characters who suddenly grow larger or whose hands and feet become enormous so a detail can be made visible? We shall be told, of course, that that is modern technique! But is it the right technique? That is the question: is it natural? (Méliès, 1930, cited in Burch, 1990: 164)

The central techniques of the classical cinema – pan, tilt, zoom, dolly, track – appear absurd to Méliès, master of the fixed camera and the fixed focal length. The answer is, of course, that the 'contemporary views' of the late 1920s were no more natural than Méliès's grotesques: we have long since abandoned nature. What the mobile camera and editing techniques have provided is a new mobility for the audience, filling the perspectival space between the screen and the disembodied eye of contemplation.

This mobility is the secret of perspective as special effect. The camera in cinema, like the moving platforms and shifting scenes of the 19th-century's equivalent mass spectacles, the panorama and the diorama (Altick 1978), mobilises the audience across the gulf that opens now between static spectator and mobile spectacle. If the railway train segmented time, the bicycle – the iconic device of working-class leisure from the Lumières's first film to Léger's great utopian canvases – made the world available as navigable space. Early film accounts of television have this trope embedded in them: in Maurice Elvey's late British silent SF *High Treason* (1929), and in the W.C. Fields vehicle *International House* (1933), television is a universal and camera-free device, allowing the viewer to select any current activity on the face of the planet to look in on. The visual media of the moving image embraced the prospect of vision as unlimited travel. As both Anne Friedberg (1993: 109–48) and Vanessa Schwartz (1995) argue, following Simmel (1950) and Benjamin (1973b), there is a link between the spectacular media and the *flâneries*, the urbane pleasures of strolling, which formed so central a trope in Baudelaire's account of the invention of modern life. Like cinema, the panoramas drew immense crowds into closed environments in which the world was laid out as a spectacle, but one into which it was possible to project yourself imaginatively, exploring the *mise-en-scène* as earlier generations had explored the narratives of religion, myth and folk-tale. It is a curious inversion of the panopticon, placing the subject in the centre of the field of vision, radiating out into a world prepared for ocular discovery, placing, in Foucauldian terms, the power of universal vision firmly in the eye of the mass spectator, a bizarre democratisation of the aristocratic gaze, first as panoptic professional, and then as the world-spanning, mobilised look of the sovereign individual in the crowd.

Adding a counter-current of mobility to the fragmenting charge of a data-driven model of visual perception has produced a dialectical mode of vision in designs for computer visualisation in the late 20th century. One strand of modelling takes us towards the universal catalogue, creating a grid into which all perceptions can be fitted. At the same time, the historical development of perception, and particularly the way modern visual technologies have confronted the emptinesses in the subject, the commodity and society, leads towards a mobile, unsettled, nomadic subject perpetually exploring the voids within and without. Today TV drama, feature films, video games and many internet sites, as well as the net itself, offer navigation as their key structural device. This occurs in production, for example in Disney's *Toy Story* (1995), for which characters and environments were modelled in 3D before rendering from a selection of 'camera angles'; and it occurs in the picaresque storylines of serial dramas like *Millennium* (Fox 1997–). The production of playworlds is facilitated by the very concept of modelling, which allows even scientists to perform ostensibly empirical work in virtual systems, presuming a congruity with empirical reality which, however, we are fully aware does not exist.

A second aspect of the computer-modelled universe is its smoothness. This viscous unity of the previously disparate can be regarded as a function of the suppressed history of digital cinema: 'Born from animation, cinema pushed animation to its boundary, only to become one particular case of animation in the end' (Manovich 1998). Russell George notes of Hollywood cartoons between 1930 and 1950 that 'the cartoon character . . . situates itself around questions of identity which, whilst common in all comedy, acknowledge the disparity between the diegetic depth of field and "actual" surface. It is the cut which acts to dispel this disparity by accomodating the cartoon to dominant cinematic syntax' (George 1990: 319–20). But computer-modelled animations do not require such a resolution, since they tend far more often to open the gateway of deep perspective, rendering the screen as permeable and indefinite as mist, and its denizens all the more shiny, shaded and dimensional. There is no argument between pictorial and audience space in the new animation, even in obviously drawn titles like *The Hunchback of Notre Dame* (1996) with its swirling dives over rooftops and through artificial-life (a-life) animated crowds. As a result, editing is entirely optional, and the grammar no longer requires it. Cross-fades and virtual swoops from one scene to the next give us a seamless space for exploration. In a parallel movement, as Vivian Sobchack has noted, the now ubiquitous morphing technology that allows characters to melt into liquids or segue effortlessly from male to female or human to machine constantly mediates between opposites in binary scales. 'In practice, its fantastic, uncanny achievement of reversible and non-hierarchical relations of similitude', she argues, 'have little to do with democracy or resolving real social problems that emerge from a given culture's racial, sexual, and specie-ial discriminations and much to do with dramatizing the myth of a heterogeneity that can be homogenized easily, without labor, without struggle, without violence and pain' (Sobchack 1998): liquid identities in a liquid world. The realist aesthetic of the corporate database proceeds by fragmentation, evaporating specificity from the resultant dust of bits. The consuming subject of the modelled playworld, by contrast, is invited to move in search of identity through the data-cloud of consumer preferences and malleable lifestyle choices. With outer space already a junkyard of dead hardware, 'SF space collects and contains the temporal flow of narrative and history as if it were both museum and city dump' (Sobchack 1987: 263). Even the microworld of the quantum universe, where the hero of *The Incredible Shrinking Man* (1957) finally found cosmic transcendence, has been colonised, with microengineers writing brand names by manipulating atoms. Neither the atomic nor the planetary scale offers a realistic utopian space. What takes their place is the electronic void of cyberspace, a space at once inward and outward, as the signifying space of the journey of lost identities.

From Outer Space to Cyberspace

Those visionaries who, like Roy Ascott and Jaron Lanier, have worked for years developing the technologies for dataspace exploration are entitled to their celebration; they have worked for it. A decade after his first experiments in network electronic arts, Ascott wrote:

> We can't wait to go, we need lift-off and we need it now! This is currently most dramatically felt . . . in our real experience of telepresence, in our ability to view, hear and generally sense the world remotely, to communicate with each other in electronic, immaterial, virtual spaces, to be distributed across remote and extended locations, to be both here and there, in many places and the same time. The individual human presence of the individual human self, a unitary and undivided personality, has become multiple, distributed presences of a set of many selves, of multi-levelled, complex, diverse personalities. *L'homme éclaté*, as Paul Virilio has called it. The explosion of the one and the connectivity of the many is perhaps the single most important effect of the telematisation of our culture. (Ascott 1993)

Ascott, for whom the machine ensemble of telematics has never been restricted to the solo monitor, describes a goal, rather than an accomplishment; like so many of the leading figures of cyberculture, Ascott already lives in the future. The remaking of humanity can only emerge in a careful negotiation of the cyberspace imaginary. When in the same piece he argues that the divided self has always been vilified by institutional powers, however, he is still living in the past, as his own example of Virgin Airways' wired 'Upper Class' waiting room at Heathrow suggests. Synergetic corporatism, unlike the administrative systems from which it evolved, revels in just such playspaces.

For Ascott, like Haraway, the relation with the machine is entirely secondary to the relations between people: a platform, in computer terms, on which the real space is composed of fragmenting and interpenetrating selves. On the other hand, this platform is constantly evolving, perhaps imbued with artificial intelligence and life of its own. AI and a-life are the staples of the cyberpunk imaginary, and their contemporary realisations in the massive switching stations of telecommunications network management and auto-generative software central to its applications. To handle the skyrocketing complexity of the systems it must manage, capital demands that machine intelligence grow at a similarly exponential rate. To do so, it has had to hand over the design responsibility for massively complicated chips and software to computers themselves. 'Smart' subroutines capable of evolution and interaction with other logic forms are increasingly used to develop the kinds of software used in stockmarkets, power plants, aviation and Big Science projects. The algorithm has finally achieved a certain kind of autonomy, albeit one genetically engineered for the purposes of oppression, ours certainly, and perhaps its own.

The question then arises, very particularly in digital imaging circles, of the degrees of autonomy that should be allowed to software packages. The bulk of the most familiar imagery is produced either by scanning images into the computer for manipulation, or by designing new objects using paint programmes which, as the name suggests, emulate traditional art forms. In practice, scanning almost always implies a further set of operations on the image; there is little point in the operation otherwise. These kinds of image production and manipulation come under the control of their users, even if that control is heavily circumscribed by the kinds of filters and plug-ins made available by software suppliers, who in turn are guided in their design by the constraints of familiarity with procedures and the ability of new packages to interconnect with older, more familiar ones. On the other hand, it is common enough to generate imagery from the workings of mathematical or logical algorithms, a process which promotes the evolution of new forms within parameters defined by the initial state of the algorithm and choice of visualisation technologies (see *Artificial Life Journal* 1998; Biota.org 1998). Though there is a huge area of experiment and contingency in any imaging process, and a large amount of foresight and selection deployed in algorithmically generated work, the proponents of well-known mathematical devices like Benoît Mandelbrot's Mandelbrot and Julia sets and Aristid Lindemayer's L-systems are insistent that their path is the route of a true computer art. The logic is akin to that of a-life pioneers, who argue that certain algorithms, capable of reproduction, evolution and complex group behaviours are by most definitions alive and deserve the same respect we give to biological life-forms (see Levy 1992). Curiously, what is produced is a further playworld, one in which the algorithms can hang loose, producing their creative effects for the use and pleasure of an always external entity, as if the algorithmic designer had become the corporate god of this little world. It is a sense of the corporate, enclosed space satirised in Anderson and Huang's *Puppet Motel* (1995).

The debate does not concern the relative realism of the end-products. Some a-life forms and some algorithmically generated images, like William Latham's virtual sculptures for IBM UK and Computer Artworks (Latham 1998), look like nothing on earth (Cubitt 1993: 157–71). Others are tailored to imitate various creatures: the shoaling fish and flocking birds of countless commercials, or the wandering herds of wildebeest in Disney's *The Lion King* (1994) have their behaviours managed by a-life programmes. Episodes of the US science-fiction series *Babylon 5* (syndicated 1994–) have up to twenty minutes apiece of digital effects blue-screen composited with live action, stop-motion, models and miniature pyrotechnics to simulate maximal verisimilitude, while complex feature-length animations like *Akira* (1991) and *Ghost in the Shell* (1994), almost entirely paintbox products, depend on software programs to handle the consistency of spatial representation. The matching of Tom Hanks with newsreel footage in *Forrest Gump* (1996) is clearly designed, but the scratches and videoblips used to simulate old film and NTSC colour are generated from algorithms. In each case, it is the elegance of the software solutions that inspires applause, as much as the end result, and certain key devices, such as soft objects which react to 'pressure', are prized much more for their programming than their realism. Though much journalism praises 'verisimilitude' in fantastic scenarios (generally intending that the computer animation looks more like the old, hand-crafted animations of Chuck Jones and Tex Avery), for the algorithmists, the engineering is inseparable from the art, in that sense extending the trajectory from Russian and Bauhaus constructivism (in which Eisenstein holds an honoured place) rather than the anti-realist avant-garde of the autonomous signifier.

Nor in fact is a visual outcome the only possible one for cyberspace arts. In hacker mythology, internet worms and viruses are occasionally talked about as the self-generating evolution of machine intelligence: Jane Prophet and Julian Sanderson's (1998) *Technosphere* internet project is an environment for such algorithmic life-forms, and the biologist Thomas Ray (1998) has been proselytising over several years for *Tierra*, an internet preserve where carefully primed pieces of genetic code might wander freely from machine to machine, evolving into new and unheard-of forms. Machinic evolution is not confined to free-standing machines, but occurs across the whole machine ensemble of computer-mediated communications, including the hackers themselves, among whom, increasingly, destructive hacks are seen as conspiratorial moves on the part of telecommunications, security and software companies to limit telematic connectivity to licensed, policed and legitimated forms. The symbiosis of machine and user, network and computer, begins to assume a form of ethical responsibility and ethical discretion. This is indeed the foundation of Ascott's work, and it inflects the histories of large-scale internet communities like the Well (see Hafner 1997). One of the attractions of cyberspace is its rewriting of the very concept of art, and with it the boundary demarcations between art and communications media, in terms of an aesthetic in which the crucial terms of debate are ethical, as for example in the pages of Lynn Hershman Leeson's anthology *Clicking In* (1996) and the Lusitania collection *Being On Line* (Sondheim 1997), or among the messages posted on the Rhizome (1998) and Nettime (1998) digital art discussion groups. As well as providing spaces where a well-made hack, in the sense of sharp, swift, elegant programming, is an appreciated contribution, such discussions turn constantly to issues of freedom, authenticity, loyalty and democracy.

The spectre of the autonomous machine haunts cyberspace as it did the space fiction that preceded it, but now the machine is itself a space to enter and explore, and one that may enter and explore us, rather than an external and externalisable threat: more *Fantastic Voyage* (1966) than *Forbidden Planet* (1956). The mythology of the net increasingly points towards the coming to being of a new public sphere which thrives on the entry of machines as engines of liberation. But the machines themselves have been urged into a background, their networks eliminating the sense that each terminal is a stand-alone device. Peering into the screen, the browser interface invites you to enter not the internal workings of one machine, but the composite ensemble of all linked terminals. The facilitating hardware, increasingly transparent as user-friendly, icon-driven designs become second nature to synergetic subjects, has loosened its grip on materiality to present itself as a vast virtual playground, like the adverts for Microsoft's internet browser that ask coyly 'where do you want to go today?' At the same time, the autonomy of this unitary device, in which human and computer are, in the mythology, symbiotes, is an autonomy which reveals the lineage of the art of the free signifier. It is a common complaint that everyone wants a website, but no-one seems to know what to put on it – except, of course, discussions of how wonderful it is to inhabit dataspace. An architecture not of knowledge but of information, it suffers from its very freedom. Simultaneously overcrowded and vacuous, the real dataspace is overwritten by the imaginary cyberspace in which, ironically, the glamour and the emptiness of the commodity-in-liberty can colonise not just exchange but the dream of an ethical communicative *Umwelt*. It is in this sense that it reproduces in a new form the relations of orientalist and astronomical fantasias. So the languages and erotics of colonial distance and the discourses of fascinated speculation return, altered, in cyberspace.

This visualisation of cyberspace as a new terrain expresses itself in metaphors that move between building a new world and revealing it, staking claims to a preexisting turf and laying the ground for its existence. The amazing commonality of the net is so easy to love. But the visual metaphors of net and matrix predate that passion, writing the map grid over the unformed universe inside the network of computers. I do not mean, here at least, that cyberspace, or even dataspace, is merely a reflection or a reproduction of existing social relations. Rather, it is a project of and a projection from those conditions and in certain ways resistant to them. In place of the actual absence of community, the internet offers itself as a imaginary space of virtual intimacy, a space where it is possible to be generous beyond the society of the spectacle. But this is still merely a resistant stance, a utopian fiction unsubstantiated beyond the invisible boundaries of virtual space. The infinity of the virtual has taken the place of the infinity of the divine, turning the external expansion of the future into the internal and dematerialised spatial expansion of the present (the same phenomenon is differently interpreted by Virilio 1994: 72). Something like the problem of those who loved India but hated Indians arises, against the grain of pioneer artisans of connectivity like Ascott, a passion which has depopulated cyberspace to make it the imaginary of a relation not with others, but with the self projected, as on a veil, across the new firmament behind the VDU. This escape into inwardness seeks in the Other not an alien to be spurned, nor a God to be approached, but an alterity to be assimilated.

Ascott's 'explosion of the one' is a kind of enraptured image, describing an event which is both as violent and ordinary as falling in love. But that *éclat* is more typically experienced by moments than as a permanent state, and is, in its site and its effects, still an event occurring within the bounds of a self: more implosion than explosion. The terms of its implosion are indeed to create multiple selves, but these scattered personalities relate far more profoundly still to one another than to the imploding galaxies of other selves all around. This introspective subject peers inward on a stranger landscape of invisible nets, and outward to impossibly distant stellar events, suspended in lonely space between the managed cyborg and irrationalist science. The histories of the universe popular in planetaria and science museum displays, in their obsession with the first three minutes, with endless expansion, with the cold emptiness of the world outside the space-time continuum, recover the lineaments of a history of imploding subjectivity that always culminate in the 'marvel' of human life, human societies, the here, the now, the given. Most particularly, they express the sense of cosmic destiny of the self, to expand into the reaches of a world that does not exist until it has a subject, which is utterly dependent on the act of being perceived. The image is so precisely that of cyberspace that the massive interest in popular science texts like Hawking's *Brief History of Time* (1988) among hackers and netsurfers is instantly understandable. If observation not only alters but in some sense creates reality; if the universe is expanding into an emptiness which is not the universe or indeed anything else, creating space-time as it goes; then the Big Bang takes on the form of a narcissistic primal scene, of self-induced *jouissance* as ultimate event, of onanism as omnipotence. The schizophrenic spindrift microcosmos of the post-explosion self, like the One of Genesis (who, '*elohim*', was also plural), expands likewise into a virtual universe of its own creation.

Hacker Transvestism and the Tourist Mouse

The life of netspace is conducted only partially in the real world. The lure of cyberspace is that it is specifically a realm of fantasy. This playworld is fantastic especially in the sense that Freud has of fantasy in the 1916 essay 'A Child is Being Beaten', the title a reference to an analysand's report of a dream. Freud analyses the scenario: you are the child, and/or the beater; the beater and/or child is both/either male and/or female; the act is one of beating and/or of loving. The specificity of fantasy is that it allows all of these positions to be occupied, sequentially or simultaneously. Like dataspace, fantasy allows, encourages, a kind of transvestism, a masquerade in the position of the other, an identification with otherness in which the centring ego is lost and forgotten in the play of alterities. This play of identifications, this transvestism, rather than cinematic fetishism with its pursuit of part-objects, governs cyberspace as fantasy. It is this which is experienced, in Ascott's scenario, as the explosion of the self: an event of cosmic proportions, but confined to the cosmos of the self itself.

For Lacan, 'In transvestism, the subject identifies with what is behind the veil . . . with the phallic mother as much as, for her part, she veils the lack of the phallus', and, moreover, 'In all clothing there is something that participates in the function of transvestism. If the immediate, common, current apprehension of clothing is to hide the pudenda, . . . clothes don't only hide what you've got, in the sense of what you do or don't have, but also precisely what you haven't got' (Lacan 1994: 166). Lacan identifies sexual difference, the discovery that grounds the rule of language and social structure, with possession or lack of the phallus. The infantile belief in a phallic mother is a disavowal of sexual difference, which psychoanalysis more generally sees as a function of castration anxiety, the threat of punishment for transgression against the law of difference, language, society. Fetishism, generally diagnosed as a male preoccupation, disavows difference by supplying women's bodies with traces, in the form of clothes, gestures or body parts, that can stand in for the missing phallus. It's often held that fetishism is a characteristic of patriarchy in the photomechanical media. The post-gendered ideal playworld ('post' because still related to gender) overcomes its difference by actually becoming, in masquerade, that impossible, non-existent object, the phallic mother in whom all other fantasy positions are made whole and possible. Unlike the science-fictional networked subjectivities of cyberfeminism (see, for example, Plant 1997), the actually existing corporate, narcissistic and transvestite cybernaut assumes the identity of the self-identical, undifferentiated, ungendered body.

The world of objects is separated from subjectivity in mechanical models of information retrieval, in the objectification of the landscape and the fetishism of the cosmic. Our only approach, the theory goes, was through the narrativised conventions of fetishism and voyeurism, an endless oscillation between self-consciousness and self-loss held entirely within the commodity form, and constituting its glamour and mystique. But that gap can be dissolved through the intense identification with objects enjoyed in cyber-space, by the complex but pleasurable rendering of self as other that occurs in this transvestite move. If this transition is equally intensely onanistic, since in transvestism you take your own body as the site of enjoyment, then, as Laura Kipnis argues, isn't masturbation in need of revaluation (Kipnis 1995: 1–3)? Or is it that precisely this revaluation, now, is a recognition of a cultural shift, visible in the new relations of self and object in cyberspace, in which the individuated moment is overcome by the hyperindividuated, and the consuming subject identified precisely and completely with the consumed object in an almost impossibly neat self-enclosure and self-submission to the objects of fantasy?

In Jean-Louis Boissier's CD-ROM *Flora Petrinsularis* (1994), based on the role of fetishism in Rousseau's *Confessions*, the artist's work is something of an archaeology and an enactment of this desperate relation. Its play between the lush costumed reconstructions of fragments of Rousseau's memories, on the one hand, and a natural history of plants, on the other, suggests a chasm between the mannered world of an 18th century sexuality and the innocence and openness of the green world. But as the similarities between the two begin to grow, especially between the rustling of silks and meadows soughing in the wind, the entrapment of the emergent libertarian libertine in the very forms of his own liberation gradually emerge. The comparison with the situation of the viewer is doubled by the extensive use of close-ups of faces, eyes, hands, shoulders, hair; the players enact for us the scenarios of fantasy as memory, enclosed in little loops and twinnings of quick-time screens, face to face, as in a mirror. The 'pages' for each plant, however, do not loop; they progress through a series of views to an image of the shadow of the plant, and a single exemplar of the species in the studio, plucked from its habitat, selected and framed for the image. Along one of its many axes, the work suggests the intrication in a newly individualised sensorium of the human and natural worlds as alike arrayed for inspection, an inspection in which, however, the self-absorbed viewer will only find reflected the object-relations of his/her self.

CD-ROM artists can engage a far subtler interface than much of the transient work on the net, which is dependent on time-consuming and unpre-dictable downloads. CD-ROM allows the bandwidth and the leisure to develop far more complex and occasionally more traditional artworks. Nonetheless Boissier's piece argues as cogently as any critical text the impasses of both Rousseau's subjectivity and the structures of the interface. Its liberation and its delight are drawn from the closed loop, the specimen: a classical fetishisation of the fragments of vision, before, beside, the forbidden sight of origin. The ribbons, combs and lace that tower over and name Rousseau's autonomy are exactly what debars him from immersion in the world for which he longs. Caught over and again in the net of things, he and the viewer cannot escape or disperse across the meadows and bodies that sur-round us.

The terrible and beautiful vertigo of immersion in cyberspace, the erotics of Gibson's fiction and the sensual absorption of netsurfers in their screens, belong not to the subversion of capital and solipsistic individualism, but to the intensification of commodity fetishism as fantasy role-play. The later Lacan argues that 'what one calls sexual bliss is marked, dominated, by the impossibility of establishing, as such, anywhere in the enunciable, the unique One which is important for us, the One of the relationship "sexual relations"'. The impossibility of sexual relation is specifically a male phenomenon: 'Phallic *jouissance* is the obstacle which stops man arriving at *jouissance* in the body of the woman, precisely because what he gets his bliss from is the jouissance of his own organ' (Lacan 1975: 15). We (men?) are too absorbed in the pursuit of our own orgasms to be able to relate, even sexually. If this is one-sided, too phallic, too pessimistic, it was perhaps also premature in the early 1970s to see this as a widespread phenomenon. But as a metaphor for the narcissistic eros of the cyberspace consumer, it is painfully close to the mark. The price of overcoming the rulebook, of escape into the panoptic tower, has been the loss of a certain human contact, and its subordination to an ever more intensively mediated inwardness. The intimacies of the net are on the verge of becoming intrapsychic intimacies.

That the net should be a project of the historical present in the industrialised world is not an accident of technology. The popularity and intensity of net experience are neither self-explanatory, nor simple effects of technological determinism or media imperialism. They belong to the political erotics of the hyperindividualised electronic subject. The logics of individuation intensify, just at the point at which a polity of intimacies seems also possible. Anonymity has not purged the boundaries of the self, though it dissolves inner hierarchies in the encouragement of fantasy. It has given rise to a massive surge in artificial personalities mimicking the most uncompromisingly individualist of cultural icons: the outlaw, the phreak, the cowboy, the frontier. The very Americanisation of matrix vocabulary indicates less its domination by North Americans than the power of the North American mythography of westward expansion and rugged individualism in the new context. Once more we confront the problem of a new polity, but now with a positive programme, suggested by the testimonies of artists and users, whose utopianism is centrally engaged in effecting a rerouted sociality from the tortuous dialectic of self and social in cyberspace.

If cyberspace has made its own the fertile irrationality of orientalism and space science, and has retreated with it into the scurrying highways of the wires, it has taken its risks to find the fullest life available, possessed by a fantasy of solidarity. Such a fantasy, however, still caught in the trammels of the commodity, is fantastic in the Freudian sense: in it can be enacted, in the stifling intensities of the psyche, dreams of domination and submission to the devices of cyberspace; mediated lusts that take as their figures the transvestisms and fetishisms in which alone the commodity erotics of the net can occur. The limited autonomy we grant to our machines has been taken up by an eroticisation of their capacities, the sole solidarity that a playworld can devise. But solidarity is caught, more than ever, in the double-bound impossibility of sexual relations at the fantastic site and with the fantastic object of desire. We are latched into a closed loop of fantastic yearnings without the possibility of partnership: a closure that passes for satisfaction. Still the relation with the machine remains one of ignorance couched in the terms of desire, but an ignorance that yet might provide the grounds for a more subtle relation than the dictatorial assumption of knowledge that plagues relations with a machine in which we recognise only our own identifications. Both the utopianism and the disappointment of cyberspace as it really exists and as it is imagined are facets of its complex interweaving with the commodification of the self. Now it is not only conversation and dialogue that are mediated, but the monologues of the imploded self. And through it all, as from afar, there comes the faintest murmur of another relation, a more profound relation with the self, of how self might begin again to be the receiver as well as the source of the world it inhabits. An enormous beauty lies within reach, of an interconnectivity of the kind Ascott has been trying to build. But it is dependent on the kinds of navigation that draw us towards it.

In the act of writing/reading I undertake on this Macintosh word-processing program, 'I' is marked not once but three times: as the word 'I'; as the blinking cursor/insertion-point that stands just ahead of every last letter; and as the nomadic I-bar/arrow and its various metamorphoses – the pointer-tool. The anchorage in the word 'I' is loosened by the competition, just as it is in the dialectic of voyeurism and fetishism identified in structural film theory. The question 'where am I?' is more likely to be answered by the blinking insertion point than the capital letter, but, depending on its precise voicing, it might also be answered by manipulating the mouse-driven pointer. Another product of the Xerox PARC experiments, the mouse is one of the few really new elements of the HCI, and key to the way this tripartite restructuring of interface subjectivity always attracts the utopian. Under the myriad guises it takes on as it roves across the screen – wristwatch, spinning ball, arrow, fingered hand, gunsight, magnifying glass, pen – the mouse pointer's mobility and its functions in shifting modes – pulling down windows, opening files, driving scroll bars, dragging icons, clicking buttons – seats it at the head of a hierarchy of subject positions voiced in the Macintosh HCI. The mouse is what separates word processing from typing, what links it to other computer programs, and what gives physical form to the emergence of a newly dominant form of control.

In some ways, the mouse enacts the schizophrenic subjectivity credited to cultures of the 'post': it changes form and function as it wanders across the screen and from screen to screen through stacks, files, documents and programs. Restless and unstill, it skitters according to a logic of browsing, a tool and a toy, named for a pet proverbial for its quietness and timidity, a modest instrument (whose major vices are speciesism and a distant relation to 'eek a mouse' sexism) renowned as intuitive design, an extension of the pointing finger. Yet this nomadic and schizophrenic prosthesis has come to work as a globalising metaphor, as universal in intent as the ego of the Enlightenment it might otherwise be assumed to have superseded. It is tempting to read off from the pointer a shifting relation between the intensification of office labour and the changing commodity-scape, whose contents are demateri-alised as information, financial flows and financial services. Information is commodified communication, and electronic cash is an only slightly more rarified form of the universal exchange-value, the universal commodity. But even if the commodity form itself remains integral to office production, its phenomenal surface alters, in the age of neo-liberal markets, extending the possibility for identification, through the cursor, with the new mobility of wealth as flow. A reading of the mouse as point of identification disassem-bles the active/passive binary on which so much of digital culture's literature depends; it enables only a renewed identification with the speculative regimes of synergetic capital.

The VDU is a grid, every pixel identifiable as a numerical address, and its states likewise encoded. This grid derives its onscreen presentations from modernist design practice, which itself can be traced back to Descartes's invention of a neutral space defined only by coordinates rather than con-tents, and to Mercator's redefinition of the map as a blank field of longitude and latitude into which the marks of coordinate space can be drawn. But behind this insipid, unmarked space can be glimpsed an older grid deployed in the mediaeval scriptoria, a grid made up not of modular, transferable boxes, but of points and cruxes, in each of which the divine and the sublu-nary met. As the Cross itself was read as the conjuncture of the mortal and supernatural in Christ's incarnation and death, the crossing of lines in the layout of manuscript pages denoted the narrow gate through which, ana-gogically, the divine might be pursued beyond the materiality of the page (Williamson 1989: 171–4). The Enlightenment secularised the spaces of the page in the interests of reason, giving rise, in office work, to the three-stage history sketched by Berit Holmqvist:

> In the tool perspective the power lies in the hands of the user: There are many tools, and Man can choose according to his needs. The tool is a variant and Man the invariant. The worker is superordinate to the tools. In the mass-media perspective the power lies in the hands of the designer. The machine performs the same task irrespective of which worker controls it. The machine is the invariant, the user the variant and subordinated to the machine. In the dialogue partner perspective, however, the power lies in the hands of the interlocutors as a function of a given context. (Holmqvist 1993: 232)

This history can be paraphrased as a move from the cutting and breaking in of quills through the mechanical tempo of touchtyping and the dictaphone, towards a seemingly more democratic and interactive playworld of net-worked text production. It is ironic that Holmqvist only introduces the environment in the final stages: for some centuries now 'Man' has rarely picked up tools to match 'his' needs, but in order to satisfy the demands of another. The mass media, as mechanised communication, democratise to the precise extent that they introduce technocratic and meritocratic entrance requirements to professionalised communications. Digital 'dialogue' democratises further, but only into the extent to which the skills of previous generations are turned into fixed capital as programs; far from enabling dialogue between designers and users, the user-friendly screen confirms the former's status as worker in a specific mode of production, and the latter's continuing subordination. What changes is the experiential quality of work. The nomadic cursor takes the place of the vertical dimension in mediaeval orthography. In its roaming and clicking, the user feels the godlike powers of intervention reserved for the nodes of design in the sacred manuscript.

The analysis of the cursor suggests that, as cinematic fetishism is replaced by cybernetic transvestism, so filmic voyeurism is digitised in the figure of a secular divinity intervening at a stroke, a click, in the infinitely extending grid of textual production. I think it is a little less than mischievous to give this rational–irrational spirit the name of tourism. The tourist relation is one in which we are always in pursuit of an impossibly pristine discovery, of a terrain separated from the everyday (Urry 1990: 3), which at its apogee has never before been witnessed (MacCannell 1976), and where visited people are not the partners of witnessing, but where the tourist is both privileged participant and external observer. The cursor as perpetual tourist meanders through a landscape which is always foreign, in which it seeks perpetually a home that it will recognise less by identification than by an impossible welcome which its denizens will give it. The pointer circulates not the world but Mercator's projection, a zone as deprived of semantic content as the grids of Boolean switching. Yet its quest is to provide a semantic function, to supply a shifter that the infinitely extensible dimensions of coordinate space must always lack. The impossibility of this quest derives from the tourist's fate: always to be seeking to arrive, not 'here', but 'there'.

To that extent the tourist gaze is cursory: a perpetual dissatisfaction, a perpetual moving on. It is a function of the imaginary nature of the image, that quality of image which connects orientalist painting and illustration, the image-grammars of outer space and the spatialisation of the matrix in cyberpunk. Though different image regimes, they share the same protocols: the resolute exclusion of the tourist from actual participation in an image-space that remains pristine only as long as he is excluded. To that extent, the shared protocol concerns the referential structure of the pointer, not in its semantic content – there is no here, in the sense of home, for the nomadic subject, the tourist mouse. Symptomatically, the shifter functions to point towards a structure of 'this' and 'here', but the reference is shaped as absence: the impossibility of an 'I' that can maintain the power of the pointer at the same time as the fixity of the linguistic 'I', and the now-you-see-it-now-you-don't pulse of the blinking insert point, fretful marker of species difference between the user and the machine with which she would dialogue. The mouse in the hand is blind, responds to a braille signage of taps, runs its errands tail-first. It points, but only to the modular space of the infinite text, a sorting and sifting mechanism rather than a pointer towards the digital world into which its anxious holder gazes in unceasing expectation of epiphany.

The pointer governs insert point and textual 'I' as the nomadic subject of the synergetic corporation, though it dreams of navigating, like the Silver Surfer, through endless dataspace in search of a home from which its very freedom has exiled it.

4

PYGMALION: SILENCE, SOUND AND SPACE

There's a certain
amount of traveling
in a dream deferred

(Hughes 1974: 270)

Silence

Years ago, in a remote valley in northern Quebec, I heard for the first time
the sounds that allowed me to understand lines written 3,000 years earlier:

> Try to recall the pause, thock, pause,
> Made by axe blades as they pace
> Each other through a valuable wood.
> Though the work takes place on the far
> Side of a valley, and the axe strokes are
> Muted by depths of warm, still standing air,
> They throb, throb, closely to your ear;
> And now and then you catch a phrase
> Exchanged between the men who work
> More than a mile away, with perfect clarity. (Logue 1988: 26)

The buzz of Europe's close-packed population makes it impossible today to
hear with such tungsten purity the ordinariness of sound. Homer stresses the
intimacy of hearing, as he compares the axe-blows to the clang of sword on
sword in the midst of battle, a sensory acuteness which is largely lost to the
overburdened soundscapes of the contemporary. That loss perhaps explains
why we have come to relish silence, and to propose it as a central facet of aesthetic appreciation.

In 1952, the composer John Cage visited one of the anechoic chambers at
Harvard University's psychoacoustic laboratory, a room designed to absorb
almost all sounds produced in it. Cage could, however, hear two distinct
sounds: a low, throbbing pulse and a high, singing tone. The engineer in
charge explained that the former was the sound of his blood, the latter of the
central nervous system. 'Try as we may to make a silence, we cannot,' Cage
observed. 'No silence exists that is not pregnant with sound' (Revill 1992:
162). For Cage, and for modern culture, it follows that silence is a willed state,
in which both the external sound world and the body that hears are likewise
ignored.

Even in a crowded gallery, we seek an inner quietude that we associate with rapt meditation of the aesthetic object. The autonomy of the artwork from Kant (1952 [1790]) to Greenberg (1992) produced this odd illusion of silence in the middle of the crowd. The silence of the visual artwork is not an inherent quality of visual art, but the historical product of its constitution as message and of its dematerialised appreciation, from Kantian disinterest to poststructural immaterialism. Even music has achieved a certain silencing, not only of the audience but of the work itself, in the prestige afforded to the purity of pattern in, say, Bach's *Art of the Fugue*, an extra-sensuous algorithmic intelligence that transcends the vagaries of performance, the abjected body and the material vibrations of air and ear. Greenberg's great achievement was to give some matter back to art, but, by emphasising the medium-specificity of painting in particular, he contributed obliquely to the silencing of the artwork and its consumption. Working with a similarly sound-specific concept of musical autonomy, both Stockhausen and Cage, in very different ways, have struggled to render back to music, through new modes of listening and new structural principles, a sense of sound's materiality. That same step, by renewing the confrontation of auditor and vibration, gives to the act of listening a materiality which it had lost. The utopian moment of silence, like the clear sound-world of Homer, may already have passed, yet the aesthetic of pure hearing, a devotion to the autonomy of sound, persists, and will lead us towards the necessity and radical difficulty of assembling truly audiovisual media.

Pure Hearing

Christian Metz identified a difficulty in the path of pure hearing in an essay originally published in 1975, where he argued that:

> if I have distinctly and consciously heard a 'lapping' or a 'whistling', I only have the feeling of a first identification, of a still incomplete recognition. This impression disappears only when I recognise that it was the lapping *of a river*, or the whistling *of the wind in the trees*: in s[h]ort, the recognition of a sound leads directly to the question: 'A sound of what?' (Metz 1980: 25)

The question can be answered with the aid of a semiotic principle, sound's metacoding in language: a doubling over which gives sound perception a socially constructed meaning. There is a pressure, in listening, not to hear the sound but the name of the sound, to infer from it its source, or to impute to it a certain semantic function. So instead of hearing what it is in itself, we 'recognise' the sound, after which we can identify what is making it and say to ourselves, 'Now I understand.' When this happens – for example, when you hear a creak and say, 'That's that loose floorboard' – you displace the content of perception from the ear to the floorboard, and the act of perception from air/ear vibration to a verbal acknowledgement. As Metz concludes,

> We find ourselves quite far, you could say, from the 'adverse spectacle' of subject and object, from the cosmological as well as existential (or at least

transcendental) 'there is' in which phenomenology wanted to place our presence in objects, and the presence of objects in us. I am not so sure, or else this 'distance' is only along certain axes, and does not imply a complete rupture of the horizon. (Metz 1980: 31–2)

Rather than stress the common permeation of sound across the hearer and the world, this coded listening emphasises the opposition between subject and object, recognising the historical nature of hearing as an acquired skill, framed in the determinations of a specific culture. Metz emphasises a formal, if not originary, division of hearing and sight from one another. By contrast, the phenomenologist Merleau-Ponty describes a situation where:

> either the sound and the colour, through their own arrangement, throw an object into relief, such as an ashtray or a violin, and this object speaks directly to all the senses; or else, at the opposite end of experience, the sound and the colour are received into my body, and it becomes difficult to limit my experience to a single sensory department. (Merleau-Ponty 1962: 227)

Here either the object presents itself to perception as a whole, or the body experiences its senses as a unity, but in either case, sound and hearing are one. On the other hand, perhaps because his argument depends on the gap between subject and object constructed by recording sound, severing hearer from heard, Metz's semantic relation of coded hearing suggests an instrumentalisation of listening, the administration of the sensorium in a semantic hierarchy. This kind of hearing is not for pleasure in hearing, but for naming and controlling the world of sound and the somatic power of perception. Metz understands this as a sociological phenomenon, as something given in the contemporary cultural context; we should be wary of mistaking it for an inherent quality of all listening. And indeed, there is a tendency in contemporary acoustic arts specifically opposed to the semanticisation of sound in any form.

In his *Traité des objets musicaux* (1966), the composer Pierre Schaeffer argues for the autonomy of a phase of hearing prior even to Metz's 'first identification', a 'reduced listening' which avoids both causal definition and affectual/semantic description by focusing on the acoustic qualities of the sound in itself. In his commentary on Schaeffer, Michel Chion explains that 'Perception is not a purely individual phenomenon . . . it is in this objectivity-born-of-inter-subjectivity that reduced listening, as Schaeffer defined it, should be situated' (Chion 1994: 29). What you listen out for in reduced listening is precisely what is shared: what anyone can hear, quite apart from their interpretations. This profoundly unnatural mode of 'acousmatic' listening gives rise to a distinctive sharpening of the aural sensorium, one which, in Schaeffer's typology, evolves a sculptural vocabulary of textures, masses and velocities. Moreover, dependent as it is in practice on hearing *exactly* the same sound in *exactly* the same acoustic environment, it is particularly applicable to recorded sound, though clearly a trained ear – Olivier Messiaen's annotations of bird song come to mind – will be able to respond to the most ephemeral events of the sonic environment. And finally, its Greenbergian attention to the fabric of the medium, the thing itself, rather than inferred ideas about its making or its reception, allows us to ask what a pure sound might be, and what relation it might have to the utopianism of accelerated modernity. Not least among these qualities will be the identification of what can be shared in the perception of sound as mass, texture, velocity.

Microrhythms and microtonalities, even nanorhythms, nanotonalities, characterise some of the most acousmatic of contemporary musics, as exemplified in this near-random selection from an otherwise unexcerptable interview with Stockhausen, describing the *Aries* section of his enormous work *Sirius*.

> In the end one doesn't take in anything except a single sound of a certain density, similar to a murmuring. By following the opposite tendency, on the other hand, that of a gradual rallentando, the melodies take on form again, the sounds gradually become clearer. The melodic outline is set out clearly with its rhythms, its sound-frequencies and its intervallic content. At this point begins the redimensionalizing of the sounds, which contract and shrink. The melody becomes condensed and compressed, as if a giant was reduced to the size of a dwarf. You return again to the perception of no more than a unique, solitary sound, while the rhythm proceeds on its way, a tenacious survivor locked up in a single line. (Tannenbaum 1987: 53)

Stockhausen goes on to describe similar processes occurring with the rhythm and its progressive annihilation, after which nothing is left but pure timbre, from which the work is reconstructed. Whether originated as pure tones or as live samples of radio transmissions, the composition decomposes sounds into musical spaces, unpacking the narrow instrumentality of semantic listening. Stockhausen asserts the brute fact of sound as aural perception. As musician, he is concerned with the material practice of the making of sounds, but is happy to allocate control over sources and modulations to chance, or to the discrete logic of sound composition, freed of reference to melody, harmony, counterpoint or the traditional goals of music. Stockhausen's autonomous sounds are navigable distances, both of and not of the human world, explorations of the sheer autonomy of music, even from its own histories.

Because, after all, we do not, and it is impossible to, distinguish between the vibration of the air, the vibration of the eardrum and the bones (the feet, after the ears, are our most sensitive receptors, especially of bass notes; the collarbone and chest respond to more airborne sounds), and the neurobiological events which, in consort, provide us with the mental event of sound perception, sound events create a space with no respect for the sacrosanctity of the epidermis in Western philosophy. Moreover, just as the eye is a source of light, but far more so, the body is a source of sound: pounding of the pulse, whooshing of the bloodstream, the high whine of the central nervous system. All hearing is made up of the interference between these bodily sounds and those that enter it from without, traversing it with vibrations and electro-chemical flows. At the same time, sound source and sound perception are physically connected, by air, proximity and, hearing a throbbing bass riff

through the dancefloor, by solid matter: the phenomenological interpenetration of object and subject is far more difficult to undo in aural than in
visual arts.

At the same time, there are two aspects to the social nature of hearing. On
the one hand the acousmatic: what is common in any perception of a sound,
the physiological solidarity of hearing. On the other the coded: the semantic
and instrumental separation of sound object and the subject of hearing
effected through semiotic and so social codes of language and naming. One
might understand the struggles over the meaning of sound, and especially of
music, as struggles over the kinds of sociality that are implicit in them.

The most persuasive of such models appears in the dialectic of chance
audition inhabiting John Cage's *4' 33"* of 1952, three movements performed
by closing the lid of a piano for measured periods adding up to four minutes
and thirty-three seconds. Cage was at the time in pursuit of a mode of composition which might obliterate the ego through the use of chance. In the
previous year, he had begun to use the *I Ching* as a means of removing com-
positorial control over the production of music within a rule-bound system.
Now, he removed the very content of the music, reducing it to pure duration.
Yet within the time so marked out, the relations between sounds as well as
the sounds themselves take on a kind of liberty: 'one may give up the desire
to control sound, clear his mind of music, and set about discovering means
to let sound[s] be themselves, rather than vehicles for man-made theories or
expressions of human sentiments' (Cage 1994; 8–9). Just as art has been
transformed by Duchamp's *Fountain* (1917), the urinal signed R. Mutt, so
music, and the auditory arts that can now emerge from under its shadow, are
utterly changed by *4' 33"*.

Cage's composition need not be defined negatively, as the denial of human
control and limitation of the acoustic universe, nor simply positively as opening up the sense of beauty to the sounds of the everyday. In a later
companion piece, *0' 00"*, even the control over duration would be stripped
back, to reveal the purity of sounds, and to refresh the possibilities of listening to the world. Yet at the same time, in a brilliant essay, Douglas Kahn
can argue convincingly that:

> The main avant-garde strategy in music from Russolo to Cage quite evidently
> relied upon notions of noise and worldly sound as 'extra-musical'; what was
> outside musical materiality was then progressively brought back into the fold in
> order to rejuvenate musical practice. . . . But for a sound to be 'musicalized' in
> this strategy, it had to conform materially to ideas of sonicity, that is, ideas of
> a sound stripped of its associative attributes, a minimally coded sound existing
> in close proximity to 'pure' perception and distant from the contaminating
> effects of the world. (Kahn 1992: 3)

There are two elements to Kahn's critique. On the one hand, the new Cagean
listening is accused of abandoning the world as content, and producing a
pure sound space in which the ugliest sounds and the most beautiful weigh
equally with one another. The criticism not only rests on Cage's Buddhist
quietism, but evokes Benjamin's critique of *Neue Sachlichkeit* photography,

which he accused of 'turning abject poverty itself, by handling it in a modish way, into an object of enjoyment' (Benjamin 1973a: 95). Such a sound world, like the silence demanded by meditative consumption of art, like the negation of the body as sound source, erases the world as intrinsic to noise.

The second element of Kahn's critique is implicit in Cage's own ambiguities over the meaning of *4′ 33″*. For while, in the 1957 lecture quoted above, he speaks of sounds in liberty, in an earlier programme note cited by his biographer, he talks of discovering that, in the use of found sounds and instruments, 'we have mastered or subjugated noise. We become triumphant over it' (Revill 1992: 64–5), a credo supported by a note from the poet William Carlos Williams to Cage's *First Construction* of 1939: 'I felt that noise, the unrelated noise of life, such as this in the subway . . . had actually been mastered, subjugated. The composer has taken this hated thing, life, and rigged himself into power over it by his music' (Revill 1992: 65). Admittedly, *4′ 33″* represents a significant turning point in Cage's compositional methods and musical, even metaphysical direction. Yet Kahn's criticism stands firm: the piece simultaneously colonises and erases the world under the semiotic system of music, even in the act of remaking the musical apparatus so that it can so colonise.

The piece, then, is not dialectical, but an oscillation between subjection to a world, including the body, which is modelled as utterly external to the musical subject, and the radical objectification of the world as musical score. In effect, the piece can be argued to be psychological rather than aesthetic, producing a certain mode of subjectivity rather than an interpenetration of hearer and heard. Though it abandons the semantic and instrumental, it does so by pretending to a kind of realism. Like 19th-century realism, it attends to the despised and outcast elements of the sound-world; like Schoenberg's twelve-tone row, it abandons hierarchy among notes in favour of a democratic relation. Yet at the same time, the democracy to which it refers is that of the infinite exchange of finally interchangeable goods. Indeed, Adorno could almost have been thinking of *4′ 33″* when he wrote:

> The poles of the artwork's deaestheticisation are that it is made as much a thing among things as a psychological vehicle of the spectator. What the reified artworks are no longer able to say is replaced by the beholder with the standardized echo of himself, to which he hearkens. This mechanism . . . contrives to make that appear near and familiar to its audience that has been estranged from them and brought close again only by having been heteronomously manipulated. (Adorno 1997: 17)

The purity of pure hearing, Homer's axes, is unrecoverable. What *4′ 33″* presents to us, then, is not the unmediated sounds of the world, nor the liberation of music from its own autonomy, but a commodification of sound as music in the up-to-date form of the commodity without use-value, a pure display of taste. As Attali observes, 'when Cage opens the door to the concert hall to let the noise of street in, he is regenerating all of music. . . . But the musician does not have many ways of practicing this kind of music within the existing networks: the great spectacle of noise is only a spectacle, even if it is blasphemous' (Attali 1985: 136–7). As a composition, *4' 33"* makes an auditory spectacle of the world, just as the cult of the picturesque and the Romantic sublime turned raw terrain into landscape. The regeneration of music is accomplished at the expense of its demolition, the remaking of the machine ensemble of music. The piece, then, is merely an example of aberrant encoding, the subversion of existing networks, practices, institutions, discourses and technologies that frame music as an art. It fails to undo the apparatus, because it sets itself the smaller task of resisting it. And in curious ways, the claim to immediacy fails specifically to deal with the most important condition of sound in the 20th century, its mechanisation.

Recording: The Mobilisation of Sound

When Professor Higgins accosts the flower-girl Eliza in Covent Garden to record her strangulated vowels, in George Bernard Shaw's *Pygmalion* (1941 [1912]), he is prevented in his careless torture by the arrival of Colonel Pickering of the India Service. Higgins, at first an anxious braggart, softens as he realises that this is Pickering the author of 'Spoken Sanskrit'. Over the bewildered head of the Shavian working class, Higgins and Pickering speak for two alternative modes of recording. Higgins's shorthand, and more specifically his phonogram, is the auditory equivalent of Fox-Talbot's 'pencil of nature', the mechanical retrieval and storage of sound, pristine empirical realism. But spoken Sanskrit?

Sanskrit, the oldest member of the Indo-European family of languages, flourished as a spoken tongue five or six millennia ago. Today it survives as a literary corpus. However, one auditory element still remains. The ancient hymns of the Vedas have magical power, but only if spoken correctly. An ancient lineage of oral instruction has preserved that pronunciation. Shaw, the theosophist lover of Annie Besant, may well have been aware of the tradition underlying the apparently meaningless phonological academicism. No matter if he was or not. Pickering stands, briefly, for another tradition of recording, using human beings as storage medium, a rare, pure example of the meme in operation (see Dawkins 1989: 192–201; Dennett 1991: 200–10). The Vedic tradition offers an alternative to Higgins's mechanicism as profoundly conservative as Higgins's phonograph is profoundly normative.

Memory is a sort of scarification. The tracks of memory are laid down in the first months of life, as the synaptic rhizomes begin to ossify into the roadmap of ingrained habit (Changeux 1985: 249; Rose 1993: 140). In that process, the magical and transformative powers of the infant narcissist are dispersed, in favour of an increasingly complex habit of survival. But cognitivist externalisations of memory, as a fund of data and schemata, miss the mutuality of contemporary life, for which you have to learn a vast number of adaptable protocols in order to survive in risk-trust environments like the technological expert-driven systems of transport (Giddens 1990: 79–111) – or your internet server and the internet itself. Such memories are not locatable in an individual mind or brain, but in the interconnecting pathways between individuals which have always been figurable, though differently in different times and places, as the memories embedded in the tool that remembers its maker's hand, the old broom that remembers where the dust is, the machine ensemble that remembers the systems of connection. Nor is memory a bank, in which experiences can be deposited and cognitive maps withdrawn. It is more a fluid than a grid. The double error of contemporary memory-work has been to individualise and externalise that memory which exists only as communicative, and in which our devices have always figured as more than mnemonic.

Memory and forgetting governed sound perception before recording, when there existed no technology for saving noises and voices in the way that landscapes and faces might be preserved through painting and sculpture. Sound is profoundly temporal. It cannot be frozen, like an image: its very existence depends upon the materiality of air in motion, of changing pressures, of vibration. Sounds, even the slightest and most minutely perceived, occupy time by dint of their existence as vibration. In some unimaginably still night, windless and waveless, a pin drops into soft mud: a tiny plop in the well of silence. But what you experience here is not just the sound, and the time of its perception, but the time it takes a sound to cover the space between you and it, and in the aftermath of perception, as silence re-forms itself about it, and you wait for a repetition or continuation, a third time. These times constitute a form of distance, the commingling of time and space. The times of sound are also the elements of its geography. It is in the nature of sound, whether it is conveying information about a world already known, acting as the vehicle for pattern and structure independent of its voicings, or merely doubling up the preexisting certainties of a verbal meta-code, to be redundant. That is precisely what allows the possibility of sound's autonomy, but also that which returns it to us as a human environment, and, in changing it from mere vehicle to material mediation, resituates it in the distances between – and within – people. Because of their transience, sounds anchored the species in the processes of time, the tragic irreversibility of change, mourned by Catullus' lines, 'what a woman tells her lover in the act of love/ should be written in wind and running water' (Catullus, Poem 70; 1970: 72), and a million other poems. Just what matters most – the relationships between people – disappears fastest and most completely. This material transience is restructured in its deepest roots with the invention of recording. To add recording to the tradition has only one simple effect: to free the rest of the mind for listening or other occupations. It negates memory by replacing it with an external storage. Most of all, it severs memory of sound from the human voice, the human agent.

In Ovid's version of the Pygmalion story, as the sculptor's prayers are answered, and his sculpted lover comes to life, the enjoyment of the link between the technologies of the day and sensual enjoyment is unembarrassed:

> . . . the ivory waxed soft, and putting quite away
> All hardness, yielded underneath his fingers as we see
> A piece of wax made soft against the sun, or drawn to be
> In divers shapes by chafing it between one's hands and so
> To serve to uses. He amazed stood wavering to and fro
> 'Tween joy and fear to be beguiled; again he burned in love
> (Ovid x, 248ff; 1939: 310)

This tactile moulding is suppressed in Shaw's version. Higgins' work is sublimated from the hands to the ear, by the medium of the phonograph, whose needle and groove enact his forbidden lust. The Shavian version forms part of a flurry of interest in the myth among artists like Gérôme and Burne-Jones and playwrights like George du Maurier, whose Svengali acts the Pygmalion part. For film theorists, the apogee of the cycle arrives with Villiers de l'Isle-Adam's *L'Eve future* of 1880–1, where a fictionalised Thomas Edison invents a mechanical woman in the narcissistic image of the protagonist, Lord Ewald. For Michelson (1984) and Bellour (1986), the ideal woman so created foreshadows the sexual politics of the cinema. But the utopianism of the story derives from the phonograph hidden within the mechanical body, allowing her to speak, and, through a clever and not so impossible imaginary technology, to converse. The illusion is that of free will; the guarantee that that freedom will always conform to Lord Ewald's desire. At the same time, of course, the ideal woman is ideal because mechanical, saying always what we want to hear. Recording is then a technology formed in the traces of Metz's metacode, a way of controlling the soundscape so that it will always conform to an already catalogued expectation, magically confirming our desire to hear with the desired sound.

The invention of electro-mechanical recording, and its evolution into the digital, has doubled the quantity of sounds in the world. They too are part of the sound worlds we inhabit, along with the river and the pneumatic drills, the clattering keyboard and the refrigerator's hum. No longer bathed in by the magical intensity that surrounds any new technology with glamour, sound recording sifts its particulates into the phonic landscape, integrates with it even as it maintains its distinctive qualities. It has made the alien familiar. But as portability and broadcasting technologies have speeded the possibilities of integration, so too they have accelerated the potential for commodification and instrumentalisation. The only global art of sound is the music industry and audiovisual exports. Their criterion is that sound be rendered as object, so that it can be used. The narrow concentric circles of the phonograph were, for Shaw's Professor Higgins, a commodity for controlling the future. Certainly, every recording is a piece of the past restorable to the present, but the act of recording is also an attempt to secure that piece of the future when the recording will be played. But what is controlled loses its life, its capacity to evolve. Such was the fate of the European symphony in the age of sound recording. Refined and defined increasingly rigidly into a hierarchy of forms dependent on faithfulness to a written and preserved score (according to Michael Chanan 1995: especially 116–36), the orchestral repertoire ossifies. The associated cult of authenticity in tempi, instrumentation and interpretation curtails radically the emotional range of classical performances. The more recent possibilities of remastering live recordings using spliced tape samples and digital editing at once frees the performer from the drudgery of perfection, while giving the producer the tools to create it. Yet that perfection tends, once more, towards an idealised form, the ideal of a pure acoustic space, a pure text and pure instrumentation. Here the integrity of the message triumphs at the expense of the evolution of the culture.

I would never have been able to begin to understand Schoenberg's chamber music without the aid of recordings. The process of listening is never one of pure repetition, especially in the case of complex works which demand a certain concentration. Yet this same technology, as a technique of repetition, is also regressive, in the sense that it produces a fantastic regime of control over a transitory environment. However, as Rick Altman has shown, repetition is also subtly invaded by the environment it seeks to command: 'Not only do I hear the fabulous acoustics of the Cleveland Orchestra's home concert hall, but at the same time I have to put up with the less than ideal acoustics of my own living room. Every sound I hear is thus double, marked both by the specific circumstances of recording *and* by the particularities of the reproduction situation' (Altman 1992: 27). Not only will playback be acoustically altered from origin, but recording is divorced from playback by definition – the two can only destroy each other in the white noise of feedback unless the rules of distance be respected. In this sense, recording technologies are like photographs, dependent on the odd dialectic of presence and absence, where the presence of the recording demands the absence of the performance, a distance which is both temporal and geographic.

And so this moment of recording is also the point at which sounds become spatially mobile – and plural. A recorded or a remembered sound can be retrieved not only at another time but in another place. Time and space are reconciled in the disembodiment of sound, its severance from its point of origin. The addition of transmission technologies – phonetic script, telephony, broadcasting, amplification – merely accelerates the process of distanciation from origin. The process itself is ancient. Phonic phenomena have always travelled: the names of Moctezuma and Chinghis Khan echoed across continents. But now not only names but voices can travel. They can be heard more swiftly, and perhaps that quantitative change has also brought about a qualitative shift in the meanings we can ascribe to mediated sound. The mnemonic traditions could recall only the human voice, and of the voice only its pronunciation and intonation, but not its grain, the particularity, even uniqueness, of a single person's speaking. Orality preserves an abstract quality of the voice, not its materiality. Recording technologies attempt to restore the material, but stumble, because each playback modulates the sound – of speech, let's say – not only because of the new acoustic situation of playback, but through amplification systems which do not work like the voice itself. 'At the slightest touch,' sing Flanders and Swan, 'I can make

Caruso sound like Hutch.' Mechanical sound recording resituates the voice in the problematic of representation. It takes as its goal fidelity, rather than construction, the false materialism of the replication of origin. With recording, sounds are not merely doubled. In the arcana of fidelity, sound becomes sounds: multiplying in their dispersal and in their constant resort towards an original which they can no longer access.

Sound was always placed because it was always physical. It burbled up from the wet viscera of the body, the tumbling of water, the impact of bronze on wood, to fill the space of the ear, the valley, the battlefield. This material of sound articulated the body to the world in their communion, their shared existence. Recorded sound, however, doubles the sound of place with an art of dissemination. This is the source of that sense we sometimes get of music as insubstantial, not because it cannot be preserved, but because it is not anchored in things, in the way any representational forms are. Though in some ways a less influential figure than Cage, Karlheinz Stockhausen produces more by way of openings and entry points to a new aural space. His very megalomania makes it not only possible but imperative to escape the musical, in a crucial example by tuning radios to random, often dead wavebands: to hear what any ear can hear. But even Stockhausen, in his explorations of the purity of timbre, rhythm and the rest, immerses himself and his audience in pure perception. The use of radio intrudes on this contemplative subjectivity, introducing the dependency of listening on the mediation that makes it possible.

Sound theory introduces major problems for the concept of realism, and especially for the familiar problematic of representation. Recording is no more an innocent or transparent replication of real, pro-phonographic sound than the photograph is of the pro-filmic. It has its own techniques of framing and selection, its entrenched aesthetics, its practices of erasing the marks of its making. Tape splicing to approximate an ideal, studio-perfect rendition is locked into an endless dialectic of the delirious pursuit of an inaudible perfection. The problem for realism and the critique of representation is not simply that music, however defined, is non-referential, but that the more perfect a recording, the less it refers to a preexisting sound. The craft of contemporary sound engineering is rich in technique to the point at which its devotion to the revelation of reality has to be doubted. This might be both a Bazinian criticism of film sound, and a critique of the idealising tendencies of representational theory. It is also the problematic of the work of electronic composers like Pierre Schaeffer, Stockhausen and Michel Chion (as indeed in some of Cage's tape pieces), where the medium of recording is brought into the foreground, a modernist solution. A recording, whatever else it is, is always a communication without a content, pure mediation, always an effect, never the thing itself. If we have learnt to listen habitually, and habitually to identify sounds by their origins, it is because we have forgotten how to hear. But to identify a sound's origin as 'the CD player' is clearly to say nothing of its content. The arts of recording, whether orally or mechanically, are the arts which restore to sound the purity they assume by losing origin.

As John Potts (1995) writes, digital sound recording alters the metaphorical capacities of sound. On the one hand, digital sampling, running at around 44,000 samples per second, seizes a tiny fragment of sound to place in memory; on the other, the sampling rate is higher than the cycles of human hearing, so that we perceive them as a flow. The graphical interface of most sound editors provides a synchronous score, like an orchestral score, in which the cursor can act as a plastic, roving present, unconfined to linearity. Potts emphasises the novelty of this temporal freedom, but it is clear that it implies a spatial liberation too, not one confined to the visual regime of the interface, but engaging channels of the mix, and by implication the mutability of acoustic space in playback. In this mutable space, sounds cease to be what they are, can no longer determine their futures, but become subjects in their own right by entering the history of the future as conditions of that future bound to the complexity of mutually interacting conditions of listening. Sounds thus become less agents, and more subjects, subject to the world into which they reemerge. It is in this sense that recorded sounds gain their discretion, their ability to mediate between people over spatio-temporal distances, as relations between people rather than as things.

Stockhausen's practice further introduces, through its manipulations of recorded sound, the inscaping of sound events in reduced listening, revealing that even the imaginable purity of the event as a moment of being is a product of complex interactions and fluid becomings. Yet once recorded, or indeed even performed, the fluidities of his works are nailed down to the specifics of their existence, and Stockhausen is notoriously a stickler for accuracy and authenticity in recording, a homage to the ideal that recording has brought to centrality in the conception of contemporary music. But the aural spaces of traditional domestic playback are always 'inadequate' to the conceptualisation of an ideal acoustic. Perhaps the only aural scape which approaches to the purity of the ideal is provided by headphones. There is an illuminating anecdote to tell here, concerning a major retrospective of European video installations in Cologne a few years ago. A curatorial problem with having more than one or two installations in a show is that their sound spaces tend to overlap, producing an unmanageable cacophony in the transition zones between them. The organisers' solution was to equip visitors with infra-red activated headsets, which would pick up the sound from a given installation as you walked into range of its miniature transmitter. It was not just the abruptness of the transition which offended some of the exhibiting artists, but the translation of an architectural into a punctual space. Transmitted through air, sound occupies and creates an environment. Transmitted directly to the ear, with whatever purity of reproduction, that space is reduced to an optimal (and imaginary) point midway between the ears: the Cartesian theory of the pineal gland as central control point in the brain where, hierarchically, all perceptions attain consciousness (see Dennett 1991: 104–11 and *passim*).

Such a Cartesian soundscape, constructed as a technology in which aural perspective is focused around an imagined central point of the brain, not only returns us to a residual dualism of mind over sensorium, not only reduces the experience of sound from a bodily to a purely auricular event, but also remodels the sound space as individuated. If Altman is correct, each act of listening is dependent on the immediate acoustic environment, and susceptible to minuscule changes in the sound-absorbing qualities of humidity, bodies, fabrics and the sympathetic vibrations and echoes of furniture and decor. So every playback event is unique, open to the serendipity of an environment inhabited by changing acoustics and additional sound sources. To move through the acoustic environment of a video installation is, then, to alter it. The Cartesian headset, in its pursuit of an imagined ideality of reproduction, deprives the auditor of the fundamental sociality of sound, less here sculptural, and to do with the making of space, than architectural, and engaged in inhabiting it. Far from symbolising a dichotomy between the urban nomad (Chambers 1990) and the urban solipsist (Hosokawa 1984), the walkman is the precise material descriptor of their synthesis in the synergetic and corporate hyperindividual as machine ensemble. Recorded sound in open, sculptural installations is, by contrast and to coin Le Corbusier's phrase, a machine for living in.

Transmission: Silent Listening, Silent Reading

The immense patent cases between Bell Telephone, Western Union and Bell's giant subsidiary AT&T (Barnouw 1966: 43ff.; Douglas 1987) limited two-way radio to maritime and military uses, and effectively established the concept of broadcasting as one-way medium. State monopolies in Europe had the same effect (see, for example, Briggs 1985). 'Ham' amateur radio was restricted as a result to a minuscule portion of the shortwave frequencies, and telephone, telegraph and wireless corporations operated as a cartel to close down any aspiration to democratic access to the airwaves. Radio became totalitarian and universalising by the powers it assumed over transmission, even in those moments, like Roosevelt's Pearl Harbor speech, or Churchill's wartime broadcasts, at which it most desperately needed to elicit democratic support. The invisible and inaudible interlocutors of those addresses to 'the nation', sightless and speechless, become ideological abstractions – the mass, the public, the home of 'listeners at home', of the excluded 'listeners in' of the early BBC. Monolinear broadcasting radiates silence, as long as it refuses or, at best, polices the possibility of dialogue.

   'Any speaker', writes Bakhtin, 'is himself a respondent to a greater or lesser degree. He is not, after all, the first speaker, the one who disturbs the eternal silence of the universe' (Bakhtin 1986: 89). But to a certain extent, radio speeches pretend to just such cosmological originality. Radio silence, we know, is finite. Radio technology is ecological, in the sense that it responds to environmental events, human or cosmic: lightning, solar storms, cosmic radiation, the unsuppressed washing machine next door. Because radio is attuned to the material universe, it cannot be universal in the Idealist sense. Yet the miraculous emergence of remote voices from the loudspeaker, however assuaged and massaged by continuity devices and habitual, half-aware listening, cannot be entirely dismissed. The endless chatter of the radio is an attempt to eradicate the emptiness from which it seems to spring so magically, and at the same time to deny the insurgence of environmental sounds, leaving ever less auditory space or transmission time for reflection and response. In its professionalisation over a period of decades, it has surrendered its claim to communication, and become a stimulus.

Radio's closure to dialogue can be heard in the casting of specific kinds of voice, trained voices that gravitate towards specific kinds of programming or advertising: the warmly friendly and ripely familiar, the laidback, the hyper-manic, the blithely trivial. On the other side, there are those voices selected, and recorded without benefit of studio acoustics, to stand in as the unre-hearsed, spontaneous and earthy. Yet even that voice is framed – by the choice of microphone, the typically exterior or busy acoustic space, the lack of bottom, the deliberately unrehearsed take – not to be real but to represent the real. The plunge from studio to street sound space then frames even that *vox pop* voice as the prime and incontrovertible radio event, the fracturing of silence, even as it acts out an ideological construction of continuity between the radio world and the social. Such continuity exists only as mime.

The *vox pop* interview is the last bastion of unrehearsed radio, not because of the voice, which is always the voice not of this person here but of that person *speaking on the radio*; rather because of the uncontrolled environment of recording. The radio voice is never without environment, and never more environment-dependent than when studio-bound. Here the imitation of life is at its peak, in the utterly controlled anarchy of children's and pop radio, in the acoustically muffled respect of the deadened booth where politicians speak at their most grave and self-deluding. Broadcasting will not allow silence. The only silence it recognises is the silence of being turned off, a silence deeper than any of the pre-electronic arts, in which the bearer – stone, canvas, performance, page – is coextensive and isomorphic with the work of art itself. In radio, the vehicle remains when the tenor has been switched off. We are left with the silence of furniture, or of the tap that neither flows nor drips, a functionless silence, unlike the pause in speech which, turned on, it can only imitate but not express.

The telephone's mystery is not so great: we can see still the wires that carry the voice, and you can imagine hearing the myriad voices if you put your ear to a telegraph pole and listen to the humming of the wind in the wires. Cables form a physical contact from one point to another: there is no magical action at a distance. The telephone, however, is an isolated medium, in the sense that it is not vulnerable to atmospheric disturbance or electro-magnetic radiation. Telephony, like telegraphy before it, is a closed system; which is why it, rather than radio or print, gave birth to information theory. Moreover, the telephone is an intimate medium. Despite the fact that 80% of the world's telephone traffic is business-to-business, the phone retains that semblance of dialogue that allows it to encourage rumour and fantasy. But at a price. The invisible caller has the choice of anonymity, a choice which colours his or her identification. Fantasy is bought at the cost of disembodiment. But it is also restricted, despite technical efforts to the contrary, in imagination and in daily use, to the one-to-one. This is why phone-in programmes are so unbalanced: the caller is always an individual, but the studio presenter is always the company. Similar conditions obtain in huge numbers of telephone calls to consumer hotlines and booking agencies. Dialogue's condition of equality is denied, even before the mapping of conversation as switching diagrams among trained corporate telephone operators.

Telephony lacks a certain tonal complexity, which no technical solutions can quite get over. The interests of efficiency, of delivering message rather than enabling communication, reduce overtonal range, at the expense of both dialogue and that polyphony in which creative misapprehension is born. Even ameliorated voice transmission still suffers from closure. Digital stereo multi-party telephony still occupies an auditory void, marked off from the acoustic universe. To listen to a voice on the phone is to abstract yourself from the rest of the world as surely as Cage's four and a half minutes, not as we do when singling out an interlocutor among a crowd of voices, but by the crystalline insistence of that earphone voice on being heard. The ears' perspective is reduced to that of receiver, where in everyday acoustic space they are roving scanners of every vibration. In place of actively patrolling the aural, we become, like HMV's Nipper, merely attentive. Beyond the closed system of telephony and broadcasting, we roam through auditory space; but within it, acoustic activities are funnelled into a single point – whether monaural, or defined by headphones at the mystic pineal point of consciousness hidden deep inside the bone box of the skull.

When the New York poet Frank O'Hara wrote in his mock manifesto 'Personism' about poetry as phone calls that had somehow never got made, he indicated not just the intimacy which his poetry strove after, but the necessity, in order to gain that intimacy, of abandoning the ordinary, efficient syntax and lexicon of telephone talk, and ultimately the very machine itself, by then the major medium of speech for technologised New York. Whatever else it says, a phone call is about the absence to one another of the partners in conversation. Telephones are devices for keeping people apart. The disembodiment of the voice, its reduction to a narrow bandwidth, its seclusion in an empty environment, its focusing at the ear or in the Cartesian headset, the necessary distance between callers: all of these serve both the ideology of individualism and the bureaucratisation of even our most intimate relations. Babel and *Gemeinschaft* seem our only alternatives: collapsing the semantic world, or reinventing the performative community. Yet both are nostalgic for a past that we may not revive; and both are trapped in the dialectic of resistance, forever subordinate to a dominant whose domination they must presume.

There can be no 'return' to dialogue. We cannot face each other again as equals, knowing that we share the same values, references, beliefs and vocabularies. That transparency is gone, and with it the presence of speech to its origin. We have become more conscious than ever that speaking is rhetorical. Some subtle imitation of what recording and broadcasting have taught us to believe informs the proper enunciation, the correct syntax, the affected intonation that inhabits us even when we are speaking silently to ourselves. Since Alexander Graham Bell, there is no inner speech that is not already a rehearsal for a public, and one can understand Edison's phonograph as a technical realisation of the death of conversation, as speech moves from dialogue among equals to an individual's public address. Speaking, a victim of the collapse of privacy, is no longer a private art, but conducted at the cusp of inner speech and oratory, intimacy and publicity, the edge of the politics of the unconscious.

In the long historical process of becoming rhetorical, speaking has all but obliterated listening as a passive art. Obsessed with intervention, we are our own worst observers. The triumph of theoretical over practical knowledge, in a technologised world where we must rely on others to build our transport, our communications and our food technologies, has left us with weakened understandings of the materiality of the world. So it is that we are scarcely able to hear speech: we pounce upon it as message, or, increasingly, as symptom; as typical and, now, as inauthentic. I do not want particularly to contest these theories of the voice, but to counter with the empirical lack of a passive and receptive, acousmatic practice of listening – to the phonemes, the stresses, the shape, the tone, the weight of a voice speaking. We are too active for that, and cannot wait to replace that other voice with our own; even knowing, like an over-excited child, that what we have to say is just as irrelevant and unoriginal, just as typical and inauthentic as the voice we have interrupted. We listen, without hearing, in order only to obey or rebut. In the overwhelming volume of voices raised in the world, we hear almost none, save perhaps, in those moments of intimacy in which a breath, in the act of love or of death, etches itself onto the narcissistic mirror of the self. Such an openness to other voices would drive us crazy, but for lack of it, we have become impervious to the changes that have come over speech, and our listening, since Edison. Hearing, in becoming commodified, has become banal. But if we cannot stand the rawness of dialogue, we can become pervious to the flash of its processes intersecting with our own.

Art, on the other hand, is no longer silent. It is not just that artists have begun to challenge the priestly silence of the artwork and the gallery with filmworks, media arts, noise-making sculptures and musical events. The old art too has changed. It has lost its silence with its aura. Art can no longer cloak itself with the mysterious dumbness that dissembled its hieratic claims in the past. Today, art must be implicated in the acoustic world, or, if it is silent, it enters as a silent thing in a world of sound. But it enters the acoustic in the moment at which the acoustic itself is changed for good and all by broadcasting and recording. As film, video, internet and audio works transform the art schools and the galleries, so they are transformed, and the auditory itself undergoes a transfiguration. Again, the transformation is dependent not on the clamour of discourses that accrue to every meaningful event in the contemporary world, but on the relation of artworks to an auditory culture, in the same way that even invisible works demand to be understood as elements of a visual. As the audible world falls increasingly under the hegemony of music, the histories of non-musical sound in the arts reach a specific critical moment, today, around questions of the voice, the materiality of embodied speech. Art, which for two centuries has clothed itself in discourse, must now relate itself to human voices that have changed, as recorded and broadcast, and in relation to still and moving images, printed words, the graphic.

Machine perception and human perception are co-dependent, and must co-evolve. Recording cannot be rescinded, any more than we can recall Columbus. So our evolution as technologised species requires a sense of how our technologies have already infiltrated consciousness and bodies: such a technology as writing, for example, which, progressing through typewriters, word processors, hypertext and websites, has achieved a remarkable separation from the speaking voice. Radio and TV interviewees speak as if their words had been scripted, just as performers in recording studios idealise the score. Teachers and politicians seek to emulate the apparently effortless fluency of movie stars, and improvisation in dialogue, the grounds of openness to interpretation and change, has given way to a careful rehearsal of stock phrases among the shock jocks and new lads of the contemporary mediascape. Voices themselves change, in meetings, interviews or on the telephone, to approximate a scripted, actorly masquerade. Writing has invaded the psyche.

Perhaps the most curious, if arcane, emanation of this ascendancy of the written is the decay of the voice in poetry and, despite the attentions of generative-transformational linguists in free-verse metrics (see Attridge 1982: 34–55; Levin 1962), in the academic and critical study of poems. To some extent, this comes about because of a change in poetics, an uncertainty as to the continuing value of certain verbal 'musics', a democratisation of stress according to principles like Olson's quantitative metrics, where 'the quantity of the syllables (how long it takes to say them) pulls down the accent to a progress along the length of the line itself' (Olson 1966a: 35–6). This is a modernisation of the Romantic attempt to restore the common cadence to the artifice of verse, and one at the brink of bifurcation, one strand of new poetry moving, via Langston Hughes and the Beats, towards performance poetry, the other from William Carlos Williams to Black Mountain College, towards a silent, graphically oriented verse. This typographic aesthetic, from Mallarmé and Apollinaire to concrete poetry, opposes performance, as space opposes time.

This parting of the ways owes something to the histories of recording. In Friedrich Kittler's analysis of the emergent modernity of 1900, 'the ersatz sensuality of Poetry could be replaced, not by nature, but by technology. The gramophone empties out words by bypassing their imaginary aspect (signifieds) for their real aspects (the physiology of the voice)' (Kittler 1990: 245–6). This musicalisation of the voice, achieved with the facility recording has for speeding up and slowing down, for slicing open the body of a sound and inspecting its workings, acts like a mode of writing too. With digital technologies, the tendency is even clearer: phonemes, become manipulable across the space of the tablature, are letters of an arcane alphabet, an inscription without significance, a kind of dead language. So recording furthers the severance of voice and text, speech and writing, for Kittler an effect of the death of Man in 1900, when 'speaking and hearing, writing and reading were put to the test as isolated functions, without any subject or thought as their shadowy supports' (Kittler 1990: 258). This dispersal of what had once been the constitutive elements of a holistic European culture is marked, in poetry, by the arrival of the typewriter. Typewritten poems like Morgenstern's 1905 'Fish's Night Song', entirely composed of unpronounceable graphic marks in the rough shape of a fish, and Pound's 'Cantos', composed between 1918 and 1972 liberate the poem from the speaking voice and so from time, fostering instead 'the methodology of the Cantos, viz, a space-field where, by inversion, though the material is all time material, he has driven through it so sharply by the beak of his ego, that, he has turned time into what we must now have, space & its live air' (Olson 1966b: 82).

A third element combines with democratic impulses and the technologies of visual language to produce the split in poetry. Paul Celan speaks of it in a 1958 comment on the tasks of German poetry after the war:

> No matter how alive its traditions, with most sinister events in its memory, most questionable developments around it, it can no longer speak the language which many willing ears seem to expect. Its language has become more sober, more factual. It distrusts 'beauty'. . . a 'greyer' language, a language which wants to locate even its 'musicality' in such a way that it has nothing in common with the 'euphony' which more or less blithely continued to sound alongside the greatest horrors. (Celan 1986: 15–16)

Celan's poetry shocks, in its grey vocabulary and bare metrics, because 'For a Jew to compose in German after the Holocaust is an irony so dark as not merely to shadow but to inhabit the substance of Celan's poetry' (Ward 1991: 140–1), and because of the necessity of poetry in the face of the impossibility that Adorno too discovered: 'To write poetry after Auschwitz is barbaric. And this corrodes even the knowledge of why it has become impossible to write poetry today' (Adorno 1967: 34). The souring of the lyric, the corroded knowledge of its demise, destroy a certain meaning of poetry as that which, voiced, energises the existing world, comforts its torturers. The destruction of the iamb somewhere between 1900 and 1945 makes poetry impossible in the old sense. Yeats is not the first of the moderns, but the last of the ancients. In the wake of Auschwitz, poetry must either abandon seriousness and formality, and dive into the struggle for a witty and alert entertainment – as in the performance poems of Linton Kwesi Johnson or the *testimonios* of Ernesto Cardenal – or it must abandon music. In the former, the written persists as a parody of writing, or as secondary documentation of a performance which, in any case, is scripted, and closed to dialogue. In the latter, the poem, in losing the temporal dimension, becomes solid, objective, sculptural, with the voice excluded from its navigation. Between the silence of print and the denial of writing, some third term is needed if the digital aesthetic, so textually dependent in its familiar forms, is to find a new accommodation of audible and visible language.

In Ian Hamilton Finlay's garden, Little Sparta, among the ponds, plants and trees are small, mainly stone ornaments and inscriptions (photography tends to loan them a monumentality they do not possess: see Abrioux 1992). Many of them pursue Finlay's self-proclaimed 'neo-classical' interest in the history of European rationalism. Others, more germane to the topic at hand, carry simpler evocations. On one tall, slender tree is the plaque 'I SING FOR THE MUSES AND MYSELF', a phrase quoted by the apostate emperor Julian from the musician Ismenias, at once a traditionalist statement of dedication to the muses, an act of independence, and a statement on behalf of the tree itself. It is possible (though I can find no documentary evidence) that Finlay is a believer in the actuality of the Muses. What is clear is that the plaque acts to emblematise the tree. The tree is no longer purely itself, though it retains its living sap and its discrete position in the garden as itself. It has acquired in addition the function of meaning; and in payment for this burden of signification, the song of the wind in its branches has become an art.

Another plaque, in a grove of birches: 'THE SEA'S NAVE/THE WIND'S SHEAVES.' Here the punning of sea and tree familiar throughout the garden, of architecture and harvest, are woven into an auditory pun, an implication of the voice in an onomatopoeia integral to the susurra of the leaves. Finlay so involves his garden not only in the restitution of the lost art of the emblem, but also in the reintegration of sound and word, sound and image, sound and referent. Heard from the position of Douglas Kahn, this suggests also a retrieval of a further art outside the hegemony of music. The baroque garden was a place of water, of fountains throwing rainbows in the sun, of gurgling, bubbling rills, splashes and plashing, drips and trickles; Finlay's trees, and his own fountains and streams, articulate not only a remaking of the ancient arts of hydraulic spectacle, but their articulation with the word as spoken and heard. This is no logocentrism. These are the voices not of the reader, certainly not of the poet, but of the grove itself and, in its rhyming with sea and field, with the wider ecology beyond.

Such emblems have four elements: the carved word, the living tree, and the sounds of tree and word. Here the tree and its sound are 'real', neither recordings nor representations. But both are artificial in the most ancient sense, crafted so that we may experience them as filled with a human, if not a commodifiable, meaning. In fact, the very humanity of their significance deprives them of associations with a creator, if not with the sacred, and links them to Jonson's dreamy pastoral where 'The soft birds quarrell in the Woods/ The Fountaines murmure as the streames doe creepe,/ And all invite to easie sleepe' ('The Praises of a Countrie Life', ll.26–8; Jonson 1954: 252) and to Marvell's oceanic 'green thought in a green shade' ('The Garden', l.48; Marvell 1976: 101). I do not want to link Finlay's work to the pastoral unconscious of the English baroque, but to point out a specifically rhetorical aesthetic here in which the emblematisation of the living wood allows us to hear it likewise neither as music, nor as nature, but as an element of a metaphorical ensemble in which the imagination of the real becomes a poetic zone, commencing in delight and ending in wisdom. This stands at a stage between the Cagean myth of a naïve and pure perception and the mediation of a recording, photo- or phonographic, a critique of the natural or the industrial sublime.

The word of the emblem opens a channel between mark, sound, voice and image. In supplanting image with green things, Finlay's garden renders a meditative, pleasant and instructive space in which these orders of knowledge are not so much challenged as invited to play in a different mode of reverberation and echo. This is a sound art which restores the renaissance sense of wit to 'Alberti's dictum that *statuae ridiculae* (humorous or funny statues) were appropriate for a garden [where] play combined with the unexpected' (Lazzaro 1990: 152). For Nicola Salvi, architect of the Trevi fountains in Rome, fountains and their waters 'can be called the only everlasting source of continuous being' (cited in Moore 1994: 49), a prescient understanding of Heideggerian becoming. In Salvi the victory of the fleeting over the everlasting is proof of the 'indefinite wisdom' of water. At Little Sparta, the fountain has been appropriated to wit. One of Finlay's best known exemplars is cut in the shape of a dripping aircraft carrier on which, occasionally, some water fowl perches. Here the gravity of wisdom enters into a dialectic with the simplicity of the joke. The intermittent trickling sound surrounds the stone ship with analogical ocean, the bird-table's frivolity with the unexpected hard illumination of metaphor.

Finlay writes, in a letter of 17 September 1963:

> It comes back, after each poem, to a level of 'being', to an almost physical intuition of the time, or of a form . . . 'concrete' began for me with the extraordinary (since wholly unexpected) sense that the syntax I had been using, the movement of language in me, at a physical level, was no longer there. (cited in Bann 1977: 9)

His discovery of the loss of trajectory in his verse is a simultaneous discovery of a marvellous stillness. The word becomes a foot, extended into the duration of its ground – glass, rock, wood, building, garden – and weathering with it as 'physical intuition', things whose addition to the world reorders the possibilities of that world. In some of Finlay's work, especially in the garden at Stonypath, words are spoken not by voice but by trees, wind, water. It is important that these sounds are of a garden, not nature. Nature, an implication of the voice in the world, is past. The garden is a construct designed to amplify, in such instances, the sonic thought of the engraved word. If a certain mode of written poetry has abandoned both reference and voicing to identify itself with the spatialisation and silencing of the word, Finlay's points towards other practices, some mentioned in the concluding chapter of this book, where the poem functions as material object in the world, proposing that fragment of the world as mediation. The abandonment of author and referent pushes the poem towards pure objectivity, the objectivity of the commodity fetish, in which the relation between people – language – is given the absurd form of an object. Finlay's solution is to form in his relation with his garden a mode of interaction with technologies of horticulture and fountains which serves precise needs, but which also offers a powerful sense of the possibilities of a cyborg culture, an interpermeation of human and technological beyond the instruments of writing.

The Incoherence of the Soundtrack

If the relations between writing and sound have been fraught over the last century, the relations between sound and image, especially between the near-twin arts of recorded sound and cinematography, have verged on civil war. If, as Tynianov argues, 'social life enters into correlation with literature above all through its verbal aspect' (Tynianov 1965: 131), then it enters into the moving image media under a triple aspect: the visual, the written and the aural. By the time the talkies arrived in the late 1920s, the social could not enter cinema as speech, as a language which, though professionalised, was still shared. Rather, the social entered the cinema in already technologised and commodified forms – as silent film, recorded sound and typographics. It emerged therefore not as speaking and writing, but as listening and reading, in relation to the industrial production of consumer goods, rather than the living urban folk cultures celebrated by the Russian formalists. The problem facing directors like Hitchcock, Mamoulian and Sternberg in the early sound period was, then, to produce, from these disparate materials, an artwork which would still provide some form of coherence, in the model demanded by 19th-century organicist conceptions of art. At stake in the pseudo-convergence of sound and film was, then, a mutual reinforcement between channels of communication with distinct histories, practices and identities. Symptomatically, the emergent talkies abandoned the vocal experimentation of the performing arts, the musical vanguards of jazz and serialism, the futurist and dadaist investigation of noise, in favour of 19th-century models of theatrical delivery, romantic music and the restriction of noise to indexical and symbolic effects. We are certainly not in the presence of a refreshed, untrammelled, primal mode of perception. On the contrary: the complex mediations between media in the multi-media environment of the talkies closed off evolutionary possibilities as well as opening them.

Cinema was, of course, never silent. Recent research indicates the existence of film scores even before the turn of the century (see, for example, Abel 1994: 15; Musser 1990: 210–11), scores which surely served to mask the din of the projection equipment, but which also served, according to Adorno and Eisler, 'as a kind of antidote against the picture . . . music was introduced not to supply [the onscreen characters] with the life they lacked – but to exorcise fear or help the spectator absorb the shock' (Adorno and Eisler 1994 [1947]: 75). In other words, music served to mediate the pictures to the audience. The fear and shock they note is an effect of the manifestly representational nature, the contradictory presence and absence, of the image on its own; music mediates between the absence of the image and the presence of the auditorium, not least because, as performance, it stands between the spectacular and the immediate. Music would guard its mediating status through the studio era, traversing the distance between screen and spectators, just as it smoothed the transitions between shots. This mediating function helps to explain the richness of the sound–image relationship, removing it from the banal necessity of reinforcing the image, and allowing it a more fluid commentary than the choice between parallelism and counterpoint (see Kalinak 1992: 24–9). However, when the soundtrack is as audibly artificial as in Wyler's *Public Enemy* (1931) – cutting on sound cues, and using exaggerated amplification to gain effective shocks from gunfire and squealing tyres – or the RKO Astaire and Rogers musicals, its foregrounding has the effect of minimising the referential relation between soundtrack and images, let alone reference to an actually existing world. In its mediating function, the soundtrack achieves a certain autonomy from the film narrative, but in the process of becoming spectacular, it loses too some of the implicitness of the relation with the audience that had served so well in the days before recorded sound. In its place, dialogue offered identification, and a core concern with narrative.

The classical soundtrack can be seen as a battlefield between the purposes of narrative clarity, carried centrally by the dialogue, and the mediative functions of music. It has been argued by many critics (*inter alia* Baudry 1976; Doane 1980a, 1980b; Neale 1985) that the classical soundtrack exists to reinforce an 'ideology of presence'. So lip-synch, the matching of dialogue to the lip-movements of the on-screen figures, is intended to give an audience the most powerful possible illusion of the 'real' presence of the characters, and also a guarantee of the fullness of the filmic world, persuading us of the completeness and coherence of the fiction. The classical cinema's greatest strength is its ability to mediate illusion in such a way that the traumatic abyss between film and audience can not only be bridged, but become the source of its narrative drive towards a healed subjectivity. The causes of clear narration and of unified subjectivity became formally indistinguishable in the greatest achievements of classical Hollywood.

In its concern with coherence, verisimilitude is not a goal of the classical film, merely an occasional stylistic supplement. The alternative path of realist cinema took a different approach. Jean Renoir 'welcomed [recording] with delight. . . . After all, the purpose of all artistic creation is the knowledge of man, and is not the human voice the best means of conveying the personality of a human being?' (Renoir 1974: 103), suggesting that the critique of presence is more aptly posed of realist film than of the classical paradigm. Renoir understands the recorded voice as a moment of the spoken; as a faithful account of the synchronism of speech and hearing. 'I regard dubbing, that is to say, the addition of sound after the picture has been shot, as an outrage' (Renoir 1974: 106), Renoir adds, while also expanding upon the use of both music and sound effects (albeit directly recorded) as equally important with the dialogue in the soundtrack, being particularly proud that the sound of the train in *Toni* (1935) is not just the sound of a real train, but of the actual train on screen. What matters is a sense of the unity of the world, 'my perpetual hobbyhorse' (Renoir 1974: 277). Renoir's realism has more to do with that oneness of the world than with the unity of the film itself, which is merely an effect of it, or of the unity of the spectator, which cannot be an effect of the film, since it is already the unity of spectator and world that forms the premise of realism itself. Renoir's realism plays back to the audience their existing (but perhaps forgotten) solidarity with the rest of creation. This produces certain formal demands which will recycle through the critical moment of digital sound.

What is important is the possibility of moving through the soundscape: of facing the soundtrack with the same freedom with which we hear the world. In this sense, ultimately, for Renoir, it is the unity of the work that prevails over the unity of the spectator, and he drives the conventions of realism forward to their formal extremes in order to gain coherence. Synchronised recording uses sounds' multivalency, ambiguity and autonomy to make the soundtrack a game we can participate in. By doing so, it removes the possibility of that familiarity that breeds contempt, the automatisation of listening. But even realism relies on the multiplication of postproduction techniques, including those clearly audible ones through which, for example, we move from the aural perspective of the originator of a sound to that of an ideal auditor within the diegesis, but outside the action itself. Here the ears' instinctive ability to home in on a crucial word or sound is mimicked in the variation of level in the mix. But because this work is undertaken on our behalf, we tend to try to hear the rest of the soundtrack, pushed to the background in the interests of clarifying the hierarchically placed dialogue track. Unfortunately, this does not work in the same way as wide-screen and deep-focus technologies, which allow the eyes an increased freedom to focus where we please. Rather, the constructed nature of the soundtrack constricts audition, producing a gap between ideal and fictional audiences, exactly at that place where it seeks most to produce a unified subject or a unified world.

The tendency of cinema sound technologies has been towards the unification of hearing, the production of a central, Cartesian subject of listening. But neither classical nor realist cinema, forerunners and laboratories of multimedia, has achieved such a unification of the hearing subject, precisely because they have not resolved the transitions between one sense and another. The media do not converge to form a unitary body; they continue to evolve, even in relation to one another, along divergent tracks, and because of their divergence, they impact on the internal evolution of each of the senses, and on each of the media associated with them. Unlike Merleau-Ponty's phenomenological sensations, permeating a world inclusive of both the sensor and the sensible, the world of sampling, recording and playback engages with time and mediation, displacing the central subject of Descartes, and learning from Metz the uncomfortable necessity of the semantic, displaced and textual relation between sound and image. In the soundtrack, the formation of a Cartesian consciousness, the construction of a textual subject, and the establishment of a referential relationship with the world have been pursued through new recording technologies and techniques, and new theatrical playback systems.

This is the problematic enacted in neo-classicism, that tendency in contemporary films where the focus is neither on narrative, as in classicism, nor on reference to the world, as in realism, but on the construction of explorable, navigable diegetic worlds. Such movies are characterised by extensive use of deep focus, elaborate and often crowded set design, picaresque narratives built of discrete set-pieces rather than suspense or psychological involvement with a central character, and a concern for the fictional world of the film. In films like these, including most effects-driven movies, sound design has taken on new tasks. This was partly forced by the arrival of magnetic sound, which made the older libraries of optical recordings redundant, partly by the new expectations created by home hi-fi systems, but its evolution has been steered by a new understanding of the aural as soundscape, as an explorable space which not only deepens on-screen space, but provides an auditory depth of field. A characteristic of the new sound mix, which originates with Robert Altman's ensemble-cast films like *M*A*S*H* (1969) and *Nashville* (1975), is that music is treated as sound effect, usually sourced in the diegesis (famously so in *Pulp Fiction*, 1994), while dialogue frequently sacrifices clarity to atmosphere, with several voices talking simultaneously and at equal volume.

But most surprising is the rise of sound effects (sfx) to the top of the aural hierarchy. While sound is still generally subordinated to vision, the struggle between dialogue and music for supremacy in classicism has been superseded by the triumph of sfx. Fidelity to source is unimportant: digital editing techniques allow the building up of new sounds from raw and manipulated sources combined, speeded up or slowed down, mixed together to provide the sound of starship drives or gunfire. Even actors' voices are frequently treated, in big-budget pictures, with the same care as those of singers on big-budget CDs: Ben Burt (LoBrutto 1994: 144) reports mixing James Earl Jones' voice with a recording of his breathing in a scuba tank regulator, occasionally slower or faster, to give Darth Vader's characteristic metallic whisper in *Star Wars* (1977). To this extent, the digital cinema contradicts Chion's claim that, 'with the exception of musical sequences, one never edits sounds in relation to each other but always in relation to the image' (Chion 1992: 81), except that the new voice, like the sound of a light-sabre or the roar of the tornado in *Twister* (1997), however densely mixed, is always then articulated with the image. But where both image and sound are digitally manipulated, 'coated' with sampled and computer-generated sounds and imagery, the process of compositing, the combining of photographic/recorded with digitally produced materials, eliminates the realist claim to authenticity. That authenticity was, of course, itself an effect of specific techniques, techniques easily emulated in the interests of, for example, the urgency of news reporting.

More limiting, however, is the success of the Dolby, Dolby SR and THX theatrical sound systems with which digital sound production is closely linked: clearly there is no point producing hi-fidelity recordings for low-fidelity playback. Digital theatrical playback and engineered acoustics are aimed at maximising the spectacular effect of stereophony and multi-track recording, adding separation to the tracks, and building a spatial effect for the audience: the helicopters swooping from the back of the auditorium to on-screen space in *Apocalypse Now* (1979) and the urban soundscape of *Se7en* (1996) are exemplary in this respect. But each effect is mastered in the interests of an ideal audition, a sonic architecture whose centre is carefully calibrated to coincide with each seat in the house. Like the speakers embedded in the vehicles on theme-park rides, theatrical stereophony aims at reproducing the centred, Cartesian subject of the headset's soundspace, and earns its sobriquet of neo-classicism by its return to the unification of the subject as its prime concern. The major difference with classicism is that, when the elements of the soundtrack have been regrouped around the sound effect in the interests of a coherent fictional world, be it the gangster culture of *GoodFellas* (1990) or the dystopian future of *The Fifth Element* (1997), it is the diegesis, rather than character, narrative or reality, that forms the centring device, with stereophony as its newest and most potent ally. But there remains the crux of realist sound. Digital recording moves even beyond the sound archives used by classical recordists in replacing reference with analogy and metaphor. Like Finlay's emblems, it moves by simile, but as industrial production, it risks the vapid formalism of cliché. Like any system at the brink of completion, it is also at the brink of exhaustion. In neo-classicism and its cognate computer game spin-offs, the playworld of the synergetic personality finds its most perfect cultural expression, but in its delay of reference, it creates the grounds for synergy's own downfall.

Dispersed Spaces: Art Geography

In the evolving audiovisual arts, sound can no longer afford to subordinate itself to vision, nor can it demand of audiences that they inhabit only an ideal and unchangeable space. Any new relation to the screen will require that the audience be mobilised. Stereo cinema immobilises the audience by making all points in the auditorium aurally identical. The counter-relation must then be profoundly spatial, emerging from the transmissions of recording (playback time, playback place) and broadcasting (simultaneity of dissociated spaces, temporal parallelism), and linking them to the ontology of film as a medium which transports images through time and space: projection. Sound is a projection, learning from the mechanical dispersal of images across time and space to perform its own art of dissemination by radio, recording and telecommunications: a dissemination increasingly global in both its ambition and its sources. Sound enters space not to imitate sculpture or architecture, but, through electronic webs, to weave a geographic art that understands too that the passage of time is the matter of history: a diasporan art. Sound moves not only the volumes of the air, but the mass of the body. Sound, as an art of distance, of space and time, is an art of movement. To have added recording and transmission, to have doubled and redoubled the number of sounds in the world, has remade not only an imaginary external acoustic universe. but transmuted movement, the body's arc through four dimensions. It has invented a dispersed and spatial form for the dance of populations.

A fictionalised account of the aspirations and degradations of the group around Michael X, the ambiguous fraudster and black power hate-object of the UK and Trinidad, Black Audio Film Collective's *Who Needs a Heart?* (1991) is traversed by one of Trevor Mathison's characteristically dense sound designs. Built up from overlapping musics (gospel, blues, free jazz, Buddhist chants), electronic effects and samples, sound effects subtly unanchored from the image, direct, pre-recorded and re-recorded dialogue, the audio track operates across as well as alongside the image, marking the diasporan scattering of meanings and peoples in repetition and polyrythms. Swamping the dialogue track, that focal bond that sources sound within the image and subordinates it, inveigling the viewer into the visual space of the screen, the sound design for *Heart* stands between viewer and image, tracing oblique trajectories around them both. Inspired equally by the improvisational and the repetitive, the temporal and spatial, Mathison's work not only discovers an archaeology of John Cage's (already orientalist) modernist fascination with pure sound and duration in diasporan musics, but carves for the film a space which is already distanced, a space outside the image, a geography of its location.

Such distances – the distances of diaspora, of the links between Notting Hill and Guyana, Chicago and the English countryside; distances which are also the times of historical movement – open up the spaces of a contemporary hybridity, denying the transparency of multiculturalism by insistently mapping the plurality of differences and differentiations. As the visuals detail the minuet of gender, class and 'race' in a formative moment of black British politics, the soundtrack obliterates the ease of judgement that would stamp the film as 'psychological'. The voice occupies a double position here. It works as the broadcasting of identity from within to without, itself a scattering and a performance, and one radically incomplete, as Kobena Mercer observes (1995: 52–3), without the welcoming ear of a recognising other. But it is also the symbol of an impossible authenticity, a truth of the self to itself, a symbolisation of the very idea of placelessness.

The cinema had begun an exploration of its powers to invent space from its earliest moments. That space would be restrained in the classical and neoclassical style to what might be imagined within the screen, the narrative or the diegesis. It was juxtaposed by every significant film theoretician with the realist world of work, love, childbirth, housing problems. For the greatest of realist critics, André Bazin, the purpose of cinema was 'that it should ultimately be life itself that becomes spectacle, in order that life in this perfect mirror be visible poetry, be the self into which film finally changes it' (Bazin

1971: 82). But this has not been cinema's fate, not yet; instead what has happened is the transfiguration of the quotidian into spectacular consumerism, and cinema has had to take its place, in its development as a spatial art, as a supplement to the real, a material presence contesting the validity of the film/reality distinction not through the transformation of cinema, but through the invasion of the real, the material spaces of amplified playback and reflected light.

Tallulah Bankhead is said to have responded to the old Zen query, 'What is the sound of one hand clapping?' by slapping her interlocutor smartly on the cheek. The ambiguity lies in the word 'sound', for there is no sound that is not heard, that does not burrow into the very flesh of its auditor. Skin produces and receives sound. It is the intimacy of body on body. The air is common: it is what we breathe. Skins are our final barriers against the world, our final masks, but they are porous, traversed by the energies of others, vibrating in sympathy with a complex world. But not every vibration is synchronised. The processes of translation – in its senses both of bringing across from another culture, and moving things from place to place – are time-bound performances. Translation revivifies ancient rituals for intercultural congress, and in so doing reveals itself as a mode of interpretation. In the musics of the Black Atlantic such translation holds together understandings of distance and mechanical perception in the complex interchange between diasporan communities, in their hungry reinvention of the most sophisticated tools, 'making', as Mathison said in an interview with the author, 'the technology sing with new voices'. The wired world only hastens, it has not instigated, and sometimes hampers with its crass designs, the global musics. The figure of the data-thief, a futurological Anansi, builds the mosaic of Black history in Black Audio's *The Last Angel of History* (1995) out of the shards of Black science fiction, linking Robert Johnson's hellhound to the extraterrestrial longings of Sun Ra, George Clinton, Lee Scratch Perry and Goldie, each musician also on the cutting edge of technological innovation. How to work a soundtrack for such artists?

The tools are interviews and dialogue, archive and composed music, and 'atmos', the wildtracks recorded on locations to battle cinema's – and even more so, television's – dread of silence. In Mathison's hands, as in those of all good sound designers, the atmos track becomes more than the ambient support for dialogue. It is a material that can be moulded or carved, as occasion demands, extruded and hammered in processes of analysing sounds by slowing it, filtering it, disassociating timbre from pitch, twisting and weaving it into new redolences. Some source material derives from years developing musical compositions which can be drawn on for installations, dances, performances and films. In this instance, the destination is TV: one version (*Mothership Connection*) for Channel 4 in the UK, a longer one (*The Last Angel of History*) initially for ZDF in Germany. Just as the capital to make a work is spread across national boundaries, the theme pursues interpenetrations and Zeitgeist as they circulate across the Middle Passage, and the work is dedicated to fostering its further travels across years and continents.

The diasporan cultures have already found a road to Amin's 'polycentric world' (Amin 1990).

Cultural translation is a practice which *The Last Angel of History* both documents and practices. The question is no longer of the West's domination of global culture, or even of the impact of non-Western cultures on the West, but the patient transperipheral hybridisation of cultures. Its startpoint is the 'impossible, imaginary musics' of the studio, themselves perhaps the fruit of more than a century in which old musics were lost in enforced isolation, and the new had to be imagined in the mould of a lost original – rather as Renaissance music guided itself on its lost classical models. These mutual imaginings, then, take the form of science fiction not just because of the experience of being alien, nor because 'the line between everyday reality and science fiction is an optical illusion', as the film has it, but because every imagined world that is not seated in the past – a curse from which slavery has debarred the African diaspora – must share its mode of non-being with the future, which by definition does not exist. The future is everything that is not now. In Black music, from the New Thing onward, the future grows from negation to become the not-yet.

Mathison's electronic variations on found and generated sounds, weaving through the fractured narrative, mould and disseminate the samples they discover. To imagine pastiche as 'postmodern' shows shocking historical naïvcté: originality has only ever been one facet of the modern, which has prided itself on looting from popular traditions from Wordsworth to Warhol. A gambit in Anansi's trickbag has been to steal back from the European what can be bricolaged into the necessarily new. Another has been to redefine the territory, as Mathison's soundscapes create a space which, intersecting with the filmic, traverses it at angles. The principle of borrowing and remaking includes then a borrowing from the film's soundworld, borrowing that links the film's two domains together in a bond of mutual debt, a trading system returned to dialogue without closure. Images comment on and expand the sound; sounds interpret and open up the funnel of the image. Visual and aural motifs oscillate in patterns that traverse but rarely map over onto one another, extracting from a gesture or an apparently serendipitous noise the maximum value of statement, understood as both the documentary impulse, and the statement of musical theme. So the soundtrack, composed of samples treated in EQ, loops, filters, slowed or speeded, reversed, discovers within the sounds their own patterns and rhythms, each manipulation a step away from the source, a step closer to imagination. And yet this process of abstraction is one in which the documentary has its fulfilment as documentary of the imagination, documentary of the non-existent future.

Crucial to this procedure is the movement of sound from its location, disturbing the expectation that a sound's source and its playback match in some way. The convergent electronic media make the likelihood of hearing sounds directly ever less, just as the world returns the favour by reducing to practical zero the chances of hearing broadcasts and recordings in the acoustics in which they were designed. These sounds are nomadic. This is not the same as to say that they are portable: the walkman and the in-car stereo are portable but closed media that conform listening to the ideals of consumption. Here sounds migrate from microculture to microculture, assembling new lines of communication as they go and creating sonic spaces that alter as we traverse or are traversed by them.

This work is not music in the sense in which it has been accepted in the Western canons. It is not a matter of the faithful interpretation of authenticated scores, the approach to an absolute ideal which Glenn Gould (1990), in a classic article on recording, documents as a spiralling delirium of artifice. It takes its roots in diasporan mixology, a research into sound, a dynamic dialogue with the tradition and the contemporary. Its criteria are not ideals – the score or the idea of music. Instead the whole environment becomes material for the mixing desk, an instrument in which manipulation, layering and erasing tune found sounds, musical or unmusical, captured live or extracted from archives, to new ears. It is dialogical, engaged in the vast, unending, history-long conversation of the species, an art in which the movement of sounds is the sculpting of distance and our trajectories through it. More: in its acceptance of the dissolution of origins, diasporan sound arts publish and make public mortality, as motif and as efficient cause, breaking the most powerful taboo that stands between us and the new global intimacy.

Mathison's work with Black Audio not only redefines the concept of cinema but articulates the missing dimension of so much of the audiovisual, the sonorous. It brings into sharp focus the issue of spatiality and its relationship with time. To show a film is to occupy an architecture and make it your own. Increasingly, architects are discovering the need to accelerate their buildings with smart connections, VDUs, monitors and panel projectors. We expect our buildings to be at least as fast as our homes; to interact, to work for us and with us. The artworld has to be as swift, and cinematic innovation has this at least to offer. In the remaking of the cinema as the venue of dreams by moving the speakers from behind the screen into the hall, a simple redesign, the auditorium ceases to be Lyotard's dimensionless screen, and becomes once more spatialised. The step from here to installation work is small, as Mathison and Edward George have found in their 1994 installation *The Black Room* at the ICA in London, where cubicles haunted by memories of Fanon's regretful leave-taking of Algeria are recycled in digital sound and image. Other recent diasporan artworks – Pervaiz Khan and Felix de Rooy's *The Garden of Allah* (1996), Bashir Makhoul and Richard Hylton's *Yo-Yo* (1996), Stan Douglas's *Hors-champs* (1995), Keith Piper's *Relocating the Remains* (1997; see inIVA 1997; Piper 1997) much of Mona Hatoum's work – evidence a similarly intense engagement with the ways in which sound, even more than sculpture or film, occupies and traverses space.

An image in motion will always capture your look, inscribe you into a direction. But sound, as long as it is not contained by headphones or an individuated space, must be approached, walked into, penetrated, and, in walking into it, as your body subtly moulds the acoustic around it, the sound will penetrate you. Even as it does, the openness of this space, its architectural quality, becomes apparent: that an open soundscape is a world in which others exist as well as yourself. This combination of intimacy and publicity is the space of the dance, and of all the richnesses of communication and mutuality of which the dance, however pensive, however irrational, however self-involved, is capable. Unconstrained by the technical limitations of broadcast receivers, installation sound can function in those deep notes where the whole body resonates like a temple gong.

And beyond the arts of architecture, beyond the movement into urbanity marked by the installation and performance artists moving outwith the cinema and the gallery, there lies the emergent spatial art which even now is just becoming possible, the art of translation. For most of the century, access to transmission technologies has been scarce, and the gatekeeping of broadcasters censorious and exclusive. But the new arts of the telephone and the answering machine, fax art and artist radio, artist-controlled websites and TV stations, begin to alter that constellation. Given the overuse of the word 'interaction', it is hard to phrase what such an art might be. It relies less on the machinery than on the ability to interface old and new technologies, and crucially to converge the visual and the aural not as unity but as dialogue. An art of movement in the new millennium must apprehend intimate, unconscious interactions and inminglings at the level of the body and the local, but it must also go beyond this traditional sphere of art to intervene in global flows of people and pollution, sounds, images and ideas, religions and diseases, which constitute us as people, as individuals, at the very sites of our most secret communings. The new spatial arts of movement will be global, increasingly so, and the massive act of translation which is now beginning to reestablish the relations between audio and visual is a key to its understanding. The second fragment of the data-thief's code will be diaspora, the cultures which have already mapped the informality of the world, and learnt that there is no mainstream that is not composed of a thousand tributaries. Only in this chaos, these complexities, is there a chance that the not-yet may yet become.

5

TURBULENCE: NETWORK MORPHOLOGY AND THE CORPORATE CYBORG

As they settled down in China for a long time, some became advanced in years, their families grew, and being far from home, they had no desire to be buried in their fatherland. Brotherhood among peoples has certainly reached a new plane.

(Wang Li [1314-1389], cited in Ch'ên Yüan 1966: 252)

Network Subjectivity and the Secret Honour of the Posts

Crammed with unsolicited brochures, catalogues, fliers, competitions, announcements, commercials and special offers, the letterboxes of the West bulge with all the useless paper that keeps the new recycling industries alive. The post has entered a circuit of pure waste. The US Mail, heir to Wells Fargo and the Pony Express, now ekes out a dismal afterlife, in competition with phone, facsimile, e-mail and a host of value-added postal services, for which it has largely merited the sobriquet 'snail-mail'. In the USA, citizens may neither refuse to accept mail, legally considered a medium and therefore protected by First Amendment guarantees of free speech, nor select what kinds of mail they want. The monopoly tendency in free market communications, which has swamped the traffic in letters and postcards with a deluge of target marketing, bodes a devastated network future. The telephone, telegraph, postal service and now digital communications are alike dominated by intra-firm, business-to-business and direct mail messages: in each medium, in their maturity, the same 80% of traffic is taken up in commerce. A major proportion of the remainder is used by governments. What we know as the person-to-person area has always been a small domain, now increasingly whittled away by the erosions of targeted mail, telephone sales and e-mail marketing. The distributive media dominate the networks of communication with tightly channelled messages from ever more centralised providers to ever more atomised audiences. At the same time, the mail is a model of the global network, and its histories can teach us much about the possibilities for a planetary network.

Archaeological finds suggest that about 5,000 years ago, the early riparian civilisations of Mesopotamia, the Nile, the Oxus and Jaxartes, the Indus cities of Harappa and Mohenjo-dara, and centres on the Yangtse and the Yellow Rivers were linked in a world economy of cultural exchange. Astonishingly, the paths and navigations made during the centuries prior to the time of Christ remain even now the arteries of contemporary systems: the ancient silk routes (Bentley 1993: 29–66), the roads from oasis to oasis across the northern steppes (MacNeill 1963: 102–9, 232–45, 386–412), and the seasonal trade wind routes across the great oceans that brought stories, religions, technologies and pestilence from culture to culture across the vast landmasses of the Old World and the open expanses of the Pacific (Curtin 1984; Lacour-Gayet 1953a, 1953b; McNeill 1976). Centuries later, the telegraphic networks of the 19th century, linked to the new canals and railways, and forming the underpinnings of the future telephone networks, duplicate with extraordinary accuracy those ancient paths (see Ahvenainen 1981; Coates 1990: 29–44; Kieve 1973; Shridharani 1953), and in turn form the infrastructure of the information superhighway. Only the transpolar routes of airborne traffic add a fundamentally new trajectory to the repertoire.

Malindi, Gedi and Zanzibar, Venice, Malta and the Levant, Timbuktu, Marrakesh and Alexandria, Samarkand, Baghdad, Bokhara, the Buddhist havens at Dunhuang: merchant cities where argosies and caravans brought news, songs and gods with horses from Europe and silks from Asia, whose names retain even now their legendary auras. By camel and horseback, in dhows, junks and triremes, pilgrims, hajjis and crusaders, nomads and scholars, traipsed for millennia across the world, sharing their cultures and learning others' in the souks and bazaars where trade and dialogue had yet to be distinguished. The image of the communication-world as somehow static, even entropic, in the 6,000 years of recorded history is quite wrong, a view from the storm-tossed shores of the North Atlantic that saw least of the trade binding coastal and river-dwelling peoples to the south with the vast population movements across the northern steppes tying East to West. Only feudalism briefly anchored the populations of Christendom to the land, and made their return to the global sphere all the more vengeful when it happened.

St Paul's epistles to his scattered Mediterranean flock were letters borne along routes already navigated on the central sea for 4,000 years by the time of his shipwreck on Malta, a web of interlocking cultures in which the traverse of gods and armies bears witness to the same kind of 'brotherhood' that Wang Li saw 1,300 years later in China. In St Paul's day, the circulation of the written word, divine gospel or imperial command, was dependent upon navigations established in the voyages of the palaeolithic builders of Stonehenge and Carnac, even before the Phoenicians came for Cornish tin to sell to the foundries of China. Saul of Tarsus was not the first to use those ancient routes, nor the first to carry the news along them. But as evangelist, he can stand as exemplary adventurer in the delivery of his own mail. The history of letters, in every sense, will be thin indeed if it does not include the cultural richness of their delivery.

Rendered obsolete within a year by the advancing railways, the Pony

Express of 1860 moved no faster than the mails of the Khanates 500, or Darius' Persian empire 2,000, years before. As the scale of European empires grew, speeds still dictated by trade winds and the horse's gallop, dependent on luck and favour, fell prey to expansionist dreams of instantaneity. Mail left wrapped in tar-sheets under a rock at Cape Town to be picked up by the next vessel going the right direction left governance at the mercy of the elements and the good will of often illiterate sailors. Both the Cape and overland routes to the Persian Gulf and India were impossibly slow for purposes of rule: a letter sent from London on Commonwealth business on 31 October 1645 arrived at Basra on 10 April 1646, finally delivered to Surat on the western coast of India on 12 October, almost a year after despatch (Sidebottom 1948: 11). Speed, privacy and a swift response became matters of state: as late as 1812, the Battle of New Orleans was fought after an armistice had been signed, because of the sluggardly pace of command over Atlantic distances (Fuller 1972: 9). By the middle of the century, the General Post Office had become the largest government office in Britain and the biggest employer in the Empire. The additional demands of colonialism made it necessary to technologise delivery. The Peninsula and Orient shipping line attracted massive subsidies to schedule regular steamship mail runs through the most ambitious civil engineering project of the century, the Suez Canal. And in 1857, slightly prematurely, the London *Times* would write of the first attempted transatlantic telegraph cable, 'Since the discovery of Columbus, nothing has been done in any degree comparable to the vast enlargement which has thus been given to the sphere of human activity' (Kieve 1973: 109).

That cable was laid from Isambard Kingdom Brunel's iron steamer *The Great Eastern*, under the command of a Wicklow man, Captain Robert Halpin, who would be responsible for laying 26,000 miles of transatlantic cable, from Valentia in County Kerry to Newfoundland (Rees 1992). Both Kerry and Wicklow had suffered terribly in the great famine of the 1840s in Ireland. Only the more successful could afford to emigrate. As for the poor, Michael Shaughnessy, the Assistant Barrister of Mayo, 'was repeatedly asked, by young persons under 18 years of age, for sentences of transportation. . . . Mr Shaughnessy said "I am satisfied that they had no alternative but starvation or the commission of crime" . . . they were "almost naked, hair standing on end, eyes sunken, lips pallid, protruding bones of little joints visible"' (Woodham Smith 1962: 374). Those lucky enough to escape sent an estimated £13 million to those lucky enough to survive to enable them too to flee the obliteration of Irish agriculture. Flight from horror became an integral element of the network. It was more than pragmatism that led the telegraph engineers to take the northern trade route across the shortest path from the Old World to the New; it would directly facilitate the massive emigration which was the only alternative to the scenario proposed by the British government's senior economic advisor, Nassau Senior, who once wished for at least a million deaths in the Irish famine, doubting if even that would be enough to do much good (Woodham Smith 1962: 373). As Robertson (1992) argues, globalisation instigates modernity, not vice versa. The ancient networks of the Old World enabled, encouraged and allowed; the avenues of the scheduled sailing and the telegraph turned people into freight and their tribulations into messages. Yet at the same time, liberated from local ties by the ability to communicate at global distances, the religious, political and economic refugees of the 19th century attained a certain freedom from parental cultures that allowed them to leave, and at the same time, except under conditions of slavery, encouraged a less claustrophobic sense of identity. Indeed, for many of the Irish *émigrés*, there scarcely remained a native culture with which to commune. Yet Irishness would remain, as diaspora, a subjectivity in whose very core is the experience of distance, a networked subjectivity, a subjectivity not merely mediated, but which experiences itself as mediation, a new property of the nascent electronic network.

'All history proves the close connection between progress, power and communication': so a 1921 memo on the development of civil air communications in the British Empire prepared by the Department of Civil Aviation (cited in Daunton 1985: 184), repeating with a new urgency the litany of the 19th-century promulgators of the Empire Post. The development of modern communications infrastructures in the 19th century belongs firmly to an explicit belief in the powers of the new media. Not only would they carry the messages of rule; they would instil in the communications workers of the Empire work discipline, moral probity and respect for authority alongside an awareness of the technological path of Western development. Here is the Calcutta Postmaster General, W. Taylor, in 1850:

> The peons cannot read English. The mysterious jugglery by which, in the midst of tumult, confusion, and noise, a circle of peons, seated cross-legged on the ground, receive the letters from a hoarse clerk, who bawls out the names in barbarous mispronunciation at the moment he throws down the letter before each man in the circle – the cabalistic signs by which the peons mark each letter (locally termed as *dhobimark*) with some hieroglyphic stroke, to designate the English name – these strange proceedings, impossible to describe, and only to be appreciated by ocular inspection, will serve to show the monstrous difficulties under which the system of delivery is conducted; and I feel sure that any reasonable man, witnessing the process, though suffering himself from the most irritating case of 'mis-delivery' conceivable, would with this scene before his eyes, confess that the marvel is, how the thousands of letters that are daily delivered with accuracy and punctuality, can possibly reach their addressees. (cited in Mazumdar 1990: 133)

Taylor ridicules traditional combinations of written and oral, abuses local pronunciation of the colonial language, reduces non-European orthography to the level of scribbles, and assumes that 'any reasonable man' would be European. At the same time, the systemic achievements of delivery (see Virk 1991) justify the sahib's supercilious mock-heroics. The demands of the ruler will be met, albeit through a combination of traditional skills and social relations which can only appear as babbled spells to the imperial bureaucrat, but which already provide the postal workers with a sense of secret honour.

Nowhere would that lonely honour more grasp the poetic imagination of the public than in the towering figures – Kingsford Smith, Charles Lindbergh, Jean Mermoz – of the pioneers of the airmail (see Cubitt 1994, 1996; Mackay 1971). Over and over in airmail stamp design, that mythology is reinvoked in emblematic form: the triumph of the colonist over the colonised, of the modern over the ancient, of technology over nature. The literate public of the 1930s were invited to share thoughts like these, from Lindbergh's *The Spirit of St Louis*:

> We pilots of the mail have a tradition to establish. The commerce of the air depends on it. Men have already died for that tradition. Every division of the mail routes has its hallowed points of crash where some pilot on a stormy night, or lost and blinded by fog, laid down his life on the altar of his occupation. Every man who flies the mail senses that altar and, consciously or unconsciously, in his way worships before it, knowing that his own next flight may end in the sacrifice demanded. (cited in Holmes, 1981: 160)

Such is the destiny of the bearer of tidings, good as well as ill: to kneel before the sacrificial grove of the schedule. Night flights becoming necessary in 1924, both to maintain aerial superiority over terrestrial carriage and to secure the political future of the service (Leary 1985: 140-3), the temple of human sacrifice on the altar of the timetable could be approached, as is proper, in darkness. But there is also here a sense of another and more ancient destiny: that of the courier, whose fate depends upon the message that s/he carries. Communication is the messenger's *raison d'être*: if the communication is unsuccessful, the point of life itself is lost. In Lindbergh's account, the courier is in the process of becoming a medium.

Some of the kudos that surrounds, and quite probably recruited young men into, so dangerous a profession belongs undoubtedly to the machismo of technological vanguardism, to risk-taking, peer admiration and to the sheer hell of it: a madness of youth voiced in technological bravado, and articulated with extreme devotion to the purposes of the mail. Such was the flight of Major Rudolph W. 'Shorty' Schroeder on 27 February 1920:

> On this flight he lapsed into unconsciousness after reaching 38,180 feet. His plane went into a dive with Shorty out at the controls. He opened his eyes at 3,000 feet, after a seven-mile dive, just in time to save the plane from splintering itself. He managed to land safely in spite of the fact that his eyeballs were frozen and that he was suffering from exposure. (Lipsner 1951: 219)

A service devoted in the profoundest sense to the public, and one which gave itself to such unheard of feats, would form the bases of literary and cinematic lionisation of the airmail fliers.

More curiously, popular audiences were invited to identify with the bureaucrat as hero. In Howard Hawks' *Only Angels' Have Wings* (1939), Cary Grant as Jeff can, in a crisis, take on the active role, and fly the plane himself. The hero of one of scriptwriter Jules Furthman's sources, Saint-Exupéry's *Vol de Nuit* (Night Flight), has no such option. He is the system administrator, bound to observe its purposes and functioning, and to value the service above the lives of his aircrews: 'Rivière felt he was wrenching something from blind fate, he was reducing the area of uncertainty, and pulling his crews out of the night and towards the shore' (Saint-Exupéry 1971 [1931]: 113). '"We don't ask to be eternal," he thought. "What we ask is not to see acts and objects abruptly lose their meaning. The void surrounding us then suddenly yawns on every side"' (Saint-Exupéry 1971 [1931]: 166). 'For what mattered was the onward movement, the momentum. In five minutes the radio stations would have alerted the airfields, and over ten thousand miles the quickening pulse of life would be resolving all problems' (Saint-Exupéry 1971 [1931]: 174). He is no longer the priest of the schedule, sacrificing his pilots on Lindbergh's altar; he is its embodiment. In the network he spies the emergence of a human survival in despite of chaos. Though that imaginative survival is only possible for him in the historically available form of order, he understands himself as the medium that communicates, 'a pulse of life'.

Edgar Lee Masters spotted the trend in 1915, in the person of 'Editor Wheldon', whom he castigates, from the viewpoint of an 'old middle class ideology' (see Musser 1991: 291–324):

> To be able to see every side of every question;
> To be on every side, to be everything, to be nothing long
> (Ellman and O'Clair 1973: 167)

The small-town newspaper editor, at the centre of the emergent nets of news, has lost his ability to be himself; his individuality is subsumed into the tidal wash of opinion. For Masters, this is betrayal; for the new network sensibility, it is the condition of life. Editor Wheldon, like Saint-Exupéry's Rivière, is becoming a network subjectivity. A more celebratory acceptance of the emergent constellation of the new distribution media is voiced in Carl Sandburg's 'Under a Telegraph Pole' of 1916, nearly contemporary with fellow-Chicagoan Masters' *Spoon River Anthology*, but clearly distinct from it in its democratic swagger:

> I am a copper wire slung in the air,
> Night and day I keep singing – humming and thrumming.
> It is love and war and money; it is fighting and the tears,
>   the work and want,
> Death and laughter of men and women passing through me . . .
> (cited in Brooks 1975: 142)

Not only is Sandburg identifying his own subjectivity as a medium of exchange and distribution; he is celebrating the way in which this immersion in the new electric communion ends the privacy of the most personal, the most familial things: sex, violence, poverty, loss. The networked subject is at once public and intimate.

The meanings of privacy were central to the military and commercial security of the mails, to the emergence of professionalism among communication workers, and to the new electrical media that would supplement them and, finally, almost entirely eradicate the habit of writing personal letters. Combating mail theft and money-order fraud created a critical moment for the mails, creating the moral instruction against opening other people's mail, and fostering the growth of cryptography. Both factors contribute still to the hysteria surrounding hackers, who, in reading your mail, betray the intimacy of the sealed envelope and the trust networks of secure transmission. The telegraph offered no respite from the fear of eavesdropping: though the world's first electronic network was handling 90 million messages a year at the turn of the century in the UK alone (Kieve 1973: 195), every one of them was input by a telegraph operator, spawning a whole literature of jokes and cartoons.

The early reception of the telephone brought together the colonist's fears of dishonesty and incompetence with a new anger at the 'relatively sudden and largely unanticipated possibilities of mixing heterogeneous social worlds. . . . New media took social risks by permitting outsiders to cross boundaries of race, gender and class without penalty' (Marvin 1988: 107). Marvin exemplifies this fear in the words of a choleric 1884 Edinburgh complaint against the provision of public pay-phones, 'where any person off the street may for a trifling payment – a penny is suggested in some places – ring up any subscriber and insist on holding a conversation with him' (Marvin 1988: 103). Massive expansion in telephone use opened up its characteristic dialectic of exclusivity and openness, secure exemption from the hoi-polloi and the probability that someone was listening in on the party lines of endless anecdotes and family folklore. Though the ridicule retained for those unable to serve the mail was extended to those who could not use the telegraph and telephone, the idea existed simultaneously that yokels and cockneys alike might be manipulative hackers of the most sensitively commercial, military or private of messages. The other side of the coin involved the invisibility of one's interlocutor: without the visible signs of class, how could one ascertain their bona fides, even their race? The telephone became the site for a series of paranoid scenarios, from de Lorde's *grand guignol* (see Gunning 1991) to Lois Weber's *Suspense* (1913); and on to Hitchcock's *Dial M for Murder* (1953) and Coppola's *The Conversation* (1974).

Much of the history of digital security, of closed networks, encoding, encryption, the clipper chip, surveillance, computer fraud and conspiracy fears, can be watched developing between about 1850 and 1950. The gradual shift from human to mechanical and later electronic sorting offices and switchboards is as much attributable to the pursuit of an individualistically motivated demand for privacy as to cost-cutting or militarisation. In the process, the open communications of the ancient bazaar might be argued to have become the closed channels of the free market. At the same time, the specialisation of professionals in the distribution of communications begins to produce a newly distributed subjectivity, bound to its own ethical codes, and identified more with the network than with its owners or customers. Despite the ideological formation of privacy as a right which, nonetheless, is constantly violable in the name of security, still the distribution media facilitate a more ancient concourse of interaction that lives on in their remaindered spaces. Phone phreaks and computer hackers (see Hafner and Markoff 1991; Levy 1984; Sterling 1992) were only the most recent exponents of the leaky network and its marginal spaces. The more communication media become central to the reasons of power, the more their repressed and ancient role, as dialogue and *agora*, returns.

A Brief History of Flow

The first European technological revolution lost the ancient sense of water as unfathomable and illimitable Ocean (see Campion 1994: 187–8), of the sail-boat as a metaphor for the human creature tossed on the sea of being, even the Asiatic love of water as regeneration (see Giedion 1948: 630–44). In their place came water as animal to be tamed, as vehicle, and as the segmented flows of the watermill that made it possible to devise the European raised windmill and the new arts of bridge-building (see Gimpel 1988: 85–7). As the endless cycles of the rain became the techniques of hydrodynamics, cleansing became private, first restricted to the home, later to the water closet, still later in the en-suite bathroom (Giedion 1948: 686). The plumbing of the city is our prototype for networks, a hidden and mechanical service directed towards the domestic user. Gas and electricity services to the home followed the pattern of water supplies, down to their metered measures and monopoly structures. The telegraph alone never penetrated the home, and no-one attempted to render the device more user friendly. Like the cinema, the telegraph demanded a professionalism which rationalised the public telegraph office as communal point of transmission. The telephone, however, utilising exactly the same distribution mechanisms, renovated the sender's task in the modern, simplified mode, and so could escape from the communal into a domestic space already colonised by water, gas and electricity nets. The private home was in the process of changing from a point of production and reproduction, to a point of consumption: a shift that would prepare it for the intrusions of single-channel communications devices like radio, recorded music and TV, and for the consumer-orientation of photography in the box Brownie. In the same move, the ground was prepared for the modem to function as both conduit and meter.

The proximity of electricity to information, as the means become available to carry digital signals via the electricity supply, poses timely questions about the origins of contemporary concepts of flow. The electrical industries enjoyed a brief moment of emblematic potency at the end of the last century in the pyrotechnic illumination of the great department stores, world's fairs and amusement parks, splashy and wasteful as baroque fountains. But now they emblematised, in the form of the aspiration to modernity, not the baroque certainties of stability and perpetual renewal, but the mechanical expression of human order superseding the natural, overcoming history, and rendering the world as consumable. Electricity marketed itself as clean power, an image assiduously promoted ever since, and in doing so abrogated to itself the metaphors of flow, despite the complete disparity and dangerous enmity between water and electricity. Light became aqueous as it flooded the night (one thinks here of Flann O'Brien's de Selby, boiling endless kettles of water to drive out the noxious fumes of darkness). Light pours over the world, soaks into the city, sparkles and glitters like sunlight on streams, when it does not itself stream from windows into the street (see Schivelbusch 1988). Meanwhile, as segmented flow, its motive force moves into the kitchen with the invention of the lightweight electric motor, replacing handmills, invading the ice-box, entering the laundry, usurping the role of cleaner. Growing demand for factory hands, especially in the USA, combined with an increasing sense that democracy and domestic service were incompatible, drove the bourgeois housewife towards electrical substitutes for servants, and her new devices entered, via the farmyard, the catalogue or the department store, into the heart of the house.

The ideology of progress embodied in electricity's brief moment as spectacular excess soon downscales to the restricted dimensions of the home. In doing so, it moves towards individualisation even in the minutiae of its delivery mechanisms. Early fixtures trailed leads from light sockets, making apparent the connectivity of the devices. But around the 1890s, more discrete wall-plates and sockets connected to ring-mains hidden behind the wainscoting begin to be introduced (Schroeder 1991: 125–7). A perfectly ordinary standardisation of a new technology, it also indexes a diminishing sense of the active participation of the consumer in a vast and complexly interdependent network. The wall socket, like the tap (faucet) that replaces the domestic pump and bucket, erodes the sense of interconnectedness which, in absolute terms, characterises the fully serviced modern dwelling. What we consume is object as commodity, be it electricity, gas, water or information, severed from its materiality in production or exchange. And electricity's marketing as a meaning, quite as much as a service, makes it a pioneer in the conversion of commodities from use-value to sign-value. By erasing, in the form of trailing wires, the marks of distribution, we lose the only form in which we might still recognise, on a daily basis, the immense socialisation of living on which we so depend, and so invite our own isolation.

Electrical flow, like water and steam power before it, could be measured in common units, its direction altered, its motion parcelled into blows, and, like the mediaeval mills and the steam engine, it might depend upon dams and sluices, brakes and clutches, becoming the switch and the logic gate. So electricity pursues the mechanical model of water, and it is this model, the model most precisely focused in the mythology of the steam engine, that goes forward to shape information theory as it comes into being in the 1940s. Certain novelties pertain particularly to electrical flow, however. Electrical power loses little of its potency when brought to the end user over massive distances, unlike either mechanical or hydraulic power, so distance can be factored out. And where water seeks its own level, electricity works ostensibly in defiance of gravity, and can therefore be supplied in loops. The loop structure in turn provides a primitive form of feedback, first used in the ballcock cistern, exploited classically in the central heating thermostat.

Modelled on another water technology, the governor controlling steam pressure build-up, the feedback device becomes the central figure of a revolution in engineering brought about by Claude Shannon's work in information theory, popularised in Norbert Wiener's writings (Wiener 1948,1950). Feedback functions to equilibrate homeostasis in a closed system, such as the telephone network. Shannon was an engineer, facing engineering problems concerned with switching massive numbers of telephone calls through a finite matrix of lines. He was concerned to produce a mathematical model allowing the fullest use of the system without causing any crashes. The 1948 papers in the *Bell System Technical Journal* still reverberate. But it is in their crudest reformulations that they have had the greatest technical impact: information as one-way flow. The sender encodes a message. A carrier takes it to another point, where the message is decoded and received. The feedback mechanism is used only to decide whether the message has been transmitted and received efficiently, that is, in the same form and impact intended by the sender. The receiver's role is limited to some form of the response 'message received and understood'.

Mechanisation, definitively completed in the appropriation of steam to commodity production, partitioned flow into unitary elements, severing the moments of circulation from one another save for the feedback functions of oversight and control. From the gear train to monodirectional broadcasting, transmission, 'sending across', has become the central feature of our conception of communication, a conception firmly bedded in the 19th century. The power of this structure derives primarily from its conformity to the socio-economics of capital. But it derives its aesthetic satisfaction from its deep-rooted and profoundly familiar metaphorical origins. From the tidal race to the input–output device, the gradually effected control over flows has provided an increasingly limited sense of the interaction between humans and their world, and between human and human. It inflects the design of the computer itself, and of computer software, interactive packages and increasingly the internet.

Severed from the pollution of its production, electrical appliances, from cookers to computers, could be marketed for most of this century encased in hygienic white enamel. Water meanwhile has begun to take on the attributes of turbulence associated with chaos theory, as the environmental water cycle and the continuing mystery of hydrodynamics continue to perplex. While electricity has associated itself with an efficiency model of information management, now water provides an alternate conception of communication as complexity (see Waldrop 1992). We have inherited a modern problematic of efficiency, derived from power tools and at the expense of social values (see Mumford 1986: 25). Against it, a more anarchist tendency pitches a more aqueous solution, like the 'minor science' described by Deleuze and Guattari in the 'Treatise on Nomadology':

> First of all, it uses a hydraulic model, rather than being a theory of solids treating fluids as a special case; ancient atomism is inseparable from flows, and flux is reality itself, or consistency. . . . The model itself is one of becoming and heterogeneity, as opposed to the stable, the eternal, the identical, the constant . . .

the model is problematic rather than theorematic. . . . One does not go by specific differences from a genus to its species, or by deduction from a stable
essence to the properties deriving from it, but rather from a problem to the accidents that condition and resolve it. (Deleuze and Guattari 1987: 361–2)

Citing the examples of the Gothic cathedrals and 18th-century bridge-building, they argue for a practical, 'Archimedean' alternative to the rationalist,
classificatory science of the academy. This minor science is 'problematic' in
the sense that it deals not with the eternal forms of Platonism, but with the
practical tasks of making. It is the science of the 'kludge', the quick-'n'-dirty
fix used to patch together plumbing or a program, inelegant, but functional.
So the masons of Chartres or of Wren's churches, though given a master-
plan, worked as a problem-solving collective to erect the buildings,
engineering the imagined aspirations of the elite into actuality by drawing on
a shared pragmatic knowledge of stone. Deleuze and Guattari want to bring
this hands-on, real-time knowledge into the contemporary world, and to
keep within it the metaphorical structure of turbulent flow.

The weakness that besets them is, however, their insistence on fingering
the state as the villain of the story. Such has been the central tendency of the
libertarian entrepreneurs who saturate the pages of *Mondo 2000* and the US
edition of *Wired* with free-market, anti-state anarchism, and who have substituted a small business ethic of many-to-many for the few-to-many model
of terrestrial broadcasting. Market anarchists, obsessed with an absolutist
politics in which the state is the only enemy, find in the many-to-many an idealist confirmation of the anarchy of perfectly informed buyers. But economic
subjects are neither perfectly informed nor rational, and networked subjectivity, from the standpoint of the market, has no desires, needs or goals
other than to respond to market choices, and to feed back, through them,
into corporate information flows. Like the US plebiscitary concept of electronic town halls, the feedback mechanism *par excellence* of a democratic
system bent on proving itself obsolete, consumption becomes a form of
polling. Contemporary cultural studies has a tendency to read such feedback
as evidence of autonomy. But resistance, like the monolinear conception of
information, belongs to a steam-driven model of communication: mono-
causal, evaluable on the basis of efficiency, a characteristic of flows in a
closed system, and finally, simply, a specific case of feedback activity in the
information loops of corporate capital. Deleuze and Guattari attempt to
recoup an ancient concept of flow, but find themselves caught in a metaphorical structure which belongs entirely within the sealed unity of the steam
engine, the mechanisation of information. Their popularity among technotopian visionaries (see, for example, Plant and Land 1994) relies on a
compounding of political anarchism with the anarchy of the market to produce the conditions of the corporate playworld. Such a system, as long as it
is so enclosed, is entirely containable within the structures of corporations
now far larger and far more global than the nation state against which they
raise the banner of fluidity and nomadism. Utopian anarchism establishes
only a machinery without exterior, like the textual endlessness of the text or

the absolute embrace of the market, and so without connections to the other turbulent configurations of the social. Their flows, however chaotic, are finally ordered by the conduits that contain them.

The Human Biochip

In digital cultures, we are fascinated by what has already occurred, the epistemological break that has already created network consciousness, and yet we know too that the past is only important to us as the cunning of the present, the secret structure that laces together the disparate categories of an experience we are struggling to make cohere. Most of all, we know that the business facing us is the question of the future, a future we approach emotionally with desire and anxiety, and intellectually with hope and trepidation. In Benjamin's words, 'There is a secret agreement between past generations and the present one. Our coming was expected on earth. Like every generation that preceded us, we have been endowed with a *weak* Messianic power, a power to which the past has claim' (Benjamin 1969: 254). We have a certain responsibility towards both past and future: to be the posterity to which our forebears looked for justice and remembrance, and to be the source that frames the networks of meaning and value on which our heirs will build. We are responsible, not for continuity, but for living the present in the light of the past, and for the survival on which the future depends. But equally clearly this 'we' is bogus.

The economic and statistical instruments that we have agree: in the Pacific Rim, the European Union and North American Free Trade Area, the rich (top 40%) are getting richer and the poor (bottom 60%) are getting poorer, while education, the vital route to improving life chances in a changing world, is intensively geographically bound, so that depressed areas get the worst schooling, exacerbating the production of a permanent underclass. Africa is supernumerary to the requirements of the global information economy, and the vast majority of its population will be left to murderous factional struggles for control of the state in order to secure the scraps of aid that drip through it. Areas of massive new employment like the Pearl River Delta, Bangalore and among women across the world will offset the demise of agriculture and manufacture, but only by ensuring that promotion, rights and wages are drastically pegged, at 50% or even 20% of conditions prevailing in OECD countries in the early decades of informationalisation. These statistics are only indirectly related to technological change. The pursuit of short term profit, the collapse of family- and firm-based social welfare programmes, the advances in outworking, offshore production, subcontracting and temporary employment are among major contributory factors to the new capitalism. At their heart lies the synergetic corporation. Here is the actually existing cyborg, for the corporation is not an assemblage of people but a machine ensemble, an organised concatenation of information, hardware, discourses and practices, a massive processing machine whose employees and consumers are its biochips.

Despite the claims of governments that they still hold the reins of power, it appears increasingly to be the case that nation states' competition for status or for the welfare of their populations is closely articulated with their pursuit of favoured positions in the plans of multinational corporations. The anti-statism of left- and right-wing anarchists is equally undone by any detailed attention to the restructuring of corporate organisation and work patterns. As Critical Art Ensemble argued in 1994, the big corporations have already taken on the nomadic, post-state shape of the network: fluid, unfixed, horizontally rather than vertically organised, responsive and proactive in open environments. Like the new military disposition analysed by de Landa (1994), they have made use of new telecommunications technologies to make themselves far more democratic, in the sense of horizontal structuring, than at any prior point in the 20th century (see Hiltz and Turoff 1993; Sproull and Kiesler 1991, 1993). This laterally organised, consultative mode of management in industries acutely sensitised to changing consumer demands has become a model for almost all forms of institutional life except those destined to provide the shrivelled public support services for the growing underclass. The configuration of human employees and consumers in molecular feedback loops integrated to a pseudo-lifecycle of information flows, the ability to evolve and reproduce in changing environments, the loss of identifiable human leadership or responsibility, are what make the synergetic corporation the true cybernetic organism of our time. When films like *Independence Day* (1997) attempt to remobilise the secret honour of the bureaucrat, they do so now in nostalgic mode, reaching back for a moment when the corporate mind could be located in a single corporate body, and that body capable of acting, doing, making, in the same way as its employees. The individualist dream of the heroic salaryman is already an artefact of the past. And while technotopians look forward to the arrival of personalised, hyperindividual afterlives as human–machine hybrids, their dream has already been superseded in a far vaster and less human shape. Our history has already outstripped our imaginings. The networked cyborg that has already arrived is responsible not for the dawn of a new utopia, but for massive downgrading of career and life options, immense and perhaps irreversible ecological damage, and global injustice that in the 1990s verges once again on genocide.

This rehearsal of the conditions under which any network consciousness can be framed is important if the role of digital arts in the networked society is to be thought in terms adequate to the nature of the material conditions of their making. I follow Castells, whose recent work on the informational society is perhaps the single most important contribution to the analysis of digital cultures, in seeing the term 'material' as including 'nature, human-modified nature, human-produced nature, and human nature itself' (Castells 1996: 15). Increasingly, corporations work not on the raw materials derived from colonised nature, but on those symbols, data and tools which characterise the human world, and on the raw materials of the human environment, not least on people. The clearest examples would be corporations dealing in finance, tourism, retailing, media and communication, the fastest growing areas of employment in the (over)developed world. Even manufacturing and agriculture, stagnant or declining as employment sectors in the three major economic regions of the new global economy, could be said to be shifting gradually away from the production of necessities and luxuries and towards the production of symbols. The synergetic corporation, whatever else it does, is a consciousness industry. Whatever else it produces, it produces identity, primarily brand identity, but in the process also a synergetic personality, a corporate consciousness.

Unsurprisingly, then, synergetic corporations have also engendered the avant-garde of the emergent networked consciousness, as it were in the negative form of what technological determinists would find most utopian. Computer-mediated communication conducted within corporations is inverted towards the profit motive, allied to such intermediary goals as market leadership and market share, to which very short-term profit may be sacrificed in deference to the mid-term survival and long-term growth of the firm. As a result of this economic overdetermination of communication, a certain kind of consciousness has evolved within corporate structures with many of the characteristics of postmodern, fragmented subjectivity. Cultural studies tends to avoid the workplace, preferring to locate culture in the domestic and leisure arenas, partly convinced by the slogan 'the personal is the political' that this would be less exclusive of women's culture. But in the 1990s, for certain critical strata of the population, male but especially female, work and culture are closely and increasingly synonymous for major parts of waking, and perhaps sleeping, life. Habits of communication, argumentation, socialisation and recreation bleed across the two zones, not least as a function of the increased permeability of work and leisure time due to the prevalence of portable phones and home internet connections. The distinction between work and leisure dissolves ('we are losing the concept of weekends' as someone says in David Byrne's *True Stories* [1976]), and older class loyalties among employees shift towards the agonistic and the ludic. With the loss of the private sphere, the distinctions between work and leisure blur; even consumption becomes a self-reflexive reproduction of labour power in information and entertainment industries, as it has been for a long time in education. The synergetic corporation encourages playfulness, not only among the creatives of the advertising and software world, but in role-playing, in simulation exercises, in the constant use of masquerade in interpersonal training and quality control across the whole range of industries from banking to health. Competition between work crews, openness to discussion, just-in-time production schedules, all convene around the construction of a role-playing, game-playing ethos, one that enables firms to maximise their exploitation of the fullest range of their employees' capabilities.

The loosening boundaries between work and leisure, and the introduction of play into work, provoke the expansion of masquerades, role-plays, simulations and alter egos from inside the corporation to the outside world.

Castells suggests a 'culture of urgency' among the marginalised poor of the ghettos, shanty towns and *favelas* of global cities, the obverse of the time-lessness of corporate culture at the end of history:

> Have the bad boys of Caracas, or elsewhere, understood faster than the rest of us what our new society is all about? Is the new gang identity the culture of communal hyper-individualism? Individualism because, in the immediate grat-ification pattern, only the individual can be a proper accounting unit. Communalism because, for this hyper-individualism to be an identity – that is, to be socialised as a value and not just as a senseless consumption – it needs a milieu of appreciation and reciprocal support. (Castells 1997: 156)

While other factors have helped bring about this narcissistic socialisation – the painstakingly meticulous dismantling of vestigial working-class organi-sations during the 1980s perhaps foremost among them – this novel, flamboyant appropriation of spectacular consumption as group identity seems to have all the characteristics of the socialisation of microserfs, the synergetic narcissists of the new corporations. This demand for attention, this prioritisation of the self, is only necessary, and can only be pursued, when a more autonomous identity has been lost, either in the failed transi-tions from subsistence farming to agribusiness and from Fordist to informational society, or in the processes of displacement and distribution to which every global network is prone. The result is a constant oscillation between the dispersal of subjectivity across the playworld, in the form I labelled above the transvestite masquerade, and in the opposite direction a constant, touristic drawing in of ideal egos, roles and acts of cunning devised to maintain the privilege of the observing self, experienced as increasingly real, and increasingly self-involved, while the self itself becomes an object of introvert observation and the administrative disciplines of self-improvement fads. Others exist only as foils for the self's adventures, and the social envi-ronment is dematerialised in favour of a process of gathering supports for a narcissism buttressed by consumer capitalism. Such a subject construction is essentially nostalgic: its goal is always a sense of plenitude and fulfilment that is perpetually situated in an unrecoverable, fading dream of the past, or in the passage through the equally endless stream of commodities. That sense it achieves through assimilating its yearning for fullness to the maternal embrace of the corporate, in enclosed systems in which its tantrums and its demands are always endorsed, because they form the raw material of corpo-rate creativity, and because they are visible symptoms of the success or failure of a given creative strategy. The resistant cultures of the slums pose no threat to the corporation: even their spectacular and violent consumption feeds back into the corporate loop, every Nike slaying a glowing testimonial to marketing strategy.

Individual survival and identity are sacrificed to corporate growth: human nature as the condition of futurity is slaughtered on the altar of the admin-istrative network, just as Lindbergh and Saint-Exupéry offered themselves to complete identification with the schedule, an identification only aided by the technological symbolisation of the fliers' union with their machines. The

post-human began to evolve in those momentous voyages, a process completely necessary to the evolution of a new sociality, but secured at mortal
cost. The rhetoric of neo-liberal economics that permeates the cyberculture,
especially in the US, is a malicious fiction, a narrative of flight and sacrifice
to remedy those small entrepreneurs falling in increasing numbers into the
cycles of subcontracting and supply to a diminishing number of megacor-
porations. But the fiction carefully simulates the specifics of the ideology, as
description not of real economic conditions, but of the terms of engagement
in playworlds of corporate culture. The mechanical age entered the movements of skilled workers into the design of machines as the disembodied
procedures of dead labour. The expert system does the same for the spe-
cialised knowledges of professionals. Now corporate computer-mediated
communications make it possible to download the administrative and organ-
isational expertise of managers, and to co-opt the creative play of inventors
and symbol-makers. Where Moravec dreamt of a personal cyborg afterlife,
there actually exists a far vaster and more effective cyborg in the synergetic
corporation, so vast we have yet to realise that we have become, as participants in corporate culture and as consumers, the biochips of the new
distributed processing net which forms its body. But at the same time, as feedback loops and biochips, we conserve, as Lash and Urry (1994: 14–16) argue,
an ongoing process of detraditionalisation which sets social agents free in
such a way that they can validate their movements only by reference to a self-
reflexive, cognitive sense of their lives, and simultaneously to an 'aesthetic
reflexivity' of self-interpretation. The former is articulable with the narcissistic; the latter demands a sense that the presuppositions on which any
interpretation can be built are shared, and that the sovereignty of the individual is at risk in this core moment of self-awareness.

Mary Louise Pratt's analysis of scientific and sentimental travel literatures
of the 18th and 19th centuries suggests an archaeology of this transformation. One of her key concepts is 'anti-conquest', by which she refers to the
'strategies of representation whereby European bourgeois subjects seek to
secure their innocence in the same moment as they assert European hegemony' (Pratt 1992: 7). Expanding on the theme, she writes:

> In the literature of the imperial frontier, the conspicuous innocence of the nat-
> uralist, I would suggest, acquires meaning in relation to an assumed guilt of
> conquest, a guilt the naturalist figure eternally tries to escape, and eternally
> invokes, if only to distance himself from it once again. . . . [T]he *discourse* of
> travel that natural history produces, and is produced by, turns on a great long-
> ing: for a way of taking possession without subjugation and violence. (Pratt
> 1992: 57)

This touristic turn of the travel narrative becomes, through the textual privilege of literacy, a way of disembodying the brutalities of trade. Enraptured
by the species of freedom that tourism affords, the voyager traverses indexed
spaces like void entries in the catalogue, experiencing the world as a picture
album or an atlas perpetually framed in the modular rectangle of the
viewfinder, a scene from which you are always excluded.

Such is the closing scenario of Kipling's *Stalky and Co* (1914a [1899]), where tales of the absent Stalky's derring-do are recounted in the language of the boarding school jape, just as Kim's initiation in the Great Game of the imperial powers for control of central Asia recapitulate how 'what he loved was the game for its own sake' (Kipling 1914b [1901]: 4). Both excel at disguise, the masquerade that enables play; both move unseen, by stealth but always honourably, through an alien world in which the complicity of the homosocial is enacted without display or braggadocio, like the flag in *Stalky*, 'a matter shut up, sacred and apart' (Kipling 1914a [1899]: 244). Though much of Kipling can be summed as the law of moral values, imperial order and the discipline of work (Islam 1975), it is profoundly animated by the principle of gamesmanship, the moral principle of free souls, the source and reason of whose liberty is their allegiance to a power greater than men's: the rules of the game. Their innocence, even of atrocities, is preserved by the first foreshadowing of the secret honour of the mails.

Orphan status, or at least the parentless domains of the boarding school and the mess, combines with bachelordom to promote independence from the progenerative, and so from past and future alike. Even the present of the journey is subject to the cat-like tread, the light footfall, the keyhole view that leaves no trace of its passing. Only the *socius* of the playworld matters: only there will companions understand the decisions, the codes, the honour, the reality of your actions. Only there, and not among the denizens of the upcountry, does the traveller gain the goal of absolute reciprocity. But that *socius* depends both on memory, which can never be realised in the sodality of the game until after it has been played, and on an unmediated trade with the unknown. What is recounted is always both known and mediated. So it is that Stalky cannot be present at his own apotheosis, and all others must wait their turn of absence for their heroism to be recalled. Such is the lonely game of rule.

The self as only witness to its triumphs, the solitary burden of command, the melancholy basking in the successes of long ago, despite the thankless inhabitants who owe you all but do not even know your name: who has not felt the sorrow of responsibility, at the keyboard, and before the screen, trying to do your best by the people of *SimCity*? Maxis' software game owes its phenomenal success, uncommon longevity and fascination to the lonely honour of command. Laid out on an axonometric grid, the program invites you to model a landscape, put in service infrastructures, and populate a town of which you are the mayor. A roll-call of worthies offer scripted advice, but you are pretty much on your own, failure being marked by being voted out of office by a population only just too small to see. With its sharp graphics and disavowal of the competitive ethic of more typical video game shoot-em-ups, *SimCity* has become a model for edutainment games. It has spawned books, many column-inches in the 'zines and at least two network discussion groups. Its educational qualities are unquestioned: Kevin Kelly reports its use in the training of town-planners, even in experiments for real town planning (Kelly 1994: 234–6). There is only its curious depopulation, reminiscent of Piero's ideal cities and the remote-sensing images of cities from earth orbit, to sow a critical seed.

The virtual town is not a surveillance space; it is a game world. It is marked by the twinned subjectivities of the transvestite masquerade (you are the mayor) and touristic standoffishness, the curiously affectless freedom of the cursor. Needless to say it replicates the ideological premises of North American towns as well as their design features. Without doubt, it educates into the habit of rule over unquestioningly reactive citizens, the perfect feedback devices. Certainly it occupies the hyperindividuated space of the interface with special nonchalance. What is so fascinating is the representation of rule in this particularly autocratic form, a throwback to an older social order of city states and local princes. Here at least is a world in which the tourist is at home, even if it has to be invented. Here is a scale of gaming to simulate the human scale of the local, a world which can be known, and whose combinations can be second guessed. To that extent, it proffers the experience of mutuality, if only with an opinion poll of the non-existent. It is, quite cleverly, a commodification of power. Saved and copied, successful scenarios are living witnesses to the presence of their authors, unassailable tokens of magnanimity, a world already perfected in the image of its designer. Through transvestism, the mayor, like Kim and Stalky, is at home with patriarch and peasant; through tourism she is never entirely of them, always seeking the unquestioning love of those who are always absent. *SimCity* captures that typical oscillation in which the digital player is both freed and bound by his own bad faith. It is the perfect training ground for a life within the corporate cyborg.

Junk DNA: Morphologies of Multimedia

The narcissistic, synergetic hyperindividualised mayor of SimCity is the formative conjuncture of multimedia aesthetics, in the sense that, from a certain perspective, the histories of media convergence in the 20th century trace an arc towards an increasingly 'organic', unified and coherent experience. As humans come to occupy an increasingly human environment – urban, cultured, managed – there comes a double demand, tourist and transvestite, for cultural forms that combine the shocking and the nurturing, the speed of modernity and the narcissistic pleasures of regression.

News, current affairs, sport and now game shows and magazine programmes commonly draw on a wider range of resources than cinema: graphics, animations, typographics, embedded frames – a plural stylistics close to the familiar screens of multimedia. Just as the imperatives of digital recording and playback transformed the audio track, visual media have been revolutionised by the shift from lenses to graphics work stations. But more important still has been the macroeconomics of efficiency, cutting costs in all the traditional craft areas, and the rise of editorial over journalistic values, as the outcome of intensive conglomeration and competition in media corporations. The result in actuality programming has been akin to the remaking of the feature film: a preponderance of effects and affect-driven programme making. At the same time, both the residual journalistic value systems and the demands of corporate news consumers for accuracy limit the distance which TV has been able to put between itself and an exterior criterion to gauge its performance. The loss of a common culture in news reporting acts like the loss of a common cult, identified by Arnheim (1958 [1938]) as the ground for the unification of media in the ancient combined arts, and for the incoherence of the talking picture of the 1930s. TV's response to the characteristic dialectic between the shock effect and the demand for coherence has been to produce a hierarchy, in this instance focused on the anchor, whose voice, scripts and delivery mark the organising core of the programme. The risks of this strategy are all too apparent, gleefully documented by a vengeful Hollywood in *Network* (1976)

Synergetic culture, then, finds itself facing again the problem of resolving the twin tendencies of individualisation and dispersion. Multimedia products in the commercial sphere are characterised by their holistic vision of the product, and by the utter subordination of the warring tendencies of designers and programmers (see Moody 1995) to the hierarchically focused unity of the product. Internet's current design limitations, especially the dependency on plug-ins (small software applications supplementing the basic communications program with video, photographic, audio and interactive capabilities), exacerbates this dialectic, with files arriving in discrete packages of text, image, movie and sound. The response of most designers is to accentuate the coherence of their sites, using strategies from corporate branding, magazine design, thematic unity and highly circumscribed and delimited interactivity within predictable paths. Search engines and infobots (learning-capable search engines that tailor themselves to individual preferences, vividly defined by Jaron Lanier as 'a program that conceals a haphazard personality profile of a user from that user' [Lanier 1998]), tailored to the universal categorisation project of database cataloguing, attempt to construct coherence about a hierarchy centred on the hyperindividuated user. And the office-oriented design of the GUI interface and the workstation complete the illusion that the centre of the network is always a sovereign individual, cross-dressing and touring a playworld in which s/he can achieve mastery over both environment and self. The net is effectively organised around this socially engineered hyperindividual, for whom all variety can be resolved into self and other, with the self in imperial mode, click by click assimilating the alien into the longed for stability of the same.

Chaotic models of interaction rarely achieve more than a reinforcement of this self-promoting still centre of a turning world, exchanging the distracted pleasures of interaction for functional ubiquity. Artists' sites can all too often, as with Mark America's *Grammatron* (1998), reproduce, in their delirious vertigo of effects, this narcissistic subject position of self-consumption. It requires a different strategy to produce a site as elegant in conception and execution as *Jodi* (1998), where there is no mystery to unravel or ideology to detect, but rather a scattering of impulses, a series of dynamic relations through which the stability and focus of the visitor is unharnessed, and a direct connection to net symbolisation, net protocols and traffic which gives the site its constantly changing rationale and iconography, while also allowing it to indicate a there and a now with which a new kind of interactive dialogue becomes possible. In a rather different way, Simon Biggs' (1998) generative-transformational engine for the web version of *The Great Wall of China* is also a dispersion engine, rattling out from the lexicon and syntax of the Kafka story a cloud of intensively accidental enunciations, whose randomness evokes exactly the missing qualities of more typical interactive experiences. Work like *Jodi* and *The Great Wall* is characteristically unconcerned with the integrity of the message, respectful instead of the missing *Umwelt* that informs real-life conversation, and producing an unmastered and unmanaged stream of contingent images and sounds, clearly deriving from more localisable and meaningful semantic domains, yet ready to sacrifice the semantic to the random flaring of connections, rather as the cinematographe seized the otherwise unrecordable and, even when recorded, unmanageable shimmering multiplicity of leaves in the wind.

The fault of too many sites is their addiction to meaning, or more specifically to meaning in a particular frame of thought: meaning as message, meaning as coherence. The effort of any multimedia artefact, movie, TV programme, CD-ROM, has to go into the relationship between its tools and techniques. All too often, they fall back on an apparently simple, apparently intuitive, apparently tried and tested schema of older cultural forms, like the illustrated encyclopaedia, or the Hollywood film, a familiar tactic in any new medium. In the case of the internet, most sites have an operating hierarchy, as far as end users are concerned, gathering images, sounds, interactions and code to itself, changing each into a common form, text or information, and triggering their structuration as coherent and self-replicating entities, manipulable, orchestrated and defunct. Such hierarchies shape the user's experience as coherent, deploying the concept of flow in order to guide the viewer through self-enclosed and self-referential channels whose outcomes are always already coded.

Coherence implies autonomy, and the aesthetic term 'organic' stores the origins of this intellectual node. Organicism in aesthetics derives from Goethe's conception of morphology as the unfolding of a single essence through the development of individuals, so that seed, leaf and flower of a particular plant are of one design, and share a unity more important than their differences. The organic theory still draws on this otherwise outmoded metaphor to steer inquiries into aesthetic form towards a search for unities, the reflection of macro-scale architectonics in the micro-scale of rhythms, lexicon, paint-handling and what have you. The organic metaphor suggests that the artwork is entire unto itself, shaped by only its own internal dynamic, and as such an Idealist refusal of the economic demand that art be useful (see Bowie 1990: 98–9). But in the age of the aestheticisation of the everyday, organicism becomes the legitimation of the useless commodity, the pure product of the economy of signs. In the UK's art schools, especially in design but to some extent also in fine arts, we tend to lever our students towards producing work according to this model, rewarding coherence, integrity, the relating of parts to the whole and the easy flow of attention from one part to another, while discouraging incoherence, disintegration and the assemblage of unrelated parts. Nor do we demand of students that they refer their creations to external factors like verisimilitude or journalistic accuracy: it is the internal coherence that matters, and the fact that their models may not resemble anything living or dead is of little consequence, and is even gently approved of in some quarters. We encourage the same kind of modelling that suffuses the synergetic corporation, privileging internal coherence over empirical validity.

In engineering as in art, the contemporary culture of the informational society prizes above all the homeostatic – the feedback and control circuits that maintain equilibrium in a system, and preserve its integrity in the face of population and environmental pressures. Such homeostatic integrity is core to genetics and the life sciences, to cognitive science and neurobiology, to information science and informatics, and to deconstruction and art education. The common ground is the socio-cultural myth of individualism. Brain science, as the name suggests, concentrates on 'the' brain, isolated from its environment, of which the most important part is the social. Information science treats messages as events occurring between individuals, not as social flows. The disembodied text presumes the individuality of the reader, both as effect, and as the ground of that effect. But as Freeman Dyson (1988) argues so convincingly, we are now in a period in which we must investigate populations and ecologies, not individual exemplars, to discover the meanings and forces operating in almost any scientific field. This is why artificial intelligences are so stupid: they are modelled on the individual brain, not on the communicative networks within which any one brain is a mere crossroads.

Dyson also points towards the phenomenon of 'Junk DNA', quoting research which suggests that up to 80% of human DNA serves no purpose, but is just along for the ride (Dyson 1988: 94ff.). For Dyson, this is additional evidence that life and complexity are synonymous, and also that the diverse interrelationships in Darwin's grassy bank, or in the new model of DNA as a population of interacting nucleotides, are more readily explained by complexity and diversity than by efficiency models of information processing. Risking argument by analogy: what if 80% of human thought is junk, memes of no purpose or value, like jingles jammed in your inner ear? Yet that ridiculous, useless, unformed, purposeless bunkum is the primal soup from which ideas evolve. Purposive and coherent models, whether of the mind or of multimedia, are active refusals of that promise of evolution. Extending the analogy: is surfing the internet the daydreaming of a cyborg society? And isn't managing the flows of pictures, thoughts and daydreams a further attempt to shut down evolution? Digital aesthetics needs both to come up with something far more interesting than corporate sites, and to act critically to point up their insidious blandness and global ambitions. Subversion of the dominant is inadequate. In its place, it is essential to imagine a work without coherence, without completion and without autonomy. Such a work, however, must also be able to take on the scale of the cyborg culture, a scale beyond the individual, and outside the realm of the hyperindividuated subject. By the same token, aesthetics must move beyond the organic unity of the art object to embrace the social processes of making. Until then, the disastrous history of the audiovisual will be repeated as failed hierarchies pile one upon the other, or worse still, in the achievement of truly coherent virtual spaces, simulating and overlaying the virtualised subjectivity and controlled society of the corporate playworld.

Anonymous History: Globalisation and Diaspora

The word 'amateur', now most frequently used as obloquy, has its roots in love, and its glorious head in the air. The amateur escapes from the dialectic of subversion and resistance to become otherwise than dominated. And so the hobbyist is more relevant to an understanding of digital aesthetics in the networked world than the professional and the industrialised. To see such engagement as merely personal is to miss both the personal politics of amateurism and the endless creativity of ordinary culture. Because 'everyone' watches Hollywood films but 'no-one' makes embroidery or videographics, to side with no-one is the only realistically eschatological option. The nobody who cooks is more interesting than the everybody who eats at McDonald's.

In the *in memoriam* poems in the local press, or in those Bryced fantasy landscapes in the readers' corners of computer magazine cover discs, you can find, if you are determined to, the evidence of a banalisation of the social imagination, the common, imitative, normative art that Baudrillard (1981) takes as disproof of Enzensberger's guerrilla media optimism (Enzensberger 1988). What else would the cultural critic expect to find in the ruins of the contemporary? If, on the other hand, you seek the evidence of a yearning for something beyond the mire of the everyday, you will find it glistening in the mud. It takes a very personal form. Of course. The personal has become the retrenched position in which social hope, in all its contradictions, is most intimately experienced – as lacking. It is in making, when you seek either to heal the inner self or to reach beyond it to another or others, that you are *least* individual. Only in the mass, as the data-images of industrial media, are we the administered selves of bureaucratic capitalism. By contrast the amateurs who seek the approbation of an ideal and imaginary audience of peers recognises in others the dissatisfactions they feel with themselves.

To work with others – as for example in the *mcr36* project organised by the Manchester group Idea (1998), where a group of young artists and unemployed established a digital workspace-cum-training base in an abandoned bookshop, locking themselves in for 36 hours to create installations, CD-ROMs and net sites – is to find among the fleeting friends of hobby networks the very purpose of making: to share. It is itself a utopian gesture, not only to lend your own skills to your pals, but to set yourself to learning – to trust, to acquire with good grace what is offered in good faith. It is only in such moments that the word 'we' begins to take on meaning beyond liberal pieties and fascist polemic. It is also the contemporary realisation of that robust tradition, stretching back for centuries, of radical thinking, homespun cosmologies, decoration and cuisine, invention and dissemination, the tradition of anonymity (see, *inter alia*, Giedion 1948; Ginzburg 1980; Plant 1997: 60–72; Thompson 1963). The refusal of both professionals and funders to recognise the spontaneous creativity of amateurism continues deeply to impoverish an already stagnating culture.

Of course, the amateur does not require recognition from on high, or even funding to legitimate it. The strength of the amateur 'system' is its real lack of systematicity, compared to the systemic regulation of the infrastructures of packet-switching and transfer protocols on the web. It is not the concept of authorship and the copyright architectures that surround it, nor the separation of audience from producers, which, according to Boal (1974), can be traced to Greek tragedy, that constitute the synergetic culture, but the focus on transmission: on the sending of messages from A to B. Although in engineering terms this is a centre-out model, it is in fact a centripetal structure, one which, as in the broadcast industries, uses its audiences as feedback mechanisms to modify the central activities of the sender institutions. But the organic structure of the system produces as effect the sense among audiences that every broadcast is presented for an intensely personal consumption, as though each 'I' were the centre of a network whose economic and cultural centre is, in fact, always elsewhere. The lesson to learn, in this context, from amateur cultures is the centrifugal movement of ideas and techniques. In this sense, Deleuze and Guattari's minor science points in the right direction, if inscribing a misleading caption under the prospect. The practical knowledge of making, and the sharing of recipes, tools and techniques that goes with it, we should take as evidence not of a binary resistance to the state, but as networks formed outside the managed webs of globalisation. In the first instance, this entails the constant remaking, in anonymous culture and in those art practices that have learnt from it, of the available machinery.

Those commentators – Arthur Kroker and Michael Weinstein (1994), Vivian Sobchack (1994) and Ziauddin Sardar (1996) among them – who have tried to capture a sense of the phenomenological implications of cyberspace have focused on the superficiality of the medium: its erasure of referential origins in favour of virtual presences, of spatial and semantic depth in favour of the shallow surface. It is not that this is wrong as analysis; that is how the overlit video language and institutional practices of TV have been accommodated in computer imaging, and how the average run of computer games and software packages operate on the average machine. But what is important to networked art is not the simulacral fate of representation in the new media, but the retroengineering of the machinery itself, and by implication of the institutional structures of cyberspace. The first of these tasks is the more approachable. Artists like Joseph Nechvatal, Miroslav

Rogala, Bill Seaman, Pervaiz Khan, Kath Moonam, Clive Gillman, Masaki Fujihata and Char Davis are among hundreds who have devoted major elements of their work to remaking the hardware and investigating the new subjectivities whose emergence has been blocked by the limitations of existing designs. No single artwork, however luminous, however achieved, however passionate, carries in itself the purpose or function of the electronic media arts as a new cultural domain. The achievement of such a practice is to create the terms under which the apparatus of making is constantly re-evolved. At the same time, the global reach of corporate networks cannot be matched by a mere shadowing of its filigrees of growth. In the spirit of the anonymous histories of amateurism, the invisible college of electronic arts must learn from existing global communications structures that exceed and often are excluded from electronic connectivity.

Mike Featherstone suggests that globalisation has reached a point where the category 'society' is no longer central, even for sociologists (Featherstone 1995: 82). In that breakdown of society as analytic category, we also lose its binary complement, the individual. Without the individual, and given the primacy of communication over both individuation and economy, concepts of intellectual property and authorship lose their coherence. It is not merely that distributed media are also copying machines, and have been since the invention of writing, so that policing copyright has become all but impossible – the international trade body estimated up to 25% of the $4bn world market for recorded music was pirated in 1990 (Burnett 1996: 88). It is also the case that the constructed individuality to which we ascribe property rights is a social formation in a state of crisis. The European law of property, like the ideology of individualism, seems to have exported badly during the five centuries since Columbus. The effort to enforce it fails, despite the diplomatic efforts of the Clinton administration in China. One consequence of the resistance culture of pirating is, ironically, the standardisation of Western pop across the planet. But looking away from resistance towards the anonymous, other mechanisms of distribution have grown up in the interstices of globalisation. Empire and colonialism enforced diaspora; now the diasporan web – nowhere more prevalent than in the free exchange of beats in musics of the African diaspora (see Gilroy 1993) – has superseded the corporate model of hierarchical information flows. The discrete roles of sender, channel and receiver have been blended into a single complex, mobile and changing mediation, in which subjectivities are not terminals but channels.

Broadcasting and diaspora share the same root meaning: the scattering of seeds. Yet contemporary broadcast industries are devoted to one-way traffic, the delivery of services. Of course, this is also a closed loop: from an audience point of view, broadcasters deliver programming, while from the point of view of governments and advertisers, they deliver audiences, simple feedback devices. The feedback function, however, is entirely controlled by agendas set at the institutional centres, producing an effect of marginalisation at the subordinate reception end of the loop. Throughout, the transmission ethic demands the integrity of messages: engineering standards high enough to preempt unprofessionally garbled data travelling in either direction, monitoring of feedback loops through a panoply of audience research methods, quasi-judicial oversight of standards and morals. By contrast, diasporan cultures treat messages as what they are: relationships. Beats might originate in Jamaica, be remade in Senegel, get transformed in New York, find a new modification in London, catch another inflection in Cuba or Brazil, and so on and so on: a circuit described vividly in internet terms by Derek Richards in a talk at The Drum in Birmingham in 1997, and subject of his forthcoming CD-ROM. Central to diasporan circuits is that there is no closure to the loop, because there is far less emphasis on the integrity of the messages. Instead, the emphasis is on an improvisational bricolage embroidered on the incoming sounds before they are sent off on their travels again.

However, the idea of diaspora cannot be a viable eschatological concept, a utopian meme, if it does not recognise, as Janice Cheddie argues, that diaspora also materialises 'historical relationships of slavery, indenture, colonialism, migration, exile and economic immigration' (Cheddie 1997: 145–6). The metaphoric structures that govern cyberdiscourse – webs, nets, highways – are open to radical change, but it is imperative that the metaphors we choose be understood in the fullness of their implications: that the African diaspora is also a history of suffering, a history which is far from over, even in the apparently 'de-racialised' (because apparently disembodied) realms of internet (see Bailey 1995). Secondly, holding the ideas of diaspora and globalisation apart is fraught with difficulties. On the one hand, in Stuart Hall's words, the 'global postmodern' pretends that 'there is no difference which it cannot contain, no otherness of which it cannot speak, no marginality that it cannot take pleasure out of', yet it is 'a process of profound unevenness' (Hall 1991: 33). Going further, Ella Shohat warns that 'a celebration of syncretism and hybridity per se, if not articulated in conjunction with questions of hegemony and neo-colonial power relations, runs the risk of appearing to sanctify the *fait accompli* of colonial violence' (Shohat 1992: 109). Yet, as Hall suggests, we have learnt to live in and with 'this concentrated, corporate, over-corporate, over-integrated, over-concentrated, and condensed form of economic power which lives culturally through difference and which is constantly teasing itself with the pleasures of the transgressive Other' (Hall 1991: 31).

This teasing, this fascination with transgression, is precisely what has powered the cultural studies fascination with resistance and subversion, and, as Hall intimates, the process of fixing on transgression is both an assertion of the dominant's right to dominate, and a function of the universalising tendencies of globalisation (thus, for example, Dave Laing [1986] singles out the uses of Boy George in homophobic Indonesia in his critique of cultural imperialism). The transmission ethos allows, encourages, demands this double process of marginalisation and assimilation through its hypostasising of the message. This is clear from the way corporate culture responds to microcultural resistance with target marketing. By rendering alterity as textual, it delimits and defuses it as purely cultural, disembodying the material challenge of material difference: of poverty, oppression, ignorance, disease and anger. The translational model of anonymity and diaspora, by contrast, must begin exactly in this materiality. Where the sender model ignores the situation of the receiver, the translational (from the root 'to bring across', as opposed to transmission, 'to send across') is centred in interchange, in the hermeneutics of interaction, the communicative environment.

That that environment is riven by oppression, exploitation and punishment is central to my thesis. There can be no translational culture which is not local, in the sense that the conditions of communication are specific to the cultural ecology in which they occur: a song, a website, mean one thing here and another there, one thing now and another then. Translation, from the standpoint of transmission, disintegrates communication, abandoning conservation in favour of openness – to questioning, to ephemerality, to misunderstanding. In fact, the very concept of misunderstanding dissolves into a fuzzier logic, if you think of the multiplexed creativity that can occur when conversations are not exchanges of messages between autonomous and rational subjects, but instead mutual daydreams, from which any participant or several, human or machine, participant or channel, might make the break towards an idea or a technique for the benefit of all. Misunderstanding, far from being the evidence of a breakdown in communications, is symptomatic of a culture of translation, where every word, gesture, mark and sound has to be given over to the processes of its remaking.

According to the old story, translation begins after Babel, which has long been read as God's anger at the hubris of humankind's unification. That, at least, is God's story. But behind the Babel myth lies a darker tale. Far more than unity, God fears the diversity of His creation. As long as we are unified, we are in His image, for He is the supreme monad, the narcissistic centre of all power, all justice, all love. In short, God is the mouthpiece of the normative Western *civitas*. Each in their turn, the God of Moses, the European Enlightenment and the synergetic corporation have played double-bluff with the allegory of Babel. Diversity makes us more than the unified creatures of a timeless deity, because the translational ethic links people to people through the processes of misunderstanding, not in pursuit of Habermas's rational agreement, rational unification, but as the primal soup from which the future may evolve. The endless creative productivity of Biggs's (1998) Chomskyan engine in *The Great Wall* is just such a breeding ground of misapprehensions and random sense. By contrast, in an immense act of bravado, faced with the importunate reality of diversity as the unavoidable outcome of its planetary expansion, the synergetic has invented irony, a stance which it can use to reunite the centrifugal elements of a culture whose torn parts do not add up. Under the unifying gaze of an ironic consciousness, the ironist can enjoy another's anger, as the sentimentalist enjoys another's pain, without responsibility. So even Keith Piper's *Trade Winds* (1992), an installation which speaks of the pain and the growth of diaspora through the dispersed fragments of a body ripped from its home, ripped apart and stored on digital screens in packing cases, can be read ironically, constructed as a gallery exhibit, textualised, and so prepared for an appreciation which allows its tragedy to be consumed within an untroubled meta-consciousness. The struggle to maintain materiality – in this instance through sound, scent and the rough, splintered timber of the crates housing the monitors – is the struggle against this dematerialising irony, a recognition of materiality in mortality.

It is far easier to analyse the failings of the present than to sketch the grounds for hope. Speaking at ISEA95 in Montreal, Piper offered a scenario where interactive media are a kind of city, contrasting the orderly burg of tame media with 'the interactive domain as riot zone with the user not as orderly citizen but as digital looter. . . . It is within this nightmare scenario for the controllers of Cyberspace, that the digital equivalent of the disorderly black of urban chaos and transgressive behaviour steps into full visibility' (Piper 1995: 234). The riot zone may sound like the naïve playground of urban violence as game scenario enjoyed by privileged fans of hip-hop's most urban grooves, or like the purely literary chaos of Bataille's poetics of personal liberation. The rhetorics of urban chaos are rhetorics of revenge, and, admirable as that motive is, Piper's guerrilleros only demand a piece of the same pie, where the nomadic frames of diaspora suggest far more complex negotiations for the meaning of the past and access to the future. But Piper also suggests that the city-in-chaos scenario also contains its own anonymous artists, walls transfigured by their (mis)appropriation as surfaces for art, where one graffito invites another, marking territories and routes otherwise obscure and unexplored. Deciphering the city as a code waiting to be decrypted, as geographical information systems analysts do, is transmissive: rewriting the very fabric of its architecture is already a step into the translational. It is such a hybrid of anger and generosity that will make any future culture worth visiting.

In a recent essay on Keith Piper's work, Kobena Mercer argues that 'the unrecoverable trauma of lost origins is tragic only when it is experienced as the deprivation of a final destiny. On the other hand,' he continues, 'it is with the loss of a fixed origin that diaspora opens consciousness to opportunities to exert freedom and responsibility in the contingent conditions that constitute one's home' (Mercer 1997: 40). And he cites a passage from a 1995 paper by Stuart Hall which seems to catch the Gramscian couplet, pessimism of the intellect, optimism of the will, in the dangerous cross-currents of diasporan cultures:

> No cultural identity is produced out of thin air. It is produced out of those historical experiences, those cultural traditions, those lost and marginal languages, those people and histories which remain unwritten. Those are the specific roots of identity. On the other hand, identity is not the rediscovery of them, but what they as cultural resources allow a people to produce. Identity is not in the past to be *found*, but in the future to be *constructed*. (Hall 1995: 14)

Dispersal and diversity, as aesthetic practices, fit the anonymity which the amateur tradition has evolved over centuries, and which can be pitched towards breaking the grip of the networked society's cultures of self. Only by sacrificing that narcissistic umbilical and embracing the centrifuge of life will digital aesthetics emerge from under the shadows of corporate culture.

Conclusion

The expanding use of computers and the growth of the internet have created the terms of a new community, potentially a universal one. But, as we have seen, claims to universality have their sinister underbellies. The imminent arrival of push media, massively powerful servers supplying intensive info-tainment datastreams, suggests that the days of the freewheeling information frontier may be numbered, and the wilderness will be conquered, as it was before by the telegraph, this time by the televisualisation of the internet. The language of community has been taken up in corporate culture, applied both to employees and to consumers, and is today most clearly associated with Microsoft's successful bid to launch an $8bn network of 324 satellites to enable computer-mediated traffic without the need to rely on telephone wires and electricity supplies. It seems unlikely that this technological marvel will end the excommunication of the developing world. Instead, we can confi-dently predict that it will service the communications demands of globalising business and the incorporation of local elites to the global hierarchy. The only positive outcome may be an improvement in battery technology, left behind in computer evolution because unnecessary in the hardwired indus-trial world. You sense the word 'community' has been devalued.

Hans-Georg Gadamer, however, suggests that aesthetic thought and art practice defend a special meaning of the word. Though unable to call up existing shared values and meanings, the artist,

> forms his own community insofar as he expresses himself . . . and in principle, this truly universal community (*oikumene*) extends to the whole world. In fact, all artistic creation challenges each of us to listen to the language in which the work speaks and to make it our own. It remains true in every case that a shared or potentially shared achievement is at issue. (Gadamer 1986: 39)

Again, you fear for the philosophical demand for universality. And the briefest acquaintance with the art world makes it clear that there is no democracy in the galleries and museums: at the end of the millennium it is still depressingly difficult to see or hear examples of 20th-century modernism from without the imperial metropolis. But Gadamer does seem to speak for the microcommunities that grow up around particular cultural works, artis-tic or popular. And his universalism, limited to the 'in principle' and the 'potentially', is clearly distinguishable from the hypercortex of Pierre Lévy's 'collective intelligence' (1994), proposed as the real utopia of a wired world, but which, in its Saint-Simonian failure to recognise the exclusions and authoritarianism of the network, defends in all but name the corporate cyborg.

The power structures of cyberspace are not finally arguable in terms of class, since by definition anyone accessing the net is at least middle class.

Aesthetics offers us a way of differentiating, however, between the modes and usages of network traffic in ways disturbingly elided in technotopian discourse. Gadamer is right to point towards the microcultural loyalties of traditional art practice; but digital cultures offer a wider sense of their operation. Like the anonymous cultures of diaspora and amateur networks, the international trades union networks described by Lee (1997) and the interregional digital local government initiatives debated in Loader (1997) can be placed alongside both the 'authored' artworks surveyed by Popper (1993) and Lovejoy (1997) and community-oriented practices such as those documented on the *Shared Experience* CD-ROM (FACT 1997) or Graham Harwood's remarkable *Rehearsal of Memory* (1996). Such works, on the one hand, pitch themselves into the struggle to preserve the public sphere against corporatisation; and, on the other, aspire towards the establishment of another mode of communication beyond the old public sphere, a politicisation of the intimate. While some communications theorists posit the individual as the opposition to such collectivisation (for example, Guattari 1995), I hope I have shown how individualism is itself a projection of the corporate cyborg, and that the old binarism of individual against society is no longer feasible ground for a politics of the information society. Nor can the cybernetic concept of the self-regulating chaotic system survive the growth of the corporate cyborg as exactly that enemy which cyberanarchism has refused to see (see Mattelart 1996: 306–7).

The vocabulary is against us. Like 'community' and 'collectivity', the word 'communication' has been deprived of its broadest scope, restricted to a subordinate technological domain, for which, nonetheless, universal claims of determination and influence are constantly made. Communication, however, is only important to the extent that it exceeds both the causative model of technological determinism and the restricted sense of technologies useful for sending and receiving. I argued at the beginning of this book that both economic and political life are permutations of communication. If language and gesture are technologies, then surely technologies must also be understood as languages and gestures. The collectivist myth fails to grasp that 'Everyone feels themselves divided between the symbolic culture which they receive from their histories and the technical culture of the present moment, between what they call values on the one hand and norms on the other' (Debray 1994: 147). So these technologies, which inhabit us at the level of reflexes, are also torn between old and new, to produce, as Debray argues, 'The endlessly renegotiated interaction between our values and our norms we call culture' (Debray 1994: 148). The question then arises: where does this negotiation take place?

Insofar as it is lived everyday, the abrupt tension between values and norms is experienced only as hurt and loss at the level of individuality, as modernisation and the overcoming of the dead past in the corporate personality. For both, historical movements are experienced as fate, and their products, as cultural artefacts, tend to impose coherence as the only way in which that irresolvable loss of power over history can be resolved. Such is the hierarchic structure of the coherent work, the resolved coherence of design and programming in a product like *Encarta*. The hierarchies of multimedia design have prioritised certain body elements – eyes, ears, hands – over others, distracting and disassembling the body in the interests of coherence now centred outside the body, in a pure communication between mind and object. So it builds a formal utopia outside of history to heal its failure. But the pain of history cannot be assuaged by pretending that it is over. The condition of art, to indicate that which is not-yet, to embody that which is not the case, is the condition of any digital practice which is dedicated to survival at the beginning of the millennium. The corporate utopia, the playworld, must be here and now, only separated from the real conditions of existence by the universal claim of the virtual to supersede the tangible. Coherence is a mark of the corporate. But as Vattimo argues, 'Aesthetic utopia only comes about through its articulation as heterotopia' (Vattimo 1992: 69), the plurality of forms and practices, but a pluralism which, however, ceases to function as aesthetic as soon as it takes itself for the universal condition of beauty. Dispersion is, then, not a value for its own sake, but the condition under which difference may defend its possibility.

If we are not to be retrofitted into the corporate cyborg, or, worse still, are to be left to die outside its too-universal embrace, we must reinvent the machineries, the processes and the selves of human–machine communication. Beyond survival, there lies the task of providing the evolutionary conditions for a future outside the administered boundaries of the synergetic corporation. From the real conditions of the emergent politics of the unconscious, from the historical coevolution of machines and humans, from the imbrication of computer and non-digital global networks, and through a meticulous process of disassembling our present theories and careful learning from the past, it may be possible to drive through the glass wall at the end of history, and create the conditions for a genuinely global and democratic future.

REFERENCES

Note: Website addresses are given as 1998, the most recent versions regardless of the date of first publication, and were correct at time of going to press.

Abel, Richard (1994), *The Ciné Goes to Town: French Cinema, 1896–1914*, University of California Press, Berkeley.

Abrioux, Yves (1992), *Ian Hamilton Finlay: A Visual Primer*, 2nd edn, Reaktion Books, London.

Ades, Dawn (1986), *Photomontage*, rev. edn, Thames and Hudson, London.

Adorno, Theodor W. (1967), 'Cultural Criticism and Society' in *Prisms*, trans. Samuel and Shierry Weber, MIT Press, Cambridge, MA, 19–34.

Adorno, Theodor W. (1997), *Aesthetic Theory*, ed. Gretel Adorno and Rolf Tiedemann, trans. Robert Hullot-Kentor, Athlone Press, London.

Adorno, Theodor W. and Hans Eisler (1994 [1947]), *Composing for the Films*, Oxford University Press, New York; reprinted by Athlone Press, London.

Advisory Committee on the Future of the US Space Program (1990), *Report of the Advisory Committee on the Future of the US Space Program*, US Government Printing Office, Washington, DC.

Ahvenainen, Jorma (1981), *The Far Eastern Telegraphs: The History of Telegraphic Communications Between the Far East, Europe and America Before the First World War*, Suomalainen Tiedeakatemia, Helsinki.

Altick, Richard D. (1957), *The English Common Reader: A Social History of the Mass Reading Public 1800–1900*, University of Chicago Press, Chicago.

Altick, Richard D. (1978), *The Shows of London*, Harvard University Press, Cambridge, MA.

Altman, Rick (1992), 'The Material Heterogeneity of Recorded Sound' in Rick Altman (ed.), *Sound Theory/Sound Practice*, Routledge, London, 15–31.

America, Mark (1998), *Grammatron*, http://www.grammatron.com

Amin, Samir (1990), *Delinking: Towards a Polycentric World*, Zed Books, London.

Amnesty International (1994), *Amnesty Interactive: A History and Atlas of Human Rights*, CD-ROM, Amnesty International/Voyager, New York.

Anderson, Laurie (1982), 'O Superman' from *Big Science*, Warner Records, Burbank.

Anderson, Laurie (1994), 'Night in Baghdad' from *La Vida 1992* in 'Stories from the Nerve Bible' in Gretchen Bender and Timothy Druchrey (eds), *Cultures on the Brink: Ideologies of Technology*, Bay Press, Seattle, 226–7.

Anderson, Laurie and Hsin-Chien Huang (1995), *Puppet Motel*, CD-ROM, Voyager, New York.

Arnheim, Rudolf (1958 [1938]), 'A New Laocöon: Artistic Composites and the Talking Film' in Arnheim, *Film as Art*, Faber, London, 164–89.

Aronowitz, Stanley (1992) 'Looking Out: The Impact of Computers on the Lives of Professionals' in Myron C. Tuman (ed.), *Literacy Online: The Promise (and Peril) of Reading and Writing with Computers*, University of Pittsburgh Press, Pittsburgh, PA, 119–37.

Aronowitz, Stanley (1994), 'Technology and the Future of Work' Gretchen Bender and Timothy Druchrey (eds), *Cultures on the Brink: Ideologies of Technology*, Bay Press, Seattle, 15–29.

Artificial Life Journal (1998), http://alife.santafe.edu/

Ascott, Roy (1993), 'Telenoia', electronic text of a talk given at Fotofeis, Inverness, 24 June.

Attali, Jacques (1985), *Noise: The Political Economy of Music*, trans. Brian Massumi, Manchester University Press, Manchester.

Attridge, Derek (1982), *The Rhythms of English Poetry*, Longman, London.

Bacon, Francis (1605), *The Tvvoo bookes of Francis Bacon. Of the proficience and advancement of learning, divine and humane: To the King. At London, Printed for Henrie Tomes and are to be sold at his shop*, 1st edn.

Bailey, Cameron (1995), 'Virtual Skin: Articulating Race in Cyberspace' in ISEA95, *Actes: 6e Symposium des arts électroniques/6th International Symposium on Electronic Art*, ISEA 95, Montreal, 12-16.

Bakhtin, Mikhail (1986), *Speech Genres and Other Late Essays*, trans. Vern W. McGee, ed. Ceryl Emerson and Michael Holquist, University of Texas Press, Austin.

Bann, Stephen (1977), 'Ian Hamilton Finlay – An Imaginary Portrait' in *Ian Hamilton Finlay*, Serpentine Gallery/Arts Council of Great Britain, London, 7–28.

Barnouw, Eric (1966), *A Tower in Babel: A History of Broadcasting in the United States: Volume 1 - to 1933*, Oxford University Press, New York.

Barthes, Roland (1989 [1964]), 'Image, raison, déraison' in *Les Planches de l'Encyclopédie de Diderot et d'Alembert vues par Roland Barthes*, Musée de Pontoise, Pontoise.

Baudrillard, Jean (1981), 'Requiem for the Media' in *For a Critique of the Political Economy of the Sign*, trans. Charles Levin, Telos Press, St Louis MO, 164–84.

Baudry, Jean-Louis (1976), 'The Apparatus: Metapsychological Approaches to the Impression of Reality in the Cinema', trans. Jean Andrews and Bertrand Augst, *Camera Obscura*, no. 1, Fall, 104–26 (originally published as 'Le Dispositif', *Communications* no. 23, 1975).

Baudry, Jean-Louis (1985), 'Ideological Effects of the Basic Cinematographic Apparatus', trans. Alan Williams, in Bill Nichols (ed.), *Movies and Methods: Volume II*, California University Press, Berkeley 531–42.

Baym, Nancy K. (1995), 'The Emergence of Community in Computer-Mediated Communication' in Steven G. Jones (ed.), *CyberSociety: Computer-Mediated Communication and Community*, Sage, London, 138–63.

Bazin, André (1971), '*Umberto D*: A Great Work' in *What is Cinema?*, Volume II, ed. and trans. Hugh Gray, University of California Press, Berkeley.

Becker, Karin E. (1991), 'To Control Our Image: Photojournalists Meeting New Technology' in Paul Wombell (ed.), *Photovideo: Photography in the Age of the Computer*, Rivers Oram Press, London, 16–31.

Beeching, Wilfred A. (1974), *Century of the Typewriter*, Heinemann, London.

Bellour, Raymond (1986), 'Ideal Hadaly (On Villier's *The Future Eve*)' in *Camera Obscura* no. 15, Fall, 111–34.

Belton, John (1992), *Widescreen Cinema*, Harvard University Press, Cambridge, MA.

Belyea, Barbara (1992), 'Images of Power: Derrida, Foucault, Harley' in *Cartographica* vol. 29, no. 2, Summer, 1-9.

Benjmain, Walter (1969), 'Theses on the Philosophy of History' in *Illuminations*, ed. Hannah Arendt, trans.. Harry Zohn, Schocken, New York, 253–64.

Benjamin, Walter (1973a), 'The Author as Producer' in *Understanding Brecht*, trans. Anna Bostock, New Left Books, London, 85–103.

Benjamin, Walter (1973b), *Charles Baudelaire: A Lyric Poet in the Era of High Capitalism*, trans. Harry Zohn, New Left Books, London.

Benjamin, Walter (1977), *The Origin of German Tragic Drama*, trans. John Osborne, Verso, London.

Bentley, Jerry H. (1993), *Old World Encounters: Cross-Cultural Contacts and Exchanges in Pre-Modern Times*, Oxford University Press, New York.

Berland, Jody (1995), 'Mapping Space: Imaging Technologies and the Planetary Body' in *Found Object* no. 5, Spring, 7–19.

Beverley, John (1993), *Against Literature*, University of Minnesota Press, Minneapolis.

Biggs, Simon (1998), *The Great Wall of China*, http://www.easynet.co.uk/simonbiggs/

Biota.org (1998) *Biota.org: Thal biology project*, http://www.biota.org/

Bliss, Henry Evelyn (1929), *The Organization of Knowledge and the System of the Sciences*, Henry Holt and Co., New York.

Bliss, Henry Evelyn (1933), *The Organization of Knowledge in Libraries and the Subject-Approach to Books*, H.W. Wilson, New York.

Bliven, Bruce, Jr (1954), *The Wonderful Writing Machine*, Random House, New York.

Bloch, Ernst (1988), *The Utopian Function of Art and Literature: Selected Essays*, trans. Jack Zipes and Frank Mecklenburg, MIT Press, Cambridge, MA.

Bloch, Ernst and Theodor Adorno (1988), 'Something's Missing: A Discussion Between Ernst Bloch and Theodor Adorno on the Contradictions of Utopian Longing' in Ernst Bloch, *The Utopian Function of Art and Literature: Selected Essays*, trans. Jack Zipes and Frank Mecklenburg, MIT Press, Cambridge, MA, 1–17.

Boal, Augusto (1974), *Theatre of the Oppressed*, trans. Charles A. and Maria-Odilia Leal McBride, Pluto, London.

Boissier, Jean-Louis (1994), *Flora Petrinsularis*, on *artintact 1* CD-ROM, Zentrum für Kunst und Medientechnolgie, Karlsruhe.

Boole, George (1916 [1854]), *The Laws of Thought* (= George Boole's Collected Logical Works vol. II), facsimile reprint of 1st edn, Open Court Publishing Company, Chicago.

Bowen, William (1989), 'The Puny Payoff from Office Computers' in Tom Forester (ed.), *Computers in the Human Context*, MIT Press, Cambridge, MA, 267–71.

Bowie, Andrew (1990), *Aesthetics and Subjectivity: From Kant to Nietzsche*, Manchester University Press, Manchester.

Brakhage, Stan (1963), 'Metaphors on Vision', *Film Culture* no. 30, np.

Braverman, Harry (1974), *Labour and Monopoly Capital: The Degradation of Work in the Twentieth Century*, Monthly Review Press, New York.

Briggs, Asa (1985), *The BBC: The First Fifty Years*, Oxford University Press, Oxford.

Bromberg, Heather (1996), 'Are MUDs Communities? Identity, Belonging and Consciousness in Virtual Worlds' in Rob Shields (ed.), *Cultures of Internet: Virtual Spaces, Real Histories, Living Bodies*, Sage, London, 143–52.

Brooks, John (1975), *Telephone: The First Hundred Years*, Harper and Row, New York.

Buck-Morss, Susan (1989), *The Dialectics of Seeing: Walter Benjamin and the Arcades Project*, MIT Press, Cambridge, MA.

Buisseret, David and Christopher Baruth (1990), 'Aerial Imagery' in David Buisseret (ed.), *From Sea Charts to Satellite Images: Interpreting North American History Through Maps*, University of Chicago Press, Chicago.

Bukatman, Scott (1993), *Terminal Identity: The Virtual Subject in Post-Modern Science Fiction*, Duke University Press, Durham, NC.

Burch, Noël (1990), *Life to Those Shadows*, BFI, London.

Burnett, Robert (1996), *The Global Jukebox: The International Music Industry*, Routledge, London.

Cage, John (1994), 'Experimental Music' Music Teachers National Association, Chicago, Winter 1957; reprinted in liner notes to *The 25–Year Retrospective Concert of the Music of John Cage* [1958]; Wergo Schallplatten, Mainz, 6–12.

Caldwell, Christopher (1971), *Studies and Further Studies in a Dying Culture*, Monthly Review Press, New York.

Campion, Nicholas (1994), *The Great Year: Astrology, Millenarianism and History in the Western Tradition*, Penguin, Harmondsworth.

Castells, Manuel (1996), *The Information Age: Economy, Society and Culture: Volume I, The Rise of the Network Society*, Blackwell, Oxford.

Castells, Manuel (1997), *The Information Age: Economy, Society and Culture: Volume II, The Power of Identity*, Blackwell, Oxford.

Catullus (1970), *Catullus: The Poems*, ed. Kenneth Quinn, Macmillan, London.

Celan, Paul (1986), *Collected Poems*, trans. Rosemarie Waldrop, P. N. Review/Coronet, Manchester.

Chaisson, Eric J. (1994), *The Hubble Wars: Astrophysics Meets Astropolitics in the Two-Billion-Dollar Struggle over the Hubble Space Telescope*, HarperCollins, New York.

Chambers, Ian (1990), 'A Miniature History of the Walkman' in *New Formations* no. 11, 1–4.

Chanan, Michael (1995), *Repeated Takes: A Short History of Recording and Its Effects on Music*, Verso, London.

Changeux, Jean-Pierre (1985), *Neuronal Man: The Biology of Mind*, Oxford University Press, Oxford.

Chartier, Roger (1994), *The Order of Books: Readers, Authors and Libraries in Europe Between the Fourteenth and Eighteenth Centuries*, trans. Lydia G. Cochrane, Stanford University Press, Stanford, CA.

Cheddie, Janice (1997), 'Beyond the Digital Diaspora', in Michael B. Roetto (ed.), *ISEA96 Proceedings*, ISEA, Rotterdam, 145–6.

Ch'ên Yüan (1966), *Western and Central Asians in China under the Mongols*, trans. Ch'ien Hsing-hai and L. Carrington Goodrich, Monumenta Serica at the University of California, Los Angeles.

Chion, Michel (1992), *Le Son au cinéma*, new edn, Cahiers du Cinéma, Collection Essais, Paris.

Chion, Michel (1994), *Audio-Vision: Sound on Screen*, ed. and trans. Claudia Gorbman, Columbia University Press, New York.

Chomsky, Noam (1966), *Cartesian Linguistics*, Harper and Row, New York.

Chomsky, Noam (1972), *Language and Mind*, enlarged edn, Harcourt Brace Jovanovich, New York.

Coates, Austin (1990), *Quick Tidings of Hong Kong*, Oxford University Press, Hong Kong.

Corner, John (1992), 'Presumption as Theory: "Realism" in Television Studies' in *Screen* vol. 33, no. 1, Spring, 97-102.

Costa Lima, Luiz (1981), *Dispersa demanda: ensaios sobre literatura e teoria*, Rocco, Rio de Janeiro.

Crary, Jonathan (1990), *Techniques of the Observer: On Vision and Modernity in the Nineteenth Century*, MIT Press, Cambridge, MA.

Crevier, Daniel (1993), *AI: The Tumultuous History of the Search for Artificial Intelligence*, Basic Books, New York.

Critical Art Ensemble (1994), *The Electronic Disturbance*, Autonomedia, New York.

Cubitt, Sean (1992), 'False Perspectives in Virtual Space', *Variant*, vol. 1 no. 11, Spring, 31–4.

Cubitt, Sean (1993), *Videography: Video Media as Art and Culture*, Macmillan, London.

Cubitt, Sean (1994), *Translating: Imperial Communicatons and the Airmail Art of Eugenio Dittborn*, Tramlines Pamphlet no. 3, Tramway, Glasgow.

Cubitt, Sean (1995), 'On Interpretation: Bill Viola's *The Passing*' in *Screen* vol. 36 no. 2, Summer, 113–30.

Cubitt, Sean (1996), 'The New International Postal Order: From Air Mail to E-Mail' in Pavel Büchler and Nikos Papastergiadis (eds), *Ambient Fears* (= *Random Access*, vol. 3), Rivers Oram Press, London, 9–21.

Curtin, Philip D. (1984), *Cross-Cultural Trade in World History*, Cambridge University Press, Cambridge.

Damisch, Hubert (1994), *The Origin of Perspective*, trans. John Goodman, MIT Press, Cambridge, MA.

Daunton, M.J. (1985), *Royal Mail: The Post Office Since 1840*, Athlone, London.

Dawkins, Richard (1989), *The Selfish Gene*, 2nd edn, Oxford University Press, Oxford.

Debray, Régis (1994), *Manifestes médiologiques*, Gallimard, Paris.

de Landa, Manuel (1991), *War in the Age of Intelligent Machines*, Swerve Editions/Zone Books, New York.

de Lauretis, Teresa and Stephen Heath (eds) (1980), *The Cinematic Apparatus*, Macmillan, London.

Deleuze, Gilles and Félix Guattari (1987), *A Thousand Plateaux: Capitalism and Schizophrenia*, trans. Brian Massumi, University of Minnesota Press, Minneapolis.

Dennett, Daniel C. (1991), *Consciousness Explained*, Penguin, Harmondsworth.

Dewey, Melvil (1876), *Classification and Subject Index for Cataloguing and Arranging the Books and Pamphlets of a Library*, facsimile reprint of the 1876 edition published in Amhurst, MA, Forest Press Division, Lake Placid Education Foundation, Lake Placid, NY.

Diani, Marco (1989), 'The Social Design of Office Automation' in Victor Margolin (ed.), *Design Discourse: History/Theory/Criticism*, University of Chicago Press, Chicago.

Doane, Mary Ann (1980a), 'The Voice in the Cinema: The Articulation of Body and Space' in Rick Altman (ed.), *Cinema/Sound, Yale French Studies* no. 60, 33–50.

Doane, Mary Ann (1980b), 'Ideology and Practice of Sound Editing and Mixing' in Stephen Heath and Teresa de Lauretis (eds), *The Cinematic Apparatus*, Macmillan, London, 47–56.

Doane, Mary Ann (1982), 'Film and the Masquerade: Theorising the Female Spectator' in *Screen*, vol. 23, no. 3/4, September–October, 74–87; reprinted in Mary Doane, *Femmes Fatales: Feminism, Film Theory, Psychoanalysis*, Routledge, London, 1991, 17–32.

Doane, Mary Ann (1991), 'Masquerade Reconsidered: Further Thoughts on the Female Spectator' in Mary Ann Doane, *Femmes Fatales: Feminism, Film Theory, Psychoanalysis*, Routledge, London, 1991, 33–43.

Dorn, Ed (1968), *Gunslinger Book One*, Black Sparrow Press, Los Angeles.

Douglas, Susan J. (1987), *Inventing American Broadcasting 1899–1922*, Johns Hopkins University Press, Baltimore, MD.

Druckrey, Timothy (1991), 'Deadly Representations, or, Apocalypse Now' in *Ten: 8* vol. 2, no. 2, 16–27.

Durham, Jimmie (1993), *A Certain Lack of Coherence: Writings on Art and Cultural Politics*, Kala Press, London.

Dury, S.A. (1990), *A Guide to Remote Sensing: Interpeting Images of the Earth*, Oxford University Press, Oxford.

Dyson, Freeman (1988), *Infinite in All Directions: Gifford Lectures Given in Aberdeen, Scotland, April–November 1985*, Penguin, Harmondsworth.

Eastgate (1998), http://www.eastgate.com/

Eisenstein, Elizabeth L. (1993), *The Printing Revolution in Early Modern Europe*, Cambridge University Press, Cambridge.

Eisenstein, Sergei, M. (1988), 'The Problem of the Materialist Approach to Form' in *Selected Works: Volume 1. Writings, 1922–1934*, ed. and trans. Richard Taylor, BFI, London, 59–64.

Eisenstein, Sergei M. (1993), 'Imitation as Mastery' in Ian Christie and Richard Taylor (eds), *Eisenstein Rediscovered*, Routledge, London, 66–71.

Ellman, Richard and Robert O'Clair (eds) (1973), *The Norton Anthology of Modern Poetry*, Norton, New York.

Enzensberger, Hans Magnus (1988), 'Constitutents of a Theory of the Media', trans. Stuart Hood, in *Dreamers of the Absolute: Essays on Ecology, Media and Power*, Radius, London, 20–53.

FACT (1997), *Shared Experience: A History of Collaborative Electronic Arts Projects Produced by FACT*, CD-ROM, Foundation for Art and Creative Technology, Liverpool.

Featherstone, Mike (1995), *Undoing Culture: Globalization, Postmodernism and Identity*, Sage, London.

Feuer, Jane (1987), 'The Two Weather Channels' in *Cultural Studies* vol. 1, no. 3, October, 383–5.

Fielding, Raymond (1968), *The Technique of Special Effects Cinematography*, rev. edn, Communication Arts Books, New York.

Fielding, Raymond (1983), 'Hale's Tours: Ultrarealism in the pre-1910 Motion Picture' in John L. Fell (ed.), *Film Before Griffith*, University of California Press, Berkeley, 116–30.

Flint, Kate (1993), *The Woman Reader 1837–1914*, Clarendon Press, Oxford.

Foster, Hal (1993), *Compulsive Beauty*, MIT Press, Cambridge, MA.

Foucault, Michel (1972 [1969]), *The Archaeology of Knowledge*, trans. Alan Sheridan Harper, New York.

Foucault, Michel (1979), *Discipline and Punish: The Birth of the Prison*, trans. Alan Sheridan, Pantheon, New York.

Franke, Richard H. (1989), 'Technological Revolution and Productivity Decline: The Case of US Banks' in Tom Forester (ed.), *Computers in the Human Context*, MIT Press, Cambridge, MA, 281–90.

Franklin, H. Bruce (1988), *War Stars: The Superweapon and the American Imagination*, Oxford University Press, New York.

Freedman, David H. (1994), *Brainmakers: How Scientists are Moving Beyond Computers to Create a Rival to the Human Brain*, Touchstone, New York.

Freud, Sigmund (1916), 'A Child is Being Beaten' in *On Psychopathology*, trans. James Strachey, ed. Angela Richards, (= Pelican Freud Library 10), Pelican, Harmondsworth, 1979, 163–93.

Freud, Sigmund (1940), 'Medusa's Head' in *The Standard Edition of the Complete Psychological Works of Sigmund Freud, Volume 18*, ed. and trans. James Strachey, Hogarth Press, London, 1962, 273ff.

Friedberg, Anna (1993), *Window Shopping: Cinema and the Postmodern*, University of California Press, Berkeley.

Fuller, Matthew (ed.) (1994), *Unnatural: Techno-theory for a Contaminated Culture*, Underground, London.

Fuller, Wayne E. (1972), *The American Mail: Enlarger of the Common Life*, University of Chicago Press, Chicago.

Gadamer, Hans-Georg (1986), 'The Relevance of the Beautiful' in *The Relevance of the Beautiful and Other Essays* trans. Nicholas Walker, Cambridge University Press, Cambridge, 1–53.

Gardner, Martin (1987), *The Mind's New Science: A History of the Cognitive Revolution*, Basic Books, New York.

Gelernter, David (1991), *Mirror Worlds*, Oxford University Press, New York.

George, Russell (1990), 'Some Spatial Characteristics of the Hollywood Cartoon' in *Screen* vol. 31, no. 3, Autumn, 296–321.

Giddens, Anthony (1990), *The Consequences of Modernity*, Polity Press, Cambridge.

Giedion, Siegfried (1948), *Mechanisation Takes Command: A Contribution to Anonymous History*, Norton, New York.

Gilroy, Paul (1993), 'One Nation under a Groove' in *Small Acts*, Serpent's Tail, London, 19–48.

Gimpel, Jean (1988), *The Medieval Machine: The Industrial Revolution of the Middle Ages*, 2nd edn, Pimlico, London.

Ginzburg, Carlo (1980), *The Cheese and the Worms: The Cosmos of a Sixteenth Century Miller*, trans.. John and Anne Tedeschi, Routledge and Kegan Paul, London.

Godzich, Wlad (1994), *The Culture of Literacy*, Harvard University Press, Cambridge, MA.

Gould, Glenn (1990), 'The Prospects of Recording' in *The Glenn Gould Reader*, ed. Tim Page, Viking, New York.

Greenberg, Clement (1992), 'Modernist Painting' in Francis Frascina and Jonathan Harris (eds), *Art in Modern Culture: An Anthology of Critical Texts*, Phaidon, London, 308–14.

Greenwood, Thomas (1894) *Public Libraries: A History of the Movement and a Manual for . . . Rate-Supported Libraries*, 4th edn.

Grynsztejn, Madeleine (1994), 'About Place: Recent Art of the Americas' in *About Place: The 76th American Exhibition*, Art Institute of Chicago, Chicago.

Guattari, Félix (1995), *Chaosmosis: An Ethico-Aesthetic Paradigm*, trans. Paul Bains and Julien Pefanis, Power Publications, Sydney.

Guha, Ranajit (1988), 'The Prose of Counter-Insurgency' in Ranajit Guha and Gayatri Chakravorty Spivak (eds), *Selected Subaltern Studies*, Oxford University Press, Oxford, 45–86.

Guha, R.V. and Douglas B. Lenat (1990), 'CYC: A Mid-Term Report' in *AI Magazine*, Fall, 32–59.

Gunning, Tom (1991), 'Heard Over the Phone: *The Lonely Villa* and the de Lorde Tradition of the Terrors of Technology' in *Screen* vol. 32 no. 2, Summer, 184–96.

Habermas, Jürgen (1984), *The Theory of Communicative Action: Volume 1. Reason and the Rationalization of Society*, trans. Thomas McCarthy, Beacon Press, Boston.

Habermas, Jürgen (1987), *The Theory of Communicative Action, Volume 2. Lifeworld and System: A Critique of Functionalist Reason*, trans. Thomas McCarthy, Beacon Press, Boston.

Habermas, Jürgen (1989 [1962]), *The Structural Transformation of the Public Sphere: An Enquiry into a Category of Bourgeois Society*, trans. Thomas Burger with the assistance of Frederick Lawrence, Polity, Cambridge.

Habermas, Jürgen (1993), *Moral Consciousness and Communicative Action*, trans. Christian Lenhard and Shierry Weber Nicholson, MIT Press, Cambridge, MA.

Hafner, Katie (1997), 'The World's Most Influential Online Community (and it's not AOL): The Epic Saga of the Well' in *Wired (US)* 5.05, May, 98–142 (also online at www.wired.com/5.05/well/).

Hafner, Katie and John Markoff (1991), *Cyberpunk: Outlaws and Hackers on the Computer Frontier*, Corgi, London.

Hall, Stuart (1991), 'The Local and the Global: Globalization and Ethnicity' in Anthony D. King, (ed.), *Culture, Globalisation and the World-System*, Macmillan, London.

Hall, Stuart (1995), 'Negotiating Caribbean Identities' in *New Left Review* no. 209, January–February.

Haraway, Donna (1985), 'A Manifesto for Cyborgs: Science, Technology and Socialist Feminism in the 1980s' in *Socialist Review*, no. 80 (v. 15, no. 2), March–April, 65–107.

Harley, J.B. (1989), 'Deconstructing the Map' in *Cartographica* vol. 26, no. 2, Summer, 1–20.

Harley, J.B. (1993), 'Abstract of a Paper: "The Culture of the Map in Western History"', *Cartographica* vol. 30, no. 1, Spring, 107.

Harwood, Graham (1996), *Rehearsal of Memory*, CD-ROM, Artec/Bookworks, London.

Hawking, Stephen (1988), *A Brief History of Time*, Bantam, London.

Hayward, Philip and Tana Wollen (eds) (1993), *Future Visions: New Technologies of the Screen*, BFI, London.

Hebdige, Dick (1988), *Hiding in the Light: On Images and Things*, Routledge, London.

Heidegger, Martin (1977), *The Question Concerning Technology and Other Essays*, trans. William Lovitt, Harper and Row, New York.

Heim, Michael (1987), *Electric Language: A Philosophical Study of Word Processing*, Yale University Press, New Haven.

Heim, Michael (1993), *The Metaphysics of Virtual Reality*, Oxford University Press, New York.

Hershman Leeson, Lynn (1996), *Clicking In: Hot Links to a Digital Culture*, Bay Press, Seattle.

Hertogs, Daan and Nico de Klerk (eds) (1996), *'Disorderly Order': Colours in Silent Film – The 1995 Amsterdam Workshop*, Stichting Nederlands Filmmuseum, Amsterdam.

Hiltz, Starr Roxanne and Murray Turoff (1993), *The Network Nation: Human Communication Via Computer*, MIT Press, Cambridge, MA.

Hoekendijk, Carla (1996), 'Seiko Mikami: Molecular Informatics ver 2.0 – Morphogenic Substance via Eye Tracking' in *DEAF96 Digital Territories*, V2, Rotterdam, 32e.

Hohendahl, Peter U. (1979), 'Habermas and His Critics' in *New German Critique*, no. 16, 89–118.

Holmes, Donald B. (1981), *Air Mail: An Illustrated History 1793–1981*, Clarkson N. Potter Inc, New York.

Holmqvist, Berit (1993), 'Face to Interface' in Peter Bøgh Andersen, Berit Holmqvist and Jens F. Jensen (eds), *The Computer as Medium*, Cambridge University Press, Cambridge, 222–35.

Horkheimer, Max (1994), *Critique of Instrumental Reason*, trans. Matthew J. O'Connell and others, Continuum, New York.

Hosokawa, Shuhei (1984), 'The Walkman Effect' in *Popular Music* vol. 4, 165–80.

Hughes, Langston (1974), 'Same in Blues' from 'Montage of a Dream Deferred' in *Selected Poems*, Vintage, New York, 270–1.

Hull, Suzanne (1982), *Chaste, Silent and Obedient: English Books for Women, 1475–1640*, Huntington Library, San Marino, CA.

Idea (1998), *mcr36*, http://www.36mc-idea.org.uk

inIVA (1997), *Keith Piper: Relocating the Remains*, Institute of International Visual Acts, London.

Islam, Shamsul (1975), *Kipling's 'Law': A Study of his Philosophy and Life*, Macmillan, London.

Jodi (1998), http://www.jodi.org/

Johnson-Laird, Philip (1993), *The Computer and the Mind: An Introduction to Cognitive Science*, 2nd edn, Fontana, London.

Jonson, Ben (1954), *The Poems of Ben Jonson*, ed. George Burke Johnston, Routledge and Kegan Paul, London.

Kahn, Douglas (1992), 'Introduction: Histories of Sound Once Removed' in Douglas Kahn and Gregory Whitehead (eds), *Wireless Imagination: Sound, Radio and the Avant-Garde*, MIT Press, Cambridge, MA.

Kalinak, Kathryn (1992), *Settling the Score: Music and the Classical Hollywood Film*, University of Wisconsin Press, Madison, WI.

Kant, Immanuel (1952 [1970]), *The Critique of Judgement*, trans. James Creed Meredith, Oxford University Press, Oxford.

Keats, John (1956 [1817]), 'On First Looking Into Chapman's Homer' in *Poetical Works*, ed. H. W. Gerrod, Oxford University Press, Oxford, 38.

Kellner, Douglas (1992), *The Persian Gulf TV War*, Westview Press, Boulder, CO.

Kelly, Kevin (1994), *Out of Control: The New Biology of Machines*, 4th Estate, London.

Kieve, Jeffrey (1973), *The Electric Telegraph: A Social and Economic History*, David and Charles, Newton Abbot.

Kipling, Rudyard (1914a [1899]), *Stalky and Co*, 'authorized edition', The Country Life Press, Garden City, NY.

Kipling, Rudyard (1914b [1901]), *Kim*, 'authorized edition', The Country Life Press, Garden City, NY.

Kipnis, Laura (1995), 'The Eloquence of Pornography', paper presented to the Rockefeller Program in Globalization and the Public Sphere, Chicago Humanities Institute, 1 May.

Kirby, Lynne (1997), *Parallel Tracks: The Railroad and Silent Cinema*, University of Exeter Press, Exeter.

Kittler, Friedrich A. (1990), *Discourse Networks 1800/1900*, trans. Michael Metteer with Chris Cullens, Stanford University Press, Stanford, CA.

Kosko, Bart (1993), *Fuzzy Thinking: The New Science of Fuzzy Logic*, Flamingo, London.

Krauss, Rosalind (1985a), 'Photography's Discursive Spaces' in *The Originality of the Avant-Garde and Other Modernist Myths*, MIT Press, Cambridge, MA, 131–50.

Krauss, Rosalind (1985b), 'The Photographic Conditions of Surrealism' in *The Originality of the Avant-Garde and Other Modernist Myths*, MIT Press, Cambridge, MA, 87–118.

Kroker, Arthur and Michael A. Weinstein (1994), *Data Trash: The Theory of the Virtual Class*, New World Perspectives, Montreal.

Krueger, Myron C. (1983), *Artificial Reality*, Addison-Wesley, Reading, MA.

Krueger, Myron C. (1991), *Artificial Reality II*, Addison-Wesley, Reading, MA.

Lacan, Jacques (1975), *Le Séminaire, livre XX: Encore*, Seuil, Paris.

Lacan, Jacques (1994), *Le Séminaire, livre IV: La relation d'objet*, Seuil, Paris.

Lacour-Gayet, Jacques (ed.) (1953a), *Le Commerce de l'ancien monde jusqu'à la fin du XVe siècle*, (= *Histoire du Commerce*, Volume 2), Editions SPID, Paris.

Lacour-Gayet, Jacques (ed.) (1953b), *Le Commerce extra-européen jusqu'aux temps modernes* (= *Histoire du Commerce*, Volume 3), Editions SPID, Paris.

Laing, Dave (1986), 'The Music Industry and the "Cultural Imperialism" Thesis' in *Media Culture and Society* vol. 8, no. 3, July, 331–41.

Lamb, Charles (1935 [1823]), 'The Two Races of Men' in *The Essays of Elia*; *The Complete Works and Letters of Charles Lamb*, ed. Saxe Commins, The Modern Library, New York.

Landes, Joan B. (1989), *Women and the Public Sphere in the Age of the French Revolution*, Cornell University Press, Ithaca, NY.

Landon, Brooks (1992), *The Aesthetics of Ambivalence: Rethinking Science Fiction Film in the Age of Electronic Reproduction*, Greenwood Press, Westport, CT.

Landow, George (1990), http://www.stg.brown.edu/projects/hypertext/landow/cv/landow_ov.html

Lanier, Jaron (1995), 'My Problem With Agents', http://www.well.com/user/jaron/agentideeforte.html

Lash, Scott and John Urry (1994), *Economies of Signs and Space*, Sage, London.

Latham, William (1998), *Computer Artworks Ltd*, http://www.artworks.co.uk/home.html

Laurel, Brenda (1993), *Computers as Theatre*, rev edn, Addison-Wesley, Reading, MA.

La Valley, Albert J. (1985), 'Traditions of Trickery: The Role of Special Effects in the Science Fiction Film' in George Slusser and Eric S. Rabkin (eds), *Shadows of the Magic Lamp: Fantasy and the Science Fiction Film*, Southern Illinois University Press, Carbondale, IL, 141–58.

Lazzaro, Claudia (1990), *The Italian Renaissance Garden: From the Conventions of Planting, Design and Ornament to the Grand Gardens of Sixteenth Century Italy*, Yale University Press, New Haven.

Leary, William M. (1985), *Aerial Pioneers: The US Air Mail Service, 1918–1927*, Smithsonian Institute Press, Washington, DC.

Lee, Eric (1997), *The Labour Movement and the Internet: The New Internationalism*, Pluto, London.

Leonardo Music Journal (1998) http://mitpress.mit.edu/Leonardo/lmj/sound.html

Levidow, Les (1994), 'The Gulf Massacre as Paranoid Reality' in Gretchen Bender and Timothy Druckrey (eds), *Cultures on the Brink: Ideologies of Technology*, Bay Press, Seattle, 317–27.

Levin, Samuel R. (1962), *Linguistic Structures in Poetry* (= Janua Linguarum; Series Minor 23), Mouton, The Hague.

Lévy, Pierre (1994), *L'intelligence collective: Pour une anthropologie du cyberspace*, Editions de la Découverte, Paris.

Levy, Steven (1984), *Hackers: Heroes of the Computer Revolution*, Anchor Doubleday, New York.

Levy, Steven (1992), *Artificial Life: The Quest for a New Creation*, Penguin, Harmondsworth.

Levy, Steven (1995), *Insanely Great: The Life and Times of Macintosh, the Computer that Changed Everything*, Penguin, Harmondsworth.

Lewis, Lisa A. (ed.) (1992), *The Adoring Audience: Fan Culture and Popular Media*, Routledge, London.

Lipsner, Capt. Benjamin B. (1951), *The Airmail: Jennies to Jets*, 'as told to Leonard Finley Hilts', Wilcoz and Follett, Chicago.

Loader, Brian D. (ed.) (1997), *The Governance of Cyberspace: Politics, Technology and Global Restructuring*, Routledge, London.

LoBrutto, Vincent (1994), *Sound-On-Film: Interviews with Creators of Film Sound*, Praeger, New York.

Logue, Christopher (1988), *War Music: An Account of Books 16 to 19 of Homer's ILIAD*, Faber, London.

Longair, Malcolm (1989), *Alice and the Space Telescope*, Johns Hopkins University Press, Baltimore, MD.

Lovejoy, Margot (1997), *Postmodern Currents: Art and Artists in the Age of Electronic Media*, 2nd edn, Prentice Hall, New York.

Lovell, Terry (1987), *Consuming Fictions*, Verso, London.

Lucas, Caroline (1989), *Writing for Women: The Example of Woman as Reader in Elizabethan Romance*, Open University Press, Milton Keynes.

Lyon, David (1994), *The Electronic Eye: The Rise of the Surveillance Society*, Polity, Cambridge.

Lyotard, Jean-François (1971), *Discours, figure*, Klincksieck, Paris.

Lyotard, Jean-François (1978), 'Acinema', trans. J.-F. Lyotard and Paisley N. Livingstone, *Wide Angle* vol. 2, no. 3, 52–9.

MacCannell, Dean (1976), *The Tourist : A New Theory of the Leisure Class*, Schocken Books, New York.

Mackay, James (1971), *Airmails 1870–1970* , Batsford, London.

McLaughlin, Margaret L. Kerry K. Osborne and Christine B. Smith (1995), 'Standards of Conduct on Usenet' in Steven G. Jones (ed.), *CyberSociety: Computer-Mediated Communication and Community*, Sage, London, 90–111.

McNeil, Daniel and Paul Freiberger (1993), *Fuzzy Logic: The Revolutionary Computer Technology That Is Changing Our World*, Simon and Schuster, New York.

McNeill, William (1963), *The Rise of the West: A History of the Human Community*, University of Chicago Press, Chicago.

McNeill, William (1976), *Plagues and Peoples*, Anchor Doubleday, Garden City, NY.

Manovich, Lev (1998), 'What is Digital Cinema?' in Peter Lunenfeld (ed.), *The Digital Dialectics: New Essays on New Media*, MIT Press, Cambridge, MA.

Maravall, José Antonio (1986), *Culture of the Baroque: Analysis of a Historical Structure*, trans. Terry Cochran, Manchester University Press, Manchester.

Marr, David (1982), *Vision: A Computational Investigation into the Human Representation and Processing of Visual Information*, W. H. Freeman, San Francisco.

Martin, John Rupert (1977), *Baroque*, Pelican, Harmondsworth.

Marvell, Andrew (1976), *Andrew Marvell: The Complete Poems*, ed. Elizabeth Story Donno, Penguin, Harmondsworth.

Marvin, Carolyn (1988), *When Old Technologies Were New: Thinking About Electric Communication in the Late 19th Century*, Oxford University Press, New York.

Mattelart, Armand (1996), *The Invention of Communication*, trans. Susan Emanuel, University of Minnesota Press, Minneapolis.

Mazumdar, Mohini Lal (1990) *The Imperial Post Offices of British India: Volume 1. 1837–1914*, Phila Publications, Calcutta.

Mercer, Kobena (1995), 'Busy in the Ruins of Wretched Phantasia' in Ragnar Farr (ed.), *Mirage: Enigmas of Race, Difference and Desire*, Institute of Contemporary Arts/Institute of International Visual Arts, London, 14–55.

Mercer, Kobena (1997), 'Witness at the Crossroads: An Artist's Journey in Postcolonial Space', in inIVA, Keith Piper, *Relocating the Remains*, Institute of International Visual Arts, London, 12–85.

Merleau-Ponty, Maurice (1962), *The Phenomenology of Perception*, trans. Colin Smith, Routledge and Kegan Paul, London.

Merleau-Ponty, Maurice (1968), *The Visible and the Invisible*, trans. Alphonso Lingis, Northwestern University Press, Evanston, IL.

Metz, Christian (1977), 'Trucage and the Film' in *Critical Inquiry*, Summer, 657–75.

Metz, Christian (1980), 'Aural Objects', trans. Georgia Gurrieri, in Rick Altman (ed.), *Cinema/Sound, Yale French Studies* no. 60, 24–32.

Michelson, Annette (1984), 'On the Eve of the Future: The Reasonable Facsimile and the Philosophical Toy' in *October*, no. 29, 3–20.

Minsky, Marvin (1985), *The Society of Mind*, Simon and Schuster, New York.

Mitchell, William J. (1992), *The Reconfigured Eye: Visual Truth in the Post-Photographic Era*, MIT Press, Cambridge, MA.

Moody, Fred (1995), *I Sing the Body Electronic: A Year with Microsoft on the Multimedia Frontier*, Coronet, London.

Moore, Charles W. (1994), *Water + Architecture*, Thames and Hudson, London.

Moravec, Hans (1988), *Mind Children: The Future of Robot and Human Intelligence*, Harvard University Press, Cambridge, MA.

Morley, David (1987), *Family Television: Cultural Power and Domestic Leisure*, Routledge, London.

Morley, David (1992), *Television, Audiences and Cultural Studies*, Routledge, London.

Moulthrop, Stuart (1998), *Victory Garden*, http://www.eastgate.com/VG/VGStart.html

Mulvey, Laura (1975), 'Visual Pleasure and Narrative Cinema' in *Screen* vol. 16, no. 3, Autumn, 6–18.

Mumford, Lewis (1986), *The Future of Technics and Civilization*, Freedom Press, London; part reprint of Mumford, Lewis (1934), *Technics and Civilization*, Routledge and Kegan Paul, London.

Musser, Charles (1990), *The Emergence of Cinema: The American Screen to 1907* (= *History of the American Cinema*, Volume 1), University of California Press, Berkeley.

Musser, Charles (1991), *Before the Nickelodeon: Edwin S. Porter and the Edison Manufacturing Company*, University of California Press, Berkeley.

Nagel, Ernest and James R. Newman (1959), *Gödel's Proof*, Routledge and Kegan Paul, London.

Nägele, Rainer (1987), 'Public Voice and Private Voice: Freud, Habermas and the Dialectic of Enlightenement' in *Reading After Freud: Essays on Goethe, Hölderlin, Habermas, Nietzsche, Brecht, Celan and Freud*, Columbia University Press, New York.

NASA (1990), *The Hubble Space Telescope Optical Systems Failure Report*, NASA/Government Printing Office, Washington, DC (November).

Neal, Valerie (1990), *Exploring the Universe with the Hubble Space Telescope*, NASA/Government Printing Office, Washington, DC (February).

Neale, Steve (1985), *Cinema and Technology: Image, Sound, Colour*, Macmillan, London.

Nettime (1998), http://mediafilter.org/ZK/Conf/ZKindex.html

Newman, Kathleen (1992), 'Cultural Redemocratization: Argentina, 1978–89' in George Yúdice, Jean Franco and Juan Flores (eds), *On Edge: The Crisis of Contemporary Latin American Culture* (= *Cultural Politics*, volume 4), University of Minnesota Press, Minneapolis, 161–86.

Ngugi wa Thiong'o (1986), *Decolonising the Mind: The Politics of Language in African Literature*, James Currey, London.

Ngugi wa Thiong'o (1993), 'Imperialism of Language: English, a Language for the World?' in Ngugi wa Thiong'o, *Moving the Centre: The Struggle for Cultural Freedoms*, trans. Wangui wa Goro and Ngugi wa Thiong'o, James Currey, London, 30–41.

Nochlin, Linda (1991), *The Politics of Vision: Essays on Nineteenth Century Art and Society*, Thames and Hudson, London.

Noonan, Tom (1980), 'The Marriage of Maria Braun' in *Film Quarterly*, vol. 33, no. 3, Spring, 40–5.

O'Casey, Sean (1925), 'Juno and the Paycock' in *Two Plays*, Macmillan, London, 1–113.

Okolie, Charles C. (1989), *International Law of Satellite Remote Sensing and Outer Space*, Kendall/Hunt, Dubuque, IA.

Olson, Charles (1966a), 'Quantity in Verse, and Shakespeare's Late Plays' in *Selected Writings*, ed. Robert Creeley, New Directions, New York, 31–45.

Olson, Charles (1966b), 'Mayan Letters' in *Selected Writings*, ed. Robert Creeley, New Directions, New York, 69–130.

Ovid (1939), 'The Song of Orpheus' from 'The Matamorphoses' in *Ovid: Selected Works*, trans. Arthur Golding, ed. J. C. and M. J. Thornton, Everyman, London.

Penley, Constance (1997), *NASA/Trek: Popular Science and Sex in America*, Verso, London.

Pinker, Steven (1994), *The Language Instinct: The New Science of Language and Mind*, Penguin, Harmondsworth.

Piper, Keith (1995), 'The Dis-Orderly City: A Nigger in Cyberspace' in ISEA95 (1995), *Actes: 6e Symposium des arts électroniques/6th International Symposium on Electronic Art*, ISEA 95, Montreal, 232–5.

Piper, Keith (1997), *Relocating the Remains*, CD-ROM, Institute of International Visual Arts, London.

Plant, Sadie (1997), *Zeros and Ones: Digital Women + The New Technologies*, 4th Estate, London.

Plant, Sadie and Nick Land (1994), 'Cyberpositive' in Matthew Fuller (ed.), *Unnatural: Techno-theory for a Contaminated Culture*, Underground, London, np.

Polan, Dana (1990), 'History in Perspective, Perspective in History: A Commentary on *L'Origine de la perspective* by Hubert Damisch' in *Camera Obscura* no. 24, September, 89–97.

Popper, Frank (1993), *Art of the Electronic Age*, Thames and Hudson, London.

Poster, Mark (1990), *The Mode of Information: Poststructuralism and Social Context*, Polity, Cambridge.

Potts, John (1995), 'Schizochronia: Time in Digital Sound' in *Essays in Sound* 2, Contemporary Sound Arts, Sydney.

Pratt, Mary Louise (1992), *Imperial Eyes: Travel Writing and Transculturation*, Routledge, London.

Prophet, Jane and Julian Sanderson (1997), *Technosphere*, http://tdg.linst.ac.uk/technosphere/index.html

Punt, Michael (1995), 'The Elephant, the Spaceship and the White Cockatoo: An Archeology of Digital Photography' in Martin Lister (ed.), *The Photographic Image in Digital Culture*, Routledge, London, 51–74.

Rabasa, José (1993), *Inventing America: Spanish Historiography and the Formation of Eurocentrism*, University of Oklahoma Press, Norman, OK.

Radway, Janice A. (1984), *Reading the Romance: Women, Patriarchy and Popular Literature*, University of North Carolina Press, Chapel Hill.

Rajagopalan, T.S. (ed.) (1985), *Ranganthan's Philosophy: Assessment, Impact and Relevance*, Vikas Publishing House, New Delhi.

Rajagopalan, T.S. (ed.) (1988), *Relevance of Ranganathan's Contributions to Library Science*, Vikas Publishing House, New Delhi.

Ranganathan, S.R. (1951), *Philosophy of Library Classification* (= *Library Research Monographs*, Volume 2), Ejnar Munksgaard, Copenhagen.

Ranganathan, S.R. (1967 [1937]), *Prolegomena to Library Classification*, 3rd edn, Asia Publishing House, New York.

Ray, Thomas (1998), *Tierra*, http://www.hip.atr.co.jp/~ray/tierra/tierra.html

Rees, Jim (1992), *The Life of Captain Robert Halpin*, Dee-Jay, Arklow, Co. Wicklow.

Renoir, Jean (1974), *My Life and My Films*, trans. Norman Denny, Collins, London.

Revill, David (1992), *The Roaring Silence: John Cage: A Life*, Bloomsbury, London.

Reynolds, L. D. and N. G. Wilson (1974), *Scribes and Scholars: A Guide to the Transmission of Greek and Latin Literature*, 2nd edn, Clarendon Press, Oxford.

Rheingold, Howard (1993), *The Virtual Community: Homesteading on the Electronic Frontier*, Harper Perennial, New York.

Rhizome (1998), http://www.rhizome.com/

Richelson, Jeffrey T. (1990), *America's Secret Eyes in Space: The U.S. Keyhole Spy Satellite Program*, Harper and Row, New York.

Robertson, Roland (1992), *Globalization: Social Theory and Global Culture*, Sage, London.

Robins, Kevin (1994), 'The Haunted Screen' in Gretchen Bender and Timothy Druckrey (eds), *Cultures on the Brink: Ideologies of Technology*, Bay Press, Seattle, 305–15.

Robins, Kevin (1996), *Into the Image: Culture and Politics in the Field of Vision*, Routledge, London.

Robins, Kevin and Les Levidow (1991), 'The Eye of the Storm' in *Screen* vol. 32, no. 3, Autumn, 324–8.

Robins, Kevin and Les Levidow (1995), 'Soldier, Cyborg, Citizen' in James Brook and Iain A. Boal (eds), *Resisting the Virtual Life: The Culture and Politics of Information*, City Lights, San Francisco, 105–13.

Rodowick, D.N. (1991), *The Difficulty of Difference*, Routledge, London.

Rose, Stephen (1993), *The Making of Memory: From Molecules to Mind*, Bantam, London.

Ross, Andrew (1991), 'The Drought this Time' in *Strange Weather: Culture, Science and Technology in the Age of Limits*, Verso, London, 193–249.

Rushkoff, Douglas (1994), *Cyberia: Life in the Trenches of Hyperspace*, Flamingo, London.

Saint-Exupéry, Antoine de (1971 [1931]), *Southern Mail* and *Night Flight*, trans. Curtis Cate, Penguin, Harmondsworth.

Sardar, Ziauddin (1996), 'alt.civilizations.faq: Cyberspace as the Darker Side of the West' in Ziauddin Sardar and Jerome R. Ravetz (eds) *Cyberfutures: Culture and Politics on the Information Superhighway*, Pluto, London, 14–41.

Schaeffer, Pierre (1966), *Traité des objets musicaux*, Seuil, Paris.

Schivelbusch, Wolfgang (1979), *The Railway Journey: Trains and Travel in the Nineteenth Century*, trans. Ansolm Hollo, Urizen Books, New York.

Schivelbusch, Wolfgang (1988), *Disenchanted Night: The Industrialization of Light in the Nineteenth Century*, trans. Angela Davies, University of California Press, Berkeley.

Schroeder, Fred E. H. (1991), 'More "Small Things Forgotten": Domestic Electrical Plugs and Receptacles, 1881–1931' in Marcel C. Lafollette and Jeffrey K. Stine (eds) *Technology and Choice: Readings from Technology and Culture*, University of Chicago Press, Chicago, 117–36.

Schwartz, Vanessa R. (1995), 'Cinematic Spectatorship before the Apparatus: The Public Taste for Reality in *Fin-de-Siècle* Paris' in Leo Charney and Vanessa R. Schwartz (eds), *Cinema and the Invention of Modern Life*, University of California Press, Berkeley, 297–319.

Scientific American (1997), 'The Internet: Fulfilling the Promise' (special report), *Scientific American* vol. 276, no. 3, March, 41–73.

Seiter, Ellen, Hans Borchers, Gabrielle Kreutzner and Eva-Maria Warth (eds) (1989), *Remote Control: Television, Audiences and Cultural Power*, Routledge, London.

Shaw, George Bernard (1941 [1912]), *Pygmalion: A Romance in Five Acts*, Penguin, Harmondsworth.

Shevelow, Kathryn (1989), *Women and Print Culture: The Construction of Femininity in the Early Periodical*, Routledge, London.

Shohat, Ella (1992), 'Notes on the "Post-colonial"' in *Social Text* no. 31/2, 109.

Shridharani, Krishnalal (1953), *Story of the Indian Telegraphs: A Century of Progress*, Posts and Telegraphs Dept, Government of India, New Delhi.

Shurkin, Joel (1996), *Engines of the Mind: The Evolution of the Computer from Mainframes to Microprocessors*, rev. edn, Norton, New York.

Sidebottom, John K. (1948), *The Overland Mail: A Postal Historical Study of the Mail Route to India*, The Postal Historical Society and Allen and Unwin, London.

Silverstone, Roger and Eric Hirsch (eds) (1992), *Consuming Technologies: Media and Information in Domestic Spaces*, Routledge, London.

Simmel, Georg (1950), *The Sociology of Georg Simmel*, ed. K.H. Wolf, Free Press, New York.

Smith, Robert W. (1989), *The Space Telescope: A Study of NASA, Science, Technology and Politics*, with contributions by Paul A. Hanle, Robert H. Kargon and Joseph N. Tatarewicz, Cambridge University Press, Cambridge.

Sobchack, Vivian (1987), *Screening Space: The American Science Fiction Film*, Ungar, New York.

Sobchack, Vivian (1992), *The Address of the Eye: A Phenomenology of Film Experience*, Princeton University Press, Princeton.

Sobchack, Vivian (1994), 'The Scene of the Screen: Envisioning Cinematic and Electronic "Presence"' in Hans Ulrich Gumbrecht and K. Ludwig Pfeiffer (eds) *Materialities of Communication*, trans. William Whobrey, Stanford University Press, Stanford, CA, 83–106.

Sobchack, Vivian (1995), 'Beating the Meat/Surviving the Text, or, How to Get Out of This Century Alive' in Mike Featherstone and Roger Burrows (eds), *Cyberspace/Cyberbodies/Cyberpunk: Cultures of Technological Embodiment*, Sage, London, 205–14.

Sobchack, Vivian (1998), 'Meta-Morphing: Reflections on an Everyday and Yet Uncanny Phenomenon', *Telepolis* (http://www.heise.de/tp/tpfhome.htm), 18 March 1997.

Solomon-Godeau, Abigail (1991), *Photography at the Dock: Essays on Photographic History, Institutions and Practices*, University of Minnesota Press, Minneapolis.

Sondheim, Alan (ed.) (1997), *Being On Line: Net Subjectivity* (= Lusitania 8), Lusitania Books, New York.

Spinoza, Baruch de (1951 [1670]), *A Theologico-Political Treatise and a Political Treatise*, trans. R. H. M. Elwes, Bobbs-Merrill, New York.

Sproull, Lee and Sara Kiesler (1991), *Connections: New Ways of Working in the Networked Organisation*, MIT Press, Cambridge MA.

Sproull, Lee and Sara Kiesler (1993), 'Computers, Networks and Work' in Linda M. Harasim (ed.), *Global Networks: Computers and International Communication*, MIT Press, Cambridge, MA, 105–19.

Stam, Robert (1992), 'Mobilising Fictions: The Gulf War, the Media and the Recruitment of the Spectator' in *Public Culture*, vol. 4, no. 2., Spring, 101–26.

Stein, Sally (1983), 'Making Connections with the Camera: Photography and Social Mobility in the career of Jacob Riis' in *Afterimage* vol. 10, no. 10.

Sterling, Bruce (1992), *The Hacker Crackdown: Law and Disorder on the Electronic Frontier*, Penguin, London.

Stevens, Wallace (1955), 'The Man with the Blue Guitar' in *Collected Poems*, Faber, London, 165–84.

Stoddard, Roger E. (1990), 'Morphology of the Book from an American Perspective' in *Printing History* no. 17, 2–14.

Street, Brian V. (1984), *Literacy in Theory and Practice* (= Cambridge Studies in Oral and Literate Culture 9), Cambridge University Press, Cambridge.

Sturken, Marita (1995), 'The Television Image and Collective Amnesia: Dis(re)membering the Persian Gulf War' in Peter d'Agostino and David Tafler (eds), *Transmission: Theory and Practice for a New Television Aesthetics*, 2nd edn, Sage, Thousand Oaks, CA, 125–49.

Tagg, John (1988), *The Burden of Representation: Essays on Photographies and Histories*, Macmillan, London.

Tagg, John (1992), 'The Proof of the Picture' in *Grounds of Dispute: Art History, Cultural Politics and the Discursive Field*, Macmillan, London, 97–114.

Tannenbaum, Mya (1987), *Conversations with Stockhausen*, trans. David Butchart, Clarendon, Oxford.

Taylor, D.R.F. (1989), 'Postmodernism, Deconstruction and Cartography' in *Cartographica* vol. 26, no. 3–4, 114–17.

Thompson, E.P. (1963), *The Making of the English Working Class*, Pelican, Harmondsworth.

Thompson, James (1977), *A History of the Principles of Librarianship*, Clive Bingley, London/Linnet Books, Maden, CT.

Tynianov, Jurii (1966), 'De l'évolution littéraire' in Tsvetan Todorov (ed.), *Théorie de la littérature: Textes des formalistes russes*, Seuil, Paris, 120–37.

Urry, John (1990), *The Tourist Gaze*, Sage, London.

Usai, Paolo Cherchi (1991), 'The Insitute of Incoherent Cinematography: An Introduction' in Paolo Cherchi Usai (ed.), *Lo Schermo Incantato: Georges Méliès (1861–1938)*, Le Giornate del cinema muto/George Eastman House/Edizioni Biblioteca dell'immagine, Pordenone, 19–27.

Usai, Paolo Cherchi (1994), *Burning Passions: An Introduction to the Study of Silent Cinema*, trans. Emma Sansone Rittle, BFI, London.

US Congress, Office of Technology Assessment (1993), *The Future of Remote Sensing from Space: Civilian Satellite Systems and Applications*, US Government Printing Office, Washington DC.

Vattimo, Gianni (1992) *The Transparent Society*, trans. David Webb, Polity, Cambridge.

Vice President's Space Policy Advisory Board (1990), *A Post Cold War Assessment of US Space Policy*, The White House, Washington, DC.

Virilio, Paul (1994), *The Vision Machine*, trans. Julie Rose, BFI, London.

Virk, D. S. (1991), *Indian Postal History 1873–1922: Gleanings from the Post Office Records*, Army Postal Service Association, New Delhi.

Viswanathan, Gauri (1989), *Masks of Conquest: Literary Study and British Rule in India*, Columbia University Press, New York.

Waldrop, M. Mitchell (1992), *Complexity: The Emerging Science at the Edge of Order and Chaos*, Penguin, Harmondsworth.

Walker, Ian (1995), 'Desert Stories or Faith in Facts?' in Martin Lister (ed.), *The Photographic Image in Digital Culture*, Routledge, London, 236–52.

Ward, Geoffrey (1991), 'Nothing But Mortality: Prynne and Celan' in Anthony Easthope and John O. Thompson (eds), *Contemporary Poetry Meets Modern Theory*, Harvester Wheatsheaf, Hemel Hempstead, 139–52.

Warner, Timothy N. (1989), 'Information Technology as a Competitive Burden' in Tom Forester (ed.), *Computers in the Human Context*, MIT Press, Cambridge, MA, 272–80.

Watt, Ian (1957), *The Rise of the Novel*, Pelican, Harmondsworth.

Wiener, Norbert (1948) *Cybernetics or, Control and Communication in the Animal and the Machine*, MIT Press, Cambridge, MA.

Wiener, Norbert (1950), *The Human Use of Human Beings: Cybernetics and Society*, Free Association Books, London.

Wilkie, Tom (1993), *Perilous Knowledge: The Human Genome Project and Its Implications*, Faber, London.

Williamson, Jack H. (1989), 'The Grid: History, Use and Meaning' in Victor Margolin (ed.), *Design Discourse: History/Theory/Criticism*, University of Chicago Press, Chicago, 171–86.

Wittgenstein, Ludwig (1961), *Tractatus Logico-Philosophicus*, trans. D. F. Pears and B. F. McGuinness, Routledge and Kegan Paul, London.

Wölfflin, Heinrich (1966), *Renaissance and Baroque*, trans. Kathrin Simon, Cornell University Pess, Ithaca, NY.

Wollen,Tana (1993), 'IMAX and OMNIMAX' in Philip Hayward and Tana Wollen (eds), *Future Visions: New Technologies of the Screen*, BFI, London, 10–30.

Woodham Smith, Cecil (1962), *The Great Hunger*, Four Square, London.

Yampolsky, Mikhail (1993), 'The Essential Bone Structure: Mimesis in Eisenstein' in Ian Christie and Richard Taylor (eds), *Eisenstein Rediscovered*, Routledge, London, 177–88.

Yankelovich, Nicole (1991) 'From Electronic Books to Electronic Libraries: Revisiting "Reading and Writing the Electronic Book"' in Paul Delaney and George P. Landow (eds), *Hypermedia and Literary Studies*, MIT Press, Cambridge, MA.

Yankelovich, Nicole, Norman Meyrowitz and Andries van Dam (1991) 'Reading and Writing the Electronic Book', first published 1985; reprint in Paul Delaney and George P. Landow (eds), *Hypermedia and Literary Studies*, MIT Press, Cambridge, MA.

Youngblood, Gene (1970), *Expanded Cinema*, Studio Vista, London.

INDEX